CHANGING TIMES
Music And Politics In 1964

CHANGING TIMES

Music And Politics In 1964

Steve Millward

Matador
9 Priory Business Park,
Wistow Road, Kibworth Beauchamp,
Leicestershire. LE8 0RX
Tel: (+44) 116 279 2299
Fax: (+44) 116 279 2277
Email: books@troubador.co.uk
Web: www.troubador.co.uk/matador

ISBN 978-1780883-441

British Library Cataloguing in Publication Data.
A catalogue record for this book is available from the British Library.

Typeset by Troubador Publishing Ltd, Leicester, UK
Printed and bound in the UK by TJ International, Padstow, Cornwall

Matador is an imprint of Troubador Publishing Ltd

MIX
Paper from
responsible sources
FSC
www.fsc.org   FSC® C013056

For Mary, Matthew, Tom and Eric

Preface

In 1964 I became a teenager. I also moved schools that year, and lived in three different towns. So it is understandable that I remember the pop music of 1964 with clarity: it was the soundtrack to what at that stage was the most eventful period of my life. But this book is not an exercise in nostalgia. On the contrary, I am able only now, with the benefit of nearly 50 years' hindsight, to appreciate the part played by pop music in the social and political changes that were encompassed by the year 1964; and not just pop music, but jazz, soul and blues, too – even classical music.

But this is also true of other years – what makes 1964 so special?

For one thing, the events of that year were momentous: a Presidential Election in the USA and a General Election in the UK within three weeks of each other; the escalation of the Vietnam War and of the struggle for civil rights in America and around the world; the removal of the Soviet Premier; the first shoots of women's liberation; the 400th anniversary of Shakespeare's birth; the Summer and Winter Olympic Games. For another, the music of 1964 though inextricably bound to its time has had extraordinary durability. I derive as much pleasure today from records like 'Baby Please Don't Go' by Them or The Zombies' 'She's Not There' as I did then.

Of course it can be argued that to concentrate on one year gives only a partial picture of the continuity and change inherent in all music, but especially that of the 1960s. It is a point of view I acknowledge, and to which I make two concessions. Firstly, I cover music both recorded and released in 1964. That may seem in effect to equate to a book about 1963-1965; however, setting aside the fact that most records in those days came out in the year they were made, I generally only include music recorded in 1964 but released in 1965 (or later) when particular events in 1964 influenced its creation. A good example would be John Coltrane's album *A Love Supreme*, made in December 1964, but released in February 1965.

Conversely I only include records made in 1963 if they had their impact in 1964. The most notable instance is The Beatles' 'I Want To Hold Your Hand' which, though cut in October 1963, spearheaded the band's breakthrough in the USA in the early part of 1964. Secondly, there are chapters on what led to the musical explosions of 1964 and where they led.

Yet at the same time there are distinct advantages on focussing on a single year, the most obvious of which is the capacity to analyse in depth. Having done so, it is crystal clear that 1964 was indeed an *annus mirabilis* for music, whether pop, jazz, blues, rhythm and blues, African, Caribbean or classical.

Fortunately I am not alone in my enthusiasm: many people have helped by contributing their interest, ideas and information. Particular thanks are due to John Greenway and Sid Toole, both of whom lent essential books and records. John was also kind enough to send me his recollections of 1964, an extract from which appears in Chapter 8. Others have helped by giving advice, feedback and comment both on the arguments contained in the book and the way they are expressed; they include Dominic Broadhurst, Sue Fletcher, Beverly Howbrook, Jeff Mills, Mary Millward and Matthew Millward. I am also grateful to Terry Compton and the team at Troubador for their unwavering encouragement and support.

While thanking people I should also mention the debt I owe Dave Hatch (1943-2009), without whom I would not be writing at all.

Contents

CHAPTER 1:

Wishin' And Hopin'

At the end of the 1950s rock and roll seemed to be in terminal decline. Don McLean, in his eulogy 'American Pie', declares the exact date of its demise to be 3 February 1959, the day that Buddy Holly was killed in a plane crash near Mason City, Iowa. Indeed, Holly epitomised the freewheeling creativity of rock and roll and appeared to be taking it into a new phase. He was not, however, the only big star lost to the music at the turn of the decade.

As critic and historian Peter Guralnick laments, 'When the treacle period of the late fifties and early sixties engulfed us we recited the familiar litany, by now grown stale from repetition: Elvis in the Army, Buddy Holly dead, Little Richard in the ministry, Jerry Lee Lewis in disgrace and Chuck Berry in jail' (*Feel Like Going Home,* p.16).

The loss of these titans was certainly grievous but the real problem was that big business, despite its initial scepticism, had started to gain control of rock and roll, thus enfeebling the small independent companies which had given it birth and nurtured it through the early years. The major labels not only lured the leading artists away from the 'indies' as they came to be known, they also began to manufacture their own performers. Forerunners of The Monkees and The Archies in the 1960s, the Stock-Aitken-Waterman roster of acts in the 1980s and the boy bands of the 1990s, a cohort of bland white male crooners flooded the airwaves, sanitising a genre which had seemed so challenging, almost threatening, just a few years before.

Outside the USA, there had been precious little rock and roll of any quality in the first place, so there was not that much to lose. Yet there were signs that rumours of the death of rock and roll may have been exaggerated. At some point in the spring or summer of 1958, a group of teenagers called The Quarry Men recorded Holly's 'That'll Be The Day' at the Phillips Sound Recording Service in Liverpool, England. As a cover version it is creditable enough but the other side of the disc is of rather more interest; 'In Spite Of All The Danger' is again sung by John Lennon, but written by two band members, Paul McCartney and George Harrison.

At that time it was highly unusual for pop singers, even when established, to write their own material. Certainly some of the top rock and roll singers had done so, but their compositions were often heavily derivative of blues or country standards and, in any case, exemplified the individuality the large companies wanted to erode. The majors were much more accustomed not only to sourcing songs for their artists but also choosing the ones that should be recorded and released and the way they should be marketed. In the studio the producer ruled supreme, though Elvis Presley, who in many other respects embodied the star-without-influence following his move from Sun to RCA, at least had some say in the management of his recording sessions.

The dominance of the producer did not necessarily diminish the aesthetic quality of the product – in most cases, quite the opposite. Left to themselves performers can become undisciplined and self-indulgent. Instances occur throughout the history of pop music: country blues singers recorded by the Library of Congress were, for example, frequently given too much leeway while the self produced albums of the prog rock and metal eras often exacerbated their already worrying tendency towards excess.

Furthermore, some producers were tantamount to artists themselves, in particular, Phil Spector and Bert Berns whose work will be discussed later. Spector was one of the first producers to exploit to the full both the technical and artistic possibilities of the recording studio. In that respect he was heir to the great Sam Phillips for whom Elvis Presley made his earliest – and some would say his best – records. Phillips's art, however, was more intuitive and less premeditated than Spector's. Few who have read about the spontaneity with which Presley's debut single, 'That's All Right', was created will ever forget it. As Richard Williams has pointed out in his biography of Spector, *Out Of His Head,* Phillips's use of tape-echo on the Presley sessions was revolutionary: 'The snare drums and string bass snapped in unison. This "presence" gave the records an indefinable lift and vitality.'(p.20)

The innovations brought about by the likes of Phillips and Spector were accelerated by the rapid progress in sound recording, itself part of the US technological boom of the 1940s and 1950s. The Ampex Corporation, for example, was founded in 1944, within a year of the invention of multi-track recording. 'That's All Right' was made by using two Ampex 350 recorders, and Spector employed their three-track machines. The first 45 rpm seven-inch vinyl discs were issued by RCA in 1949, a development that was especially crucial for the independent record companies – and hence for rock and roll – as, unlike the larger and more brittle 78 rpm records, they were light and durable enough to be hawked around the radio stations of the South. These modern discs, or 'singles', became emblematic of the new music.

The rapid advances in technology stemmed from the manufacture of huge amounts of arms and related equipment that followed the entry of the United States into the Second World War on 8 December 1941. By 1945 the output of the US was twice what it had been in 1929 and with low unemployment and no war damage it was experiencing the highest standard of living it, and possibly any other country, had ever known. Technological advancement was now focussed on cars, entertainment and labour-saving devices for the home, all of which appealed to a population with more disposable income than ever before. There was also a surge in the birth-rate: the childhood of the 'baby boomers', born post-1945, was dominated by these products – at least if you were white and middle-class.

There was also enormous foreign demand for American goods and Britain was no exception. In fact the policies of the Conservative Government made it one of the easiest countries for the US to export to.

The Tories had been returned in 1951 with Winston Churchill as Prime Minister, an advocate of free trade for over 50 years. The resultant influx of consumer products helped brighten the gloom of post-war Britain and was swiftly followed by the associated manifestations of popular culture. Much of this was aimed at young families and fairly innocuous, but films like *The Wild One* (1954) and *Rebel Without A Cause* (1955) seemed to have a more sinister, nihilistic purpose, and caused a frisson of excitement, especially among the young. But this was as nothing compared with the impact of rock and roll.

Bill Haley first hit the British chart in 1954 with 'Shake, Rattle And Roll', and while his version bowdlerised the Big Joe Turner original it captured the imagination of British teenagers and prepared the ground for its unforgettable follow-up, 'Rock Around The Clock'. Though a number one hit on both sides of the Atlantic this record had a particular resonance in Britain: it has re-entered the UK chart on no fewer than five occasions and during showings of the eponymous film, starring Haley, Teddy Boys ripped up cinema seats with abandon. Needless to say, his British tour of 1958 was accompanied by riots.

The significance of all this was not lost on cultural commentators. In his visionary book, *The Uses Of Literacy* (1957), Richard Hoggart bemoans the imposition of mass popular culture by the media and entertainment moguls, and Theodor Adorno found further evidence for his theory that capitalism force-fed people such stuff in order to render them passive and acquiescent. Certainly both points of view are difficult to challenge when faced with the pop music scene of 1959.

But such sweeping arguments support an ideology that is at times faulty. At key moments of change, impact is created by music which, far from being packaged up by the Establishment, comes directly from – and is nourished by – the people. What is undeniably true is that these upheavals are inextricably linked to political developments. Take, for example, the British punk rock explosion of 1976, created by bands who had come up through the strikes and three-day weeks of 1973 and the huge growth in youth unemployment in 1975, or the glossy, consumer-friendly UK pop of the 1980s – a response to the market-led policies of the Thatcher Government.

Mention the link between pop and politics to most people and they will immediately think of 'political' pop singers: the likes of Bob Dylan, John Lennon and the participants in the Rock Against Racism and Red Wedge initiatives, and indeed a number of erudite studies, including Robin Denselow's *When The Music's Over* (1989), have described their activities at some length. Fewer in number are the attempts to connect politicians to pop or to attribute musical development, directly or indirectly, to their decisions. But as the examples cited above show, such influences are equally important to the context in which pop music is made, its purpose, content and execution. In the end, both standpoints are valid: there is a *reciprocal* relationship between music and politics, at no time more dynamic than in 1964.

★ ★ ★ ★ ★

In late autumn 1963, US President John Fitzgerald Kennedy visited Dallas, Texas. His Vice President, Lyndon Baines Johnson (or – more popularly – LBJ), was from the Lone Star State and this had helped deliver it, along with six other former Confederate States, to the Democrats in the Presidential Election of 1960. This was a crucial contribution in a traditionally conservative part of the country and hugely assisted Kennedy's victory. On this occasion, however, Kennedy was not there to woo Republicans but to deal with a rift in his own party between left and right. The former faction centred on the fiercely liberal Don Yarborough and his namesake but no relation, Senator Ralph Yarborough, who rode with LBJ in the Presidential motorcade which crossed the city that day. Governor John Connally represented the right and sat in the same car as Kennedy. The date of this visit, 22 November 1963, is etched on to the collective consciousness of Americans as well as millions of people elsewhere in the world, for it was when the motorcade passed through Dealey Plaza that John F Kennedy was assassinated.

During the furore and confusion that followed, Johnson acquitted himself admirably. Standing next to Kennedy's widow, Jacqueline, he was sworn in as President the same day as he travelled back to Washington aboard Air Force One, and immediately struck the right balance between outrage, reverence for Kennedy and determination to keep the country on track. In truth he had disliked Kennedy and resented his ascendancy but as a seasoned politician, he saw the need to promote continuity at a time when despair and panic were in the air. In one of his first public utterances as President, he declared, 'As he [Kennedy] did not shrink from his responsibilities, but welcomed them, so he would not have us shrink from carrying on his work beyond this hour of national tragedy' (cited in Robert Dallek, *Lyndon B Johnson: Portrait Of A President*, p. 146). But it was not long before he took the opportunity to introduce some of the reforms he had been contemplating since his earliest days in politics – in some cases even before that.

For someone who became so reviled as a warmonger and the very epitome of reactionary inflexibility, LBJ had good credentials as a liberal. He was born on 27 August 1908 into a political family. His father, Sam Ealy Johnson Jr, was what was known as an 'agrarian liberal' – an advocate of farmers' rights, who retained something of the distrust of government and big business embodied in the pro-farmer and anti-monopoly Greenback Party of the late nineteenth century. He was elected to the House of Representatives in 1906, but continued to live the lifestyle of a frontiersman and as a child Lyndon experienced the kind of poverty that he later resolved to stamp out.

Though a rebellious teenager, he trained as a teacher and again came across deprivation and poverty first-hand when he began work at the Mexican-American grade school at Cotulla, Texas, in September 1928. Here he organised and motivated children who were at the very bottom of the economic heap, setting up extra-curricular activities such as debates and spelling bees, introducing sports and music and establishing a parent-teacher group. It was in Cotulla that he developed his enduring belief in the power of education to combat social disadvantage. But Johnson did not stay long in teaching: in November 1931 he became secretary to Democratic congressman Richard Kleberg, elected to replace the recently-deceased Harry M Wurzbach.

Johnson brought enormous energy, enthusiasm and not a little arrogance to his work for Kleberg, all of which helped him build a reputation for himself. At the same time he was learning the darker political arts of ingratiation, nepotism, patronage and the calling-in of favours, all of which became essential features of his character alongside his idealism and crusading spirit. It was this latter, more positive side to Johnson that prevailed when, in July 1935, he was appointed by President Franklin D Roosevelt as the Texas Director of the National Youth Administration (NYA). This was an important part of Roosevelt's New Deal strategy and to be given such a responsibility at 26 was quite an honour for Johnson. Nationally, youth unemployment was running at around 20% and there was a real risk that the resultant disaffection and alienation would do permanent damage to the country's social and political fabric. Indeed, some Americans were looking enviously at the Soviet Union and Germany where everyone seemed to have a job. The problems in Johnson's home state were more acute owing to its size and complexity, yet in his eighteen months in the post, over 30,000 young people entered education and employment programmes funded by the NYA.

In contrast Johnson's efforts to become a congressman were tainted by skulduggery, with well-founded allegations of illegal payments, both to influential benefactors and to the farmers on whom he relied for support. On the surface, however, it was his New Deal zeal and tireless campaigning that won the day and propelled him into the House of Representatives. In his new role Johnson brought all his attributes to bear, particularly in his fundraising activities, and he was thus able to assist individuals as well as the Democratic Party as a whole. His election as a Texas senator in November 1948 was welcomed in Washington: sure, his campaign had been characterised by questionable tactics and harsh words for his opponents and for the Dallas press, but these were considered tantamount to virtues when it came to the wheeling and dealing required on Capitol

Hill. When combined with Johnson's addiction to hard work, his ability to ingratiate himself with those in power and his physically dominating presence, the result was formidable.

These days we are so used to the careful grooming of our politicians in matters of appearance, behaviour and utterances that Johnson's blunt, in-your-face style might seem archaic. But in the Washington of the early 1950s it had considerable impact, so much so that within three years of his arrival he became Leader of the Democratic Party in the Senate – at the age of 44, the youngest they had ever had. Two years later, as the Democrats took over, he became the youngest majority leader in the history of the Senate.

Naturally he began to be spoken of as a future President of the United States. While a supremely skilled politician, Johnson was, however, no longer identified with any particular causes. Throughout his career he had shown strong support for the underprivileged but had stopped short of speaking out on behalf of African-Americans. Indeed in the late 1940s, according to Robert Dallek (*ibid.*), 'on Civil Rights ... he unequivocally went along with the opposition of most Texas voters' (p. 56) and

> Opponents of the President's [Truman's] [Civil Rights] program who wrote Johnson received ... only assurances that he had "voted against all ... anti-lynching and FEPC [Fair Employment Practices Commission] legislation since I came into Congress and expect to continue to do so." (p. 57)

Then, towards the end of the decade, he attached himself to the campaign for Civil Rights; it would seem that either this or his former stance was driven by political expediency rather than sincerely held beliefs.

A third option is that he had genuinely changed his mind on the issue, but this is hard to believe given his reputation for Machiavellian manoeuvring. Another explanation is that he could not afford to be wrong-footed on Civil Rights in the race for the Democratic nomination to contest the 1960 Presidential election. Among the contenders was John Fitzgerald Kennedy who – in spite of the fact that his record on Civil Rights had barely been superior to Johnson's – was younger, more glamorous and very much the coming man in the Party.

Johnson detested Kennedy but also made the fatal mistake of underestimating him. At the Democratic convention in July 1960, Kennedy polled almost double the number of votes that Johnson received and hence secured the nomination at the first attempt. When the question of a running-mate came up, Kennedy shrewdly put any antipathy for Johnson aside, recognising that his experience and, more importantly, his ability to deliver Texas and other Southern States, made him the ideal foil for Kennedy's own youthful appeal, liberal image and North-Eastern origins.

So it proved: Kennedy won an election in which the Democrats gained from the Republicans Alabama, Arkansas, Georgia, Louisiana, North Carolina, South Carolina and, though only just, Texas. Johnson was not especially happy to be Vice President but he made the best of it. One responsibility he was content to assume was the Committee on Equal Employment Opportunity (CEEO). This put him in the forefront of Civil Rights development at a critical moment and reflected his longstanding belief in the regeneration of communities through education and work. His new job entailed a good deal of international travel, promoting the new Administration and spreading goodwill. One notable stop on his itinerary was Saigon where he made a memorable impression, extolling the virtues of American democracy to any South Vietnamese prepared to listen, and to some who were not.

By late 1963 the clamour for Civil Rights was becoming deafening and Kennedy was concerned that the CEEO was achieving nothing; he was also increasingly worried about new revelations concerning his Vice President's shady dealings. It was therefore no surprise when rumours began to circulate that he might be looking for another running-mate for the Presidential election of 1964. Johnson's fortunes were at a low ebb. But, as we have seen, they soared following Kennedy's assassination in November – and not just because of his unforeseen promotion. Johnson almost immediately established himself as a statesman to be reckoned with, considered – now by others as well as himself – to have the potential to be a great President. He began 1964 hoping, indeed almost expecting, that it would not be long before that potential was realised.

★ ★ ★ ★ ★

At the time President Kennedy's death was announced, The Beatles were about to perform at the Globe Cinema, Stockton-on-Tees, County Durham. Despite the trauma engulfing the Western world, there is no record of any interruption to the proceedings at Stockton. In truth neither The Beatles, nor their fans, were as yet connected in any way to international events, although just eighteen days previously they had played at the Royal Command Performance in the presence of the Queen Mother and Princess Margaret. For many entertainers this would have been the pinnacle of their career and while they appeared only seventh on a bill of nineteen (including such disparate acts as Marlene Dietrich and the puppets Pinky and Perky) they attracted the greatest attention. For the band were transcending their status as Liverpudlian teenage idols to appeal across the divides of age and class: to be performing for Queen Elizabeth The Queen Mother, then 63 years of age, was the ultimate proof of that. According to Bill Harry:

> After the show the Beatles were presented to the Queen Mother in the Royal lounge. She told them she'd enjoyed the show and asked them where they would be performing next. They told her, 'Slough.' 'Ah,' she said, delighted, 'That's near us.' When she was asked to comment on the Beatles she said, 'They are so fresh and vital. I simply adore them.'
>
> (The Beatles and Royalty – www.triumphpc.com/mersey-beat)

The Beatles had come a long way since we met them earlier in this chapter as The Quarry Men. As Paul McCartney (*The Beatles Anthology*, p. 82) has explained, it had been a gradual and arduous journey:

It was never an overnight success. It started in pubs; we went on to talent contests and then to working men's clubs. We played Hamburg clubs, and then we started to play town halls and night clubs, and then ballrooms. There could be as many as 2,000 people in a ballroom, so if you did a gig there the word really got round. Next up from that was theatres, and Brian took us through all these steps.

The role played by Brian Epstein in guiding The Beatles to success cannot be over-exaggerated. By the time of the Royal Command Performance he had been their manager for just under two years and taken them from uncouth, leather-clad roughnecks to the upper echelon of what early 1960s British entertainment had to offer. This was all the more remarkable since by today's standards (and indeed those of the time) he was almost obsessively scrupulous. The fact that in late 1963 they were still playing venues like the Globe Cinema in Stockton shows that he never went back on a contract even when it was clear that The Beatles were rapidly becoming one of the show business phenomena of the 20th century. His relationship with the band was perfectly calibrated: they retained their creativity and cheery, cheeky image while he brought them protection and organisation. George Martin, as we shall see, performed a similar role in the recording studio.

Prior to Epstein's first encounter with the band, at the Cavern on 9 November 1961, there had been little evidence of their potential. True, they wrote some of their own songs but these were heavily outweighed by standards, covers of rock and roll and latterly rhythm and blues material – a wide-ranging mixture which appealed to the equally heterogeneous clientele of the Hamburg clubs they played between 1960 and 1962. It was here that the principle of broad appeal, later to have such profound consequences, was first established.

Not that it helped them much at their first audition for a major record label, Decca, on 1 January 1962. A lot has been made of the band's failure that day. Dick Rowe, head of singles A&R at the label, became notorious as 'the man who turned down The Beatles' (even if, apparently at George Harrison's suggestion, he did sign The Rolling Stones and many other bands who came to prominence in 1964). But then anyone, on listening to the tapes of the session, would have to ask themselves: 'Would *you* have signed them?'

There is no doubting The Beatles' enthusiasm but they come across as a lightweight covers band characterised by an annoying silliness. 'Searchin'' is a particularly gruesome example, with its deliberately over-articulated vocals and unnecessary interjections, and the mock-foreign accents in 'Three Cool Cats' are unfunny and sound racist to the modern ear. While not entirely devoid of attempts at comedy, their own compositions fare better, especially 'Hello Little Girl', the first song ever written by John Lennon and featuring the neat interplay between lead and backing vocals that was to become so familiar.

When, five months and five days later, they entered EMI's Abbey Road studios for the first time the results were far more satisfying though none saw the light of day commercially. For one thing, they took the session seriously. This time three of the four numbers taped were Lennon-McCartney numbers, with the probable consequence that the comic vocal effects were relegated to the one non-original, 'Besame Mucho'. Instead the focus was on singing and playing to the best of their ability.

For another, the great 'Love Me Do' was included. The lyrics of this song are admittedly basic but this suits the driving, elemental melody. John Lennon's harmonica was, according to Mark Lewisohn in his sleeve notes to the CD *The Beatles Anthology* (p.16), influenced by Delbert McClinton's playing on 'Hey! Baby' by Bruce Channel (fifteen days later, The Beatles were to share the bill with both men at the Tower Ballroom, Wallasey). Whatever the case, it adds a crucial rawness that makes 'Love Me Do' quite unlike any other British pop song of the period. On hearing the issued version for the first time many listeners thought it was the work of a black group, or at least of an American one. It was, in fact, 'Love Me Do' that prompted engineer Norman Smith to go and get George Martin, whose assistant, Ron Richards, had been supervising the session up until then – thus beginning a relationship between band and producer that has never been equalled.

What made it so fruitful was that it was by no means one-sided. Martin's expertise was unquestioned but he was prepared to listen to what the band had to say, too, as The Beatles' next visit to Abbey Road, on 4 September 1962, illustrates nicely. Still accustomed to the tradition whereby professional songwriters provided artists with material, Martin had the band record Mitch Murray's 'How Do You Do It', with the intention of making it the A-side of their first single. The Beatles succeeded in persuading him to go for 'Love Me Do' instead. For such an inexperienced band to change the decision of a respected producer like George Martin was extraordinary; it certainly had important consequences for both parties in the short and the long term. 'Love Me Do' became a Top 20 hit, the first in an unbroken sequence of eighteen over the next seven years while the basis of mutual co-operation between the producer and produced had been established.

The Beatles' first album, *Please Please Me*, released on 22 March 1963, confirmed what 'Love Me Do' had hinted at – here was a significant new act on the British pop music scene. In terms of content it was a very different mix to that offered at the Decca audition. Now eight out of thirteen songs were originals, compared with just three of fifteen, and the hard rock and roll had disappeared altogether in favour of contemporary rhythm and blues. The result was a record right at the cutting edge of modern pop music: not only were the Lennon-McCartney compositions new to listeners but the cover versions were of songs by artists who at that stage meant little in the UK – The Isley Brothers, The Shirelles, and Arthur Alexander among them.

In some cases these transcended mere copies: The Beatles' version of The Isleys' 'Twist And Shout', for example, is considerably slower than the original, giving it additional punch. Compare this with The Hollies' rendition of Maurice Williams and The Zodiacs' 'Stay', recorded the same year. Though their energy is commendable the Manchester band take the number at a breakneck tempo, thereby losing the lilting sensuality of the original. Their second album, *With The Beatles*, brought more of the same. The version of The Miracles' 'You Really Gotta Hold On Me' again slows down the original, giving it a more soulful, gospel feel – for a British outfit to achieve this on a song direct from black, inner-city Detroit was scarcely credible and completely without precedent. Their account of Barrett Strong's 'Money' was not far behind, with Lennon's rasping vocals, the intensity of the instrumentation and the pounding riff all anticipating heavy rock.

It is no exaggeration to say that The Beatles re-fashioned such numbers to make them their own; even more remarkable was that there was no perceptible gap in quality between the pieces being covered and those composed by Lennon and McCartney. Over the course of the first two albums the band used material by the likes of Gerry Goffin and Carole King, Smokey Robinson, Berry Gordy and Janie Bradford, Chuck Berry, Phil Medley and Bert Berns, Brian Holland, Luther Dixon, Hal David and Burt Bacharach – all of them in the first rank of contemporary pop song writing. Yet there was a perfect fit with 'I Saw Her Standing There', 'Love Me Do', 'Please Please Me', 'There's A Place', 'It Won't Be Long', 'All I've Got To Do', 'All My Loving' and others. In this way these albums are organic Beatles records – not with an overall *concept*, as later releases would be, but with an overall *conception* that is unified and coherent.

In terms of singles, Lennon and McCartney hit on a formula, consciously or otherwise, which afforded direct communication, even intimacy, with the listener. A personal pronoun in the first or second person – that is, the words 'I', 'me', 'we' or 'you' – is used in the title of thirteen of the sixteen songs that comprise their first eight singles releases (the exceptions being 'This Boy', 'A Hard Day's Night' and 'She's A Woman'). These spanned the period 5 October 1962 to 27 November 1964 and hence are of fundamental importance for the arguments contained in this book. For, together with the day-to-day language used throughout the rest of the songs, they reinforced the appeal of The Beatles to *everyone*, irrespective of age, class, race or culture. The techniques may have been simple, but they were hugely effective, drawing the listener right into the little melodramas that unfolded in each piece. The 1964 releases will be examined later so we shall take an earlier song as an example for now.

14

'Please Please Me' begins in a striking way, with the singer recounting what he told his girlfriend the previous night. How easy it would have been to have him speaking directly to the young woman concerned – but the introduction of a third party to whom the singer relates his complaint about the relationship lends an additional element to the narrative and helps legitimise his subsequent plea for reciprocation. Personal pronouns are employed throughout – 25 times in all – and there are some clever uses of assonance ('complaining'/'raining', 'pleasing with you'/'reason with you') where the use of commonplace language renders the effect especially subtle.

Of course it was not just the lyrics that made The Beatles' records so potent: their musical structures were correspondingly straightforward yet deployed for maximum effect. With respect to 'Please Please Me', Ian MacDonald (*Revolution In The Head*, p. 55) notes that

> Restricting the verse to virtually one chord, the group had gone all out for impact … Tension mounted graphically through a syncopated bridge of call and response between Lennon and a powerfully harmonised McCartney and Harrison, before exploding in three parts on the chorus.

This interplay between voices was a key feature of The Beatles' sound and was tantamount to having three singers on call to use in various combinations. As well as giving distinctiveness to their music, it also helped establish Lennon, McCartney and Harrison as individual personalities yet somewhat inexplicably it was drummer Ringo Starr who received the most fan mail. In any case, all members of the band became recognisable, quadrupling the appeal of a band with only one 'front man.'

In terms of image, Epstein had trained the band to be smart but still convey rebelliousness through their long hair and irreverent attitude to the establishment. This had a direct counterpart in their music – belligerent, edgy material like 'Twist And Shout' and 'Money' was balanced by songs the older generation would enjoy such as 'A Taste Of Honey' and

'Till There Was You'. The Beatles' own songs were, ambiguously, in the middle and could go either way.

The net effect of all of these factors was that The Beatles were the biggest thing to hit British show business for many a year. Unfortunately British show business in the early 1960s was a fairly drab and restricted environment. Things were especially bleak for young people – there was no commercial radio until 1964 and even then the station concerned, Radio Caroline, was based on a boat off the British coastline in order to avoid the broadcasting laws. Radio Luxembourg played the right sort of music but the reception was sometimes erratic (though, miraculously, it always became clear when advertisements were broadcast). Commercial television had just one programme for teenagers, ABC's *Thank Your Lucky Stars* (a grimly appropriate title), which began in September 1961 and was presented by Brian Matthew. Associated-Rediffusion's ground-breaking *Ready Steady Go!* did not launch until August 1963.

As for the BBC, it restricted pop music on the radio to the Light Programme's *Saturday Club* and *Easy Beat*, both presented by Matthew; on television there was just *Juke Box Jury*, a copy of the American show in which celebrities commented and voted on new releases.

Those aged over 20 were better served, in terms of quantity if not quality. While there were innovations in some aspects of light entertainment such as comedy and drama, most variety shows were stuck in a format established in the vaudeville era and this carried over into summer season shows at Britain's holiday resorts and pantomimes at Christmas. Thankfully, The Beatles never had to appear in either of these settings, but they did reach the summit of the variety show scene in late 1963, topping the bill on ATV's live *Sunday Night At The London Palladium* on 13 October and the aforementioned spot at the Royal Command Performance exactly three weeks later.

But after that, where was there to go? The only answer was – America. It was a daunting prospect. British acts had been notoriously unsuccessful there: at that point, only three (Vera Lynn, Acker Bilk and The Tornados) had ever reached number one on the singles chart. Even Cliff Richard, who by the end of 1963 had 26 UK hits to his name, failed to make much of an impression in the US. But Epstein had a panoramic vision for the band that encompassed not just America but the rest of the world. His plans for the year ahead included a three-week residency at the Olympia Theatre, Paris and a tour of Australia and New Zealand. Furthermore in October 1963, he had signed a contract with United Artists for their first feature film, on which work was due to commence in March. So as 1964 approached, both Brian Epstein and The Beatles themselves were wishing for, perhaps anticipating, the international success that had seemed a remote prospect only a year before.

★ ★ ★ ★ ★

The rise of The Beatles did not go unnoticed by Harold Wilson, Member of Parliament for the Liverpool constituency of Huyton and leader of the Labour Party. In a sense Wilson was already linked with The Beatles: his emergence as a household name coincided with theirs and his accession as leader occurred on 14 February 1963, a month after the single 'Please Please Me' was released. He also benefited from the spotlight that now fell on Liverpool as a whole. Following The Beatles' success, the city was, for a brief period, the capital of the pop music world, with a large number of local acts – Cilla Black, The Searchers and Billy J Kramer among them – looking to follow in their footsteps, and a posse of record company executives keen to sign them up.

There is no evidence that Wilson was a particular fan of pop music, though he became a keen supporter of the British film industry when President of the Board of Trade in the late 1940s. However, as his career to date had shown, he knew a good thing when he saw one, especially when it might prove advantageous to his own prospects.

Many of Wilson's actions and activities as Party Leader and, in time, as Prime Minister, can be traced to his background and upbringing. There is nothing unusual in this, but for a politician who was often accused of expediency and, at times, duplicity, it is unexpected. For example, his father Herbert was an industrial chemist but found it hard to compete for jobs after becoming unemployed in December 1930. For almost two years he was unable to find work and even when he did so he was forced to move to Bromborough, near Liverpool, some forty miles from the family home in the Colne Valley. His father's experience made an indelible impression on Wilson – he claimed that it led directly to his interest in politics – but there was more to it than straitened family circumstances, with which many people were coping in the early 1930s. More pertinent was the fact that his father, a scientist who had come up through the vocational education route, had been looked down on by 'the professional classes'.

> Herbert felt a strong resentment towards "academic" chemists who, armed with university degrees, carried a higher status within the industry.
>
> (Ben Pimlott, *Harold Wilson*, p.15)

There is an unmistakable echo in the Labour Manifesto of 1964:

> In far too many firms, technicians and technologists, designers and production engineers, are held back by the social prejudices and anti-scientific bias of the "old boy" network.
>
> (*Let's Go With Labour For The New Britain*,
> subsection – *A Modern Economy*)

It may seem ironic that Wilson himself gravitated to one of the centres of the network, Oxford University, but he came at his studies from the perspective of his father's experiences, specialising in economics and the supply and demand of labour. In 1936 he won the Gladstone Memorial Prize for his paper *The State And Railways 1823-1863*. Upon graduating he took a post as researcher for the distinguished social scientist Sir William Beveridge and subsequently worked as an economist in the Mines

Department before being returned as MP for Ormskirk at the 1945 General Election. Just over two years later he was in the Cabinet, as President of the Board of Trade.

As noted above, Wilson took an interest in the film industry and increased the quota of British films to be shown here from 30% to 45%. He also introduced the National Film Finance Corporation, a funding agency which benefited independent film-makers in particular. It was finally abolished in 1985, having supported the production of several hundred films, including one of the most highly-rated of all time, *The Third Man*. Distinguished directors such as Ridley Scott and David Puttnam owe their start in the business to the NFFC.

What motivated Wilson's interest in film? By no stretch of the imagination can he be considered a connoisseur. His opinions, quoted in Pimlott's biography (p. 120) from a speech in the House of Commons, are on the contrary naive and somewhat prudish: he was dismissive, for instance, of 'the gangster, sadistic and psychological films of which we seem to have so many, of diseased minds, schizophrenia, amnesia and diseases which seem to occupy so much of our screen time.' Fortunately, the likes of Alfred Hitchcock took no notice.

Certainly he enjoyed the company of those who made, and acted in, films, though that is as far as the intimacy went – unlike some politicians. The Conservative MP John Profumo, for example, whose downfall had such a bearing on Wilson's accession as Prime Minister, married the actress Valerie Hobson in 1954.

What is most likely, however, is that he was attracted to film because of its popularity. In the immediate post-war period, going to the cinema was an important leisure activity in the UK – as it had been the decade before. Television was in its infancy: the first broadcast had only taken place as recently as 1936 and transmissions were, in any case, suspended during the war. Dancing was still a prevalent pastime, but musical fashions were changing and the era of the pop star had begun; but pop music was exclusively for teenagers and they had no vote. What his advocacy of British film gave Wilson was an association in the public mind between a politician and an important aspect of popular culture, a link which he would forge to yet greater effect fifteen years later.

For many people, trips to the cinema represented a bright spot in the otherwise gloomy aftermath of the Second World War. In fact, Britain's economy was still on a wartime footing with food rationing and controls on the production of goods still in place. Yet signs of recovery were in the air and Wilson, sensing that the public were chafing at the continued privations three years on from the end of the war, came up with his 'bonfire of controls', which began on 5 November 1948. This, in effect, was the gradual removal over the succeeding months and years of all the restrictions on industry, commerce and consumer spending imposed since 1939 – perhaps a predictable and prosaic action put in that way. But for Wilson it was a PR triumph which he was careful to spin out well beyond the Guy Fawkes Day launch. For example he introduced a consumers' committee to report back to him on the effectiveness of the measures and sought the views of ordinary people, in particular working-class women, through what today would be called focus groups.

But Wilson's populist initiatives did not endear him to his Labour colleagues, especially Hugh Gaitskell, whose influence within the Government was growing. Following the resignation, due to ill health, of Sir Stafford Cripps, he became Chancellor of the Exchequer in October 1950. Gaitskell was on the right wing of the Party and was keen to ensure that the British armed forces in the Korean War were adequately funded. This meant cuts in other areas of expenditure, including the National Health Service. It was Gaitskell's introduction of charges for NHS prescriptions in his 1951 budget that proved too much for the left-winger Aneurin Bevan who, as Minister of Health, had established the NHS in the first place. Bevan resigned from the Government on 22 April; the following day Wilson joined him.

Whether Wilson was acting on a point of principle or recognised the popularity to be gained by an anti-war stance is not clear. Certainly the peace movement was growing, especially among younger people. The World Peace Council was founded in 1949 and presented the first

International Peace Prize at the inaugural World Congress of Peace which took place in Paris that April. The following year the Congress was held in Sheffield, Yorkshire, the county of Wilson's birth, and attended by notables such as Pablo Picasso, who had reinforced the relationship between art and politics with his 1937 painting *Guernica*.

In any event Wilson's action accurately reflected the public mood: after the General Election of October 1951 Labour were out of office, and remained so until Wilson led them to victory thirteen years later.

Gaitskell took over as Party Leader in December 1955 following another defeat and, although Wilson had supported his candidature, he remained somewhat suspicious of him. Nevertheless he recognised Wilson's abilities and appointed him to the vital post of Shadow Chancellor in which he engaged in frequent and lively debate with his opposite number, Harold Macmillan. It was during this period that Wilson established his reputation as a witty and incisive speaker, a good match for Macmillan who possessed similar skills and respected them in his adversary – he was known to pass notes of congratulation to Wilson after performances of particular brilliance.

Unexpectedly Labour lost the General Election of 1959 while Gaitskell suffered defeat at the Party Conferences of 1959 and 1960 on the issues of commitment to Clause IV of their constitution (and therefore nationalisation) and nuclear disarmament – both of which he opposed. All of these eventualities encouraged Wilson to challenge for the leadership, but he was curiously equivocal on the nuclear question, perhaps not wishing to alienate the Right from supporting him. Whatever the case he was unsuccessful, and he failed, too, in his bid for the deputy leadership, losing out to the incumbent right-winger, George Brown. By now Wilson was Shadow Foreign Secretary, an important post but not where he wanted to be: the re-selection of Brown, another specialist in economics, was an obstacle to his ambition of becoming Chancellor of the Exchequer if Labour were returned to power at the next General Election, scheduled to take place in 1964.

However the picture changed with the sudden death of Hugh Gaitskell in January 1963. In the contest to replace him, Wilson was the candidate of the Left. Though seen as something of an opportunist, he supported the correct causes, had been a member of a serving Cabinet and, at 46, was relatively young. George Brown was the obvious right-wing figurehead, but there were problems. Not only did he lack Wilson's experience but his gregariousness and forthright opinions which, on a good day, gave him charisma, had their darker side – he was a notorious drunk. He also gave the impression that he would not serve Wilson if he was elected, whereas Wilson had gone out of his way to declare the opposite. This was seen as disloyal to the Party and opened the way for James Callaghan, whose candidature had previously been viewed as divisive, to enter the race. But Callaghan's entry did split the vote in Wilson's favour. When he dropped out of the election after the first ballot Wilson required only eight of his votes to win: in the end he received nineteen and defeated Brown by 41 votes.

Wilson attracted enormous attention in his first months as Party leader, his age and humble origins (of which much was made, not least by Wilson himself) contrasting sharply with the Prime Minister, Macmillan, who was 69 and distinctly upper-class. Macmillan was also beset with difficulties: unemployment was on the increase and the Profumo affair – which linked the Secretary of State for War to a Russian spy, via his mistress, Christine Keeler – was about to break. Wisely, Wilson did not use the scandal to score political points. This helped him seem above it all and – in any case – letting the whole story unravel of its own accord was destructive enough to the Government's prospects.

Compared with Macmillan, Wilson came over as untainted, youthful and dynamic: he seemed to epitomise changing social attitudes whereby the old aristocratic order was no longer to be trusted. He was also enormously popular with people of all ages and backgrounds: when he appeared in a party political broadcast in February 1963, he attracted the highest-ever audience for a British television programme. He conversed easily and candidly with the press who, in turn, responded with favourable coverage.

In terms of policies, the new Labour leader emphasised the importance of science, for the benefit both of the country as a whole and of individuals. He envisioned new jobs in new industries with access to opportunities based on merit rather than social class. He warmed to this theme in his speech to the 1963 Labour Party Conference at Scarborough, connecting the primacy of science with a proposed growth in the number of universities, including an Open University, and the abolition of selective education at eleven.

In all our plans for the future we are redefining and we are restating our socialism in terms of the scientific revolution. But that revolution cannot become a reality unless we are prepared to make far-reaching changes in economic and social attitudes which permeate our whole system of society. The Britain that is going to be forged in the white heat of this revolution will be no place for restrictive practices or for outdated methods on either side of industry... For the commanding heights of British industry to be controlled by men whose only claim is their aristocratic connection or the power of inherited wealth or speculative finance is as irrelevant to the twentieth century as would be the continued purchase of commissions in the armed forces by lordly amateurs.

Exactly one week after the conference had ended, the Conservative Party announced that their new leader, and hence the new Prime Minister, would be the 14th Earl of Home, son of Charles, Lord Dunglass and Lady Lillian Lambton, daughter of the 4th Earl of Durham.

★ ★ ★ ★ ★

In February 1960 Wilson was still to take up the post of Shadow Foreign Secretary, but will not have been unaware of Macmillan's speech to the South African Parliament on the third of the month in which he stated

The wind of change is blowing through this continent. Whether we like it or not, this growth of national consciousness is a political fact.

Many didn't like it, especially the right wing of the Conservative Party who formed the Monday Club in response. Wilson, who had been a member of a Labour Government which had begun to decolonise after the Second World War, was no doubt more sanguine.

But this was not just a matter for the British Government. France controlled a number of important colonies, four of which constituted French Equatorial Africa (AEF) with a federal capital of Brazzaville, in Middle Congo. Just across the Congo River from Brazzaville was Léopoldville, capital of the Belgian Congo.

Both Middle Congo and the Belgian Congo achieved their independence in the months following Macmillan's speech; to avoid confusion between the two new Republics of the Congo, they were popularly known as Congo-Brazzaville and Congo-Léopoldville, the latter sometimes just as the Congo. What seemed the solution to the issue of nomenclature came in 1971 when, in the interests of Africanisation, the name of the latter was changed by President Mobutu to Zaïre, and its capital re-titled Kinshasa. However Mobutu was ousted in 1997 and the new President, Laurent Kabila, changed his country's name to the Democratic Republic of Congo.

The DRC is the twelfth largest country in the world, seven times bigger than its neighbour, the Republic of Congo, and having 20 times the population; Kinshasa has ten million residents, Brazzaville one million. Despite these glaring differences, the two countries have been closely linked, linguistically and politically. Their labyrinthine histories intertwine, resulting in a rich cultural heritage and some of the most vibrant music not only in Africa, but in the world.

Back in the colonial days of the mid-1950s there was an easy interaction between the countries and some of the leading bands contained musicians from both sides of the river. OK Jazz, for example, were founded by clarinetist Jean Serge Essous from Brazzaville and Léopoldville guitarist François Luambo Makiadi, better known as Franco. Inevitably the studios were owned by Europeans, but not necessarily from France or Belgium; a number of Greek entrepreneurs had settled in Léopoldville and diversified into the recording business. The local music infrastructure ran on an informal, almost amateur basis, with musicians more likely to make money playing in the clubs of both cities than through any records they may have appeared on. In terms of repertoire, they played in a variety of genres including swing and highlife, though the dominant style was the Central African variant of rumba, a sensual, hip-swaying dance that had its origins in Cuba and in time became re-titled soukous.

The giant of 1950s Congolese music was singer Joseph Kabasele, known by a variety of nicknames, the most common of which was Le Grand Kalle. Kabasele put together the band African Jazz which included some of the best young musicians in Léopoldville: the three guitarists Nicolas Kasanda ('Nico'), his brother Charles Mwamba ('Dechaud')and Tino Baroza; bass player Augustin Moniana ('Roitelet'); saxophonist Isaac Musekiwa; and singers Roger Izeidi and Pascal Tabou, later known as Rochereau and, ultimately, Tabu Ley.

'Ambiance Kalle Catho', recorded in 1954, exemplifies their early sound – plaintive, sweet voices interspersed with bright and breezy contributions from saxophone and guitar. Nico soon became the instrumental star of the band, his reputation in Léopoldville matched only by Franco, whose OK Jazz came together in 1956. Two of their recordings from the following year show how far the teenage guitarist had already progressed. His incandescent playing illuminates the otherwise lilting 'Musica Tellema', and on 'Aya La Mode' he adroitly alternates staccato phrases with long, flowing lines. 'Merengue', from 1957, typifies his hard-edged, almost metallic intonation and rippling improvisations.

African Jazz were still the city's leading band, however, and their standing was enhanced by a purple patch of releases between 1957 and 1960. Kabasele introduced new textures – riffing saxophones, trumpet and flute – while Nico continued to improvise with imagination and verve: his power-packed solo on the pulsating 'Table Ronde' from 1960 is little short of breathtaking.

'Table Ronde' was itself an indicator of how Congolese music, and indeed the wider political scene, had changed. The easygoing, carefree culture was transforming into militancy. It had begun with musicians complaining about fees and payments: one of the stars of the early 1950s, Henri Bowane, had been briefly imprisoned for insisting on his royalties and Roitelet had organised a couple of strikes at the Loningisa and Esengo studios. There was also the occasional political comment in song: Adou Elenga fell foul of the authorities in 1953 with his 'Mokili Ekobaluka' ('The World Is Going To Change'). As the decade progressed such outbursts became more frequent, even if veiled by an apparently innocuous narrative. Seeking out the double meaning in songs became a full-time occupation for the Léopoldville police.

In 1956, responding to demonstrations in Léopoldville, the Belgians had allowed a measure of African representation in local government. Political organisations were starting to form, including ABAKO, led by Joseph Kasavubu, and the MNC, founded by Patrice Lumumba. In the mineral-rich province of Katanga, Moïse Tshombe formed CONAKAT; this did not prevent riots there in 1958, which spread to Léopoldville itself early the following year.

In December 1959 it was announced that a conference of Congolese and Belgian leaders was to be held in Brussels on 20 January of the following year to accelerate progress towards independence. Both African Jazz and OK Jazz were invited to play at the Round Table Conference. Franco couldn't make it but allowed two members of his band, bass player Brazzos and vocalist Victor 'Vicky' Longomba, to join Kabasele's group, which by then consisted of Nico, Dechaud, Izeidi and drummer Pierre 'Pierrot' Yantunla. Kabasele himself took part in the negotiations and worked with his musicians to write and record two songs to celebrate the conference – the aforementioned 'Table Ronde' and 'Indépendance Cha Cha'. Where the former had been assertive, almost aggressive, the latter was jubilant. It is moving even now to listen to the joyous vocals, the unswerving rhythm sections and Nico's sparkling guitar, his innovatory playing symbolic of the new era.

However within a matter of months hopes of a peaceful transition had been dashed. Independence had been granted on 30 June, with Kasavubu as President and Lumumba as Prime Minister but almost immediately the Army revolted against the Belgian hierarchy and a move towards secession began in the mining areas of the south. In response Lumumba made two fateful decisions. The first was to appoint Joseph-Désiré Mobutu as Army Chief of Staff to quell the dissatisfaction in the ranks. Mobutu would come to rule the country for over 30 years, maintaining a relationship with its leading musicians which, even if occasionally stormy, was generally of mutual benefit. Secondly Lumumba obtained military aid from the Soviet Union, therefore alienating Western governments and compromising their support for the new regime. In the ensuing furore, Kasavubu dismissed Lumumba and each ordered the other's arrest. In September Mobutu took over the country in a coup backed by the USA and Belgium. To placate the West he kept Kasavubu on as President but arrested Lumumba. Four months later Lumumba escaped, but was captured by a team of Katangan soldiers and Belgian paratroopers and assassinated. A period of chaos and confusion ensued that was not to end for another three years.

★ ★ ★ ★ ★

Macmillan's 'wind of change' speech was received with antipathy by its immediate audience, the members of the South African Parliament, not because it wasn't true – there was ample evidence of unrest within their own country – but because it indicated that the British Government were no longer prepared to condone apartheid:

> As a fellow member of the Commonwealth it is our earnest desire to give South Africa our support and encouragement, but I hope you won't mind my saying frankly that there are some aspects of your policies which make it impossible for us to do this without being false to our own deep convictions about the political destinies of free men to which in our own territories we are trying to give effect.

Far from complying with Macmillan's exhortations, Dr Hendrik Verwoerd and his National Party Government were intensifying segregation and restrictions on the movement of black South Africans. In response, the African National Congress (ANC) called for protests to begin on 31 March 1960, but their rival organisation, the Pan-Africanist Congress (PAC) pre-empted this by organising their own demonstration ten days earlier in the township of Sharpeville, near Johannesburg. Although the protest began peacefully the atmosphere deteriorated when low-flying aircraft were used to disperse the crowd. This led to stone-throwing and scuffles and as the crowd approached the police, they were fired on. A total of 69 people were shot dead by the police, including ten children, and 180 were injured.

The Sharpeville Massacre, which took place just six weeks after Macmillan's speech, ignited a fierce reaction internationally: the United Nations Security Council adopted Resolution 134, referring to 'the large-scale killings of unarmed and peaceful demonstrators against racial discrimination and segregation in the Union of South Africa'. Within the country Verwoerd declared a state of emergency and interned some 18,000 black South Africans; on 9 April he survived an assassination attempt by David Pratt, a white South African opposed to apartheid. The PAC was banned, as was the ANC which had been a thorn in the Government's side ever since its rejuvenation fifteen years previously.

Throughout its history the ANC has valued music, recognising its potential both to inspire individuals and to re-Africanise the culture. But in the 1940s the bond was particularly strong. Two successive ANC presidents, Pixley Seme and Dr AB Xuma, had day jobs managing bands, while the policies of self-awareness and cultural pride influenced musical developments. As Gwen Ansell (*Soweto Blues*, p.59) has written:

By the late 1940s, bands were consciously seeking to define and add African elements to their work ... One term for what they were producing was mbaqanga. "We called it African stomp," said critic Doc Bikitsha, "because there was this heavy beat ... of the Zulu traditional"... Although in this early period [mbaqanga] was used interchangeably with other terms for the new African jazz, it came over the years to be applied largely to neotraditional music with jazz-styled instrumentation.

The development of mbaqanga dovetailed with the decline of marabi, the music of the urban black working classes of the 1920s. Huge numbers of people had migrated to the cities during the first two decades of the 20th century, bringing with them rich and varied musical traditions. Marabi took shape when these were applied to Western instrumentation and chord-structures, and in time it dominated recreational activity to such an extent that the term was used to denote the whole culture of inner-city black South Africa. Often the music was played on an organ or piano for the entertainment of customers frequenting shebeens, the informal, unlicensed bars that pervaded the ghettoes during this era.

Marabi was considered degenerate, both by whites and by the aspiring middle class within the black community, so its musicians were seldom invited to the recording studios. One who did make it was pianist Thomas Mabiletsa, and his 'Zulu Piano Medley No. 1' seems to typify the genre. With echoes of both stride and boogie woogie, the cadences here lend themselves easily to dancing, reinforced by a percussive left hand and a rhythm more akin to rumba. The featured melodies are distinctly indigenous.

The year in which 'Zulu Piano Medley No. 1' was made, 1944, saw the formation by Anton Lembede of the ANC Youth League, the membership of which included Walter Sisulu, Oliver Tambo and Nelson Mandela. Their agenda was still more radical, comprising demonstrations, strikes and boycotts, all of which were invoked by Mandela in response to the Group Areas Act of April 1950 that classified and segregated blacks and whites and banned the Communist Party. This spirit of protest was reflected, albeit in more covert form, in many of the records made by black South Africans during the 1950s. A particularly interesting example is 'Meadowlands', written by Strike Vilakazi and recorded on 10 May 1955 by Nancy Jacobs and her Sisters. The song concerns the enforced removal of the residents of Johannesburg's Sophiatown suburb to the new Meadowlands township in Soweto and while the verses in Zulu and Sotho express contentment with the new location ('You'll hear white people saying, "Let's go to Meadowlands"'), those in the Tsotsitaal argot are much less positive: 'You'll hear the Tsotsies saying, "We're not leaving, we're staying right here in this beautiful place"'. 'Meadowlands' found favour with everyone: those against the development saw the positive sentiments as ironic and were pleased to get the coded message of solidarity; Vilakazi was also praised by the Peri-Urban Areas Health Board who organised the moves – as a reward he was allocated the first four bedroomed house in Diepkloof, Meadowlands' twin township within Soweto.

The Sharpeville Massacre and its aftermath had the effect of hastening South Africa's departure from the Commonwealth of Nations and the creation of the Republic of South Africa in 1961. By then Mandela was head of the ANC's military wing and he duly initiated a campaign of sabotage and disruption. He was eventually arrested in August 1962 and two months later was sentenced to five years in prison for initiating a strike the previous year.

South African pop music was still a vehicle for social comment, notably The Four Yanks' 'Msenge' of 1962, which bemoans 'the young men who have been killing one another', and The Young Stars' 'Ulova' of the same year, a warning to the loafer of the title that, 'The police may be coming, you'll be arrested for not working' But by now it was South African jazz that seemed most to embody the struggle for freedom. An interesting session took place in 1959 under the leadership of American pianist John Mehegan but featuring top black South African musicians Hugh Masekela on trumpet, trombonist Jonas Gwangwa and alto saxophonist Kippie Moeketsi. 'Lover Come Back To Me' is pretty much a showcase for the leader but 'Ole Devil Moon' demonstrates the skills of the local players: Gwangwa is characteristically robust, Masekela is bright and imaginative. But Moeketsi is the star of the show with his warm sound and apparently effortless command of his instrument. Though there were no political overtones in the music, the idea of a white American playing alongside black South Africans was anathema to the authorities and Mehegan was admonished accordingly.

The Jazz Epistles' 1960 recording 'Scullery Department' was, however, another matter altogether. The title denotes the fact that black musicians were not allowed to mix with the white patrons for whom they performed and thus would often have to go through the scullery when taking or leaving the stage. The theme, written by Moeketsi, recalls the work of Charles Mingus in its compelling urgency and provides the springboard for punchy contributions by Masekela, Gwangwa and the composer. Pianist Dollar Brand contrives to combine fluency with spiky, angular phrasing.

The Blue Notes, formed by white pianist Chris McGregor in 1962, included some of the best black African talent, in particular saxophonists Dudu Pukwana and Nick Moyake, trumpeter Mongezi Feza, bass player Johnny Dyani and drummer Louis Moholo. Some idea of their luxuriant sound can be obtained by listening to 'Switch', recorded the same year under the name of The Castle Lager Big Band. The brooding theme and unusual ensemble textures are offset by an expansive, assertive alto solo from Pukwana, resulting in a sophisticated, complex but highly accessible piece of music.

But The Blue Notes were shortly to leave South Africa, following a trend begun in 1959 by singer Miriam Makeba. By 1964, Hugh Masekela, Jonas Gwangwa and Dollar Brand (who was to rename himself Abdullah Ibrahim) had also emigrated. These musicians clearly hoped and believed they could fight the repressive regime of their homeland more effectively from beyond its shores.

★ ★ ★ ★ ★

The wind of change was also blowing outside Africa, nowhere more strongly than in the Caribbean. In January 1958 a number of British colonies had formed the West Indies Federation in order to create an independent state, on the Canadian/Australian model. But internal conflicts, resulting partly from the challenges posed by the need to co-ordinate the political activity of 24 islands, led to its demise four years later. Jamaica, for example, was several hundred miles away from the other members; it had joined the Federation in the belief that independence would be granted but three years in there was still no sign of that. In September 1961, a referendum was held there to determine if it should secede from the Federation – the consensus, by a narrow margin, was that it should. Just under a year later, Jamaica achieved independence in its own right.

By then there had been a long tradition on the island of political comment through music. As early as the 1930s, street singers wrote about current affairs and sold the lyrics to passers-by. In Trinidad this practice became formalised as calypso which, during the 1950s, went on to become renowned internationally for its wit and perspicacity. Jamaica had its own musical style, mento, which, though it took on much of what calypso offered, including the aristocratic monikers of its leading performers, had a different past and a very different future. So while Lord Laro's 'Referendum Calypso' (1960) might be seen as a clear example of appropriation, Lord Lebby's 'Etheopia' looks forward from 1955 to the centrality of Rastafarianism within the reggae of the 1970s.

Mento was a folk-based music with its roots in rural communities so it was hardly surprising that it became sidelined following the mass migration to the island's capital, Kingston, after the Second World War. As the manifestation of a comparable urban culture, the tougher sound of American rhythm and blues was more to the taste of the new city-dwellers and it began to dominate the dancehalls, not through live music but the sound systems that supplanted it. Initially these were no more than a single record deck, amplifier and speaker, but in time they became behemoths, with the disc jockeys, or 'sound men', assuming the status previously accorded to bandleaders.

Their profile was further enhanced by the growth in availability of radios and, in 1959, the formation of the state-owned Jamaican Broadcasting Corporation. The JBC's mission was to reflect the island's creativity and the tastes of its population so it wasn't long before the sound men were being looked to as arbiters of both. American R & B morphed into Jamaican R & B during the mid-1950s as a generation of local musicians worked on their own approaches. The shuffle beat of New Orleans rhythm and blues was especially influential: it is not difficult to see the seeds of ska, rocksteady and ultimately reggae in records like Fats Domino's 'Boogie Woogie Baby' (1950) or Dave Bartholomew's 'My Ding-A-Ling' (1952).

Sound system owners such as Coxsone Dodd, Duke Reid and Prince Buster were also in the vanguard of new developments and it was allegedly at a recording session financed by Reid that ska was created when Buster asked guitarist Jerome 'Jah Jerry' Hinds to adapt the New Orleans shuffle beat by emphasising the second and fourth beats of the bar (the 'off' beats).

Producers Leslie Kong, Edward Seaga and Chris Blackwell were other important figures in the gestation of ska. Blackwell formed Island Records, which became the biggest independent record company in the world; Seaga entered politics in 1959, becoming leader of the Jamaican Labour Party in 1974 and his country's fifth Prime Minister six years later. Leslie Kong produced Bob Marley's first single 'One Cup Of Coffee'/'Judge Not' as well as Jimmy Cliff's 'Miss Jamaica', one of several releases to celebrate the country's independence in the summer of 1962, including Derrick Morgan's 'Forward March' and the record chosen to mark the occasion officially, Lord Creator's 'Independent Jamaica'.

In 1963 there seemed much to look forward to in Jamaica. Despite a horrific clash at Easter between Rastafarians and the military, the advent of independence had been largely trouble-free; the economy was growing; and, on the music scene, a vibrant new style, called ska, was announcing itself across the Caribbean and to the rest of the world.

★ ★ ★ ★ ★

Further north, on the US mainland, the struggle for African-American Civil Rights was coming to a head, and blues and jazz artists were beginning to vent their frustration through their music. In one sense there was nothing new in that: the black community had used music as a release since the era of slavery. But up until the 1960s song lyrics, even at their most militant, bemoaned the consequences of oppression rather than the politics behind it. More commonly there was a tendency towards passive acceptance and fatalism. Spirituals had been primarily concerned with deliverance in the next world, there being no chance of it happening in this, while secular songwriters might complain about their individual circumstances but seldom take on wider issues. One of the very few exceptions was blues singer Big Bill Broonzy's 'Get Back (Black, Brown And White)', recorded in Chicago on 8 November 1951, which gave a witty account of the racial hierarchy.

When politicians were mentioned at all, it was with approval. Franklin D Roosevelt was particularly popular. Ella Fitzgerald's 'FDR Jones' (1938), for example, has a baby being called after him, and his New Deal programmes attracted approval – above all the Works Project Administration and Public Works Administration:

> Now you're in, Mr President, and I hope you're there to stay, but whatever changes you make, please keep the PWA (Jimmy Gordon, 'Don't Take Away My PWA', 1936)

There was plenty of insurrection in jazz but, initially at least, it was internal to the music. The 25 years that followed the first-ever jazz recording (arguably Wilbur Sweatman's 'Down Home Rag', made in December 1916) saw a succession of styles: ragtime, New Orleans, Dixieland, swing and bebop. Each claimed to have evolved from its predecessor, with the gap widening at every stage – especially between the latter two. Bebop musicians, predominantly young, gifted and black, saw their music as a radical alternative to big band swing which, though originated by African-Americans like Fletcher Henderson and Duke Ellington, had been popularised by white musicians such as Benny Goodman, Artie Shaw and Glenn Miller. The greatest change brought about by bebop was that jazz was no longer music to dance to – it was played in clubs and, ultimately, in theatres to a seated audience – a situation that has persisted to the present day. As far as one can tell, its creators, Charlie Parker and Dizzy Gillespie, were apolitical but the self-confidence, assertiveness, and elitism of bebop were, coming from African-Americans in the 1940s, tantamount to a political manifesto.

More changes were on the way – West Coast, cool jazz, hard bop and, towards the end of the 1950s, avant-garde or free-form jazz – and the radicalism implied by bebop began to take shape. In 1952, in order to avoid the artistic compromises required by major record labels, the leading bebop drummer Max Roach formed Debut Records with bassist Charles Mingus and his wife, Celia. Both men were among the first in jazz to make direct and uncompromising political comment through their music.

In 1957, the Governor of Arkansas, Orval E Faubus, brought in the National Guard to stop African-American students from attending Little Rock Central High School; the incident sparked off a crisis, and President Eisenhower intervened to withdraw the National Guard and order the 101st Airborne Division to protect the students. Faubus then closed the city's high schools for a whole year. Mingus's response was 'Fables Of Faubus', which mocked the Governor with a plodding two-beat figure recalling Kurt Weill's satirical slant on pre-War Nazi Germany. His subsequent compositions included 'Cry For Freedom (Prayer For Passive Resistance)' (1959), 'Non-sectarian Blues' and 'Suite Freedom' (both 1961).

Mingus also recorded for Candid Records, run by the white jazz critic and Civil Rights activist, Nat Hentoff. Candid aimed to feature a cross-section of jazz, but its most significant release was its third, Max Roach's *We Insist! Freedom Now* suite, recorded in New York on 31 August and 6 September 1960. Of the five pieces in the suite, two were written by

Roach – the self-explanatory 'Triptych – Prayer/Protest/Peace' and 'Tears For Johannesburg'. The other three – 'Driva' Man', 'Freedom Day' and 'All Africa' – were collaborations between Roach and Oscar Brown Jr, the son of a Chicago lawyer and senior figure in the National Association for the Advancement of Coloured People (NAACP). A talented singer, actor and writer, Brown had made history at the age of 21 by hosting the first-ever African-American radio news programme, *Negro Newsfront*.

'Driva' Man' concerns the brutality of slavery, with vocals by Roach's wife, Abbey Lincoln, and a terse tenor saxophone solo by Coleman Hawkins; 'Freedom Day' conveys the elation that followed the Emancipation Proclamation of 1863. On 'All Africa', Lincoln intones the names of African tribes while percussionist Babatunde Olatunji recites a saying from each on the subject of freedom. The whole package is completed with a liner note by Hentoff linking the record to the Civil Rights movement and a cover photograph portraying a lunch counter sit-in.

A month after the suite was recorded, Brown was back in the studio making his debut album, *Sin And Soul*. Bringing together contrasting subjects, styles and angles, it provides an overarching vision of African-American life. Among the more radical tracks are the unaccompanied 'Bid 'Em In', a sequel to 'Driva' Man' in which Brown plays the part of an auctioneer selling a female slave, and 'Work Song', where he adds lyrics depicting a chain-gang to Nat Adderley's hard bop theme.

Sin And Soul was a commercial success, and the multi-faceted Brown seemed set for a glittering future, not just in jazz but in the wider entertainment world. Mingus and Roach, too, were emboldened to continue to advocate for Civil Rights – Roach even had the temerity to interrupt a Miles Davis concert in May 1961 by conducting an on-stage protest. Davis left the stage, but was not unaffected by the incident, both in his music and in his outlook: it was an uncomfortable reminder that his work appealed more to white intellectuals than to the African-American community. It also added to the pressure he was under from the burgeoning jazz avant-garde – musical iconoclasts like Ornette Coleman, Cecil Taylor and his former tenor saxophonist, John Coltrane.

So as 1964 drew closer, many in the jazz community – artists, critics and fans – were anticipating more change, but this time a revolution that would go beyond the music and into the wider realms of ideology and politics.

By that stage, blues musicians were also beginning to become more political. Big changes had taken place since the 1930s, largely brought about by the migration from the Southern States, where blues had germinated, to the industrialised Northern cities. Chicago was an especially popular destination, so much so that the term 'Chicago blues' was used synonymously with 'urban blues' to describe the post-war incarnation of the music. Now the acoustic, largely solo setting had been replaced by bands with drums and electric guitars: the music was harsher, too, and more uncompromising.

Typical of the new breed of musician was JB Lenoir who was born in Monticello, Mississippi, in 1929 and moved to Chicago at the age of 20. But Lenoir was more outspoken than most – as early as April 1954 he was recording 'I'm In Korea' and 'Eisenhower Blues'. The latter was particularly trenchant, stating for example,

My money's gone, my fun's gone –the way things look, how can I be here long?

and it created such a stir that Lenoir was forced to remake it as 'Tax Paying Blues'.

Other artists like Otis Rush – who also came to Chicago in 1949 – complained of living conditions and unemployment in songs like 'Double Trouble' (1958) and although Buddy Guy's 'First Time I Met The Blues' (1960) has no specific political references, it is hard to believe that its savagery is not a product of hostility towards his environment.

But the biggest contribution made by Chicago blues to the events of 1964 was indirect. Diametrically opposed in geography, race and social class, a blues scene had developed in London, largely through the efforts of Alexis Korner, a former guitarist with Chris Barber and his Band. Barber himself was a trad jazz trombonist who had brought to the UK leading

African-American blues artists such as Big Bill Broonzy and Muddy Waters. Korner, though, was more interested in building a local variant and established the London Blues and Barrelhouse Club, fronting it with the band he co-led with harmonica player Cyril Davies, Blues Incorporated.

On 21 July 1962, Blues Incorporated were due to play the Marquee club but had to cancel in order to appear on BBC radio's *Jazz Club*. In their place a new band named after a record by Waters made their debut – Elmo Lewis (guitar), Keith Richard (guitar), Ian Stewart (piano), Dick Taylor (bass), Mick Avory (drums) and Mick Jagger (vocals) – The Rolling Stones.

Taylor subsequently formed The Pretty Things; Elmo Lewis was a pseudonym for Brian Jones, who continued the band with Jagger and Richard. Former drummer Tony Chapman brought in Bill Wyman on bass but then went off to form The Preachers, allegedly because he found The Stones 'too way out'. Avory's replacement was Charlie Watts, who joined in January 1963. As for Stewart, a burly Scotsman, he was considered by Andrew Loog Oldham, who became the band's manager in April 1963, to have the wrong image, and was relegated to road manager/occasional backing piano player.

The Rolling Stones' first single, released in June 1963, was a cover of Chuck Berry's 'Come On' which, although it was a hit, failed to please the band. A year previously, just before their Marquee debut, Jagger had told *Jazz News*, 'I hope they don't think we're a rock and roll outfit', a reflection of their desire to be seen as authentic purveyors of a style of music beginning to make waves in London. It was something new and undiscovered, a contrast to commercial pop music in that it wasn't about making money but expressing real and heartfelt emotion.

But Oldham saw he was on to a goldmine and carefully moulded the band to rival The Beatles, a sort of sinister alternative to their charm and gregariousness. He very much wanted them to write their own songs but towards the end of the year the best idea anyone could come up with as a follow-up to 'Come On' was, ironically, a cover of Lennon and McCartney's 'I Wanna Be Your Man'.

★ ★ ★ ★ ★

In 1963 the struggle for Civil Rights affected the one-eighth of the US population categorised as black. The same year saw the publication of a book which proposed the emancipation of 50% of its citizens – women. Betty Friedan's *The Feminine Mystique* analyses how, by the early 1960s, American women had come to value getting married and having children above all other priorities and how their educational, intellectual and occupational growth had become stunted in the process. Her research among college students, graduates and teaching staff revealed a contrast in outlook and behaviour between contemporary women and those of even a generation before, who were more independent and career-minded but equally, if not more, fulfilled when they took up traditional female roles.

Friedan finds a number of causes for women's decline into passive domesticity, including the negative influence of Freudian precepts and the over-reliance on the functionalist theories of anthropologist Margaret Mead. Her book caused something of a sensation, among both readers and critics; according to *The New York Times* obituary of Friedan in 2006, it 'ignited the contemporary women's movement in 1963 and as a result permanently transformed the social fabric of the United States and countries around the world'.

Feminism was by no means a new concept, but *The Feminine Mystique* catapulted it into a new era; the year after it was published, 1964, the term 'Women's Liberation' was used for the first time. The feelings of optimism experienced by women were, however, part of a much wider sense that momentous events were imminent – not the World Wars that had devastated the youth of previous generations, but positive, progressive developments that would improve the lot of mankind.

Albeit unfocussed as yet, these feelings pervaded social, political and cultural environments across the globe from the lofty heights of The White House to the smallest Congolese village. And underpinning it all, arguably driving much of it, was music – blues, jazz, classical, pop, rock – about to enter a golden age never seen before or since.

CHAPTER 2:

I'm Into Something Good

On Wednesday 1 January 1964, The Chants released 'I Could Write A Book', a record which in many ways represented the high water mark, but also the beginning of the end, of Mersey Beat. Its irrepressible energy, tight arrangement and touch of humour epitomised the qualities that had attracted fans like a magnet. But at the same time it exposed the limitations of the genre: a queasy, anachronistic organ solo and a reliance on material from a previous generation (Richard Rodgers and Larry Hart had written the song for the 1940 musical, *Pal Joey*). The Chants were an all-black vocal group, a very welcome development in a white dominated pop scene. But this immediately rendered them old-fashioned since it linked them to their American counterparts from the 1950s – The Flamingos, The Coasters and the mixed-race Marcels, on whose 1961 version of 'Blue Moon' 'I Could Write A Book' was modelled. So inevitably The Chants faded from the picture, as did many of the Mersey Beat acts that had broken through in 1963.

Gerry and The Pacemakers, for example, whose first three singles all made number one on the UK chart – a feat not repeated until 21 years later, by Frankie Goes To Hollywood – had no number ones in 1964: even the anthem 'Ferry Cross The Mersey' only made number eight. Their final two hits were in 1965 and neither reached the Top Ten. Billy J Kramer and The Dakotas had three records in the Top Five in 1963 – all written by Lennon and McCartney – but only one chart-topper, 'Little Children', in 1964, and beyond that, just two further hits.

Other Mersey Beat groups had a little more staying power. The Searchers had broken through the previous year with the lively 'Sweets For My Sweets' and 'Sugar And Spice' and consolidated their position in the pop music hierarchy with five big hits in 1964. Two of these were associated with the US singer/songwriter Jackie De Shannon: 'Needles And Pins', written by Jack Nitzsche and Sonny Bono – and a minor American hit for her in 1963 (though it reached number one in Canada) – and her own composition, 'When You Walk In The Room', which The Searchers turned into one of the best singles of 1964. Already an excellent song with well-crafted, emotive lyrics, it surges from verse to verse, fortified by close harmonies, a propulsive rhythm section and the jangly guitar sound that subsequently became the trademark of American folk-rock bands such as The Byrds. Almost as good were their versions of two other songs by female writers, Sharon McMahan's 'Some Day We're Gonna Love Again' and the anti-nuclear 'What Have They Done To The Rain' by Malvina Reynolds.

One of the few solo singers to transcend Mersey Beat was Cilla Black. A former cloakroom attendant at the Cavern, she signed with Brian Epstein in September 1963 and a month later had a minor hit with 'Love Of The Loved', a Lennon-McCartney number performed by The Beatles at the Decca audition. Within the first five months of 1964 she had two UK number ones: 'Anyone Who Had A Heart' and 'You're My World'. Both have melodramatic, sweeping melodies, well suited to her powerful, if at times rather metallic, vocal style, but even better was the follow-up, It's For You' (on which its composer, Paul McCartney, plays piano): this time her attack was moderated by an attractive tenderness. At the end of the year she recorded 'You've Lost That Lovin' Feelin', written by Phil Spector, Barry Mann and Cynthia Weil. While it made number two on the chart, it was eclipsed aesthetically and commercially by The Righteous Brothers' original. Subsequently Black became a durable and popular all-round entertainer, a unique feat for a Mersey Beat artist, although comedian Freddie Starr had sung with Howie Casey and The Seniors and fronted his own band, The Midnighters, neither of whom had made much impression outside Liverpool.

At the beginning of 1964 Black had few rivals among British female singers and her example was soon followed by the likes of Lulu and Sandie Shaw. But there were still fewer counterparts among the men: if you were male, you were in a group. So, at least in the UK, there was a different dimension to the pop music of 1964 than to any era that preceded it. This was especially remarkable given that only a couple of years previously the scene had been dominated by male singers. Cliff Richard, Frankie Vaughan, Danny Williams, Frank Ifield and Mike Sarne had all reached number one, while the big names from America, alongside Elvis, included Roy Orbison, Pat Boone, Bobby Vee, Bobby Darin, Frankie Avalon and Brian Hyland. Most of these were unable to weather the Beat Group storm, and even those who did, like Elvis and Cliff, suddenly looked terminally old-fashioned.

All of the above developments were embodied in a new television show, transmitted for the first time on 1 January 1964. Originally broadcast from Studio A, Dickenson Road, Manchester, *Top Of The Pops* was soon to become the BBC's flagship pop programme and destined to survive the psychedelic, prog rock, punk and rap eras before being laid to rest in July 2006. The line-up for this inaugural edition was telling:

- The Rolling Stones – I Wanna Be Your Man
- Dusty Springfield – I Only Want To Be With You
- The Dave Clark Five – Glad All Over
- The Hollies – Stay
- The Swinging Blue Jeans – Hippy Hippy Shake
- The Beatles – I Want To Hold Your Hand

As we have seen, Liverpool groups were on the wane. Each major British city had now come up with its own equivalent to The Beatles, and London had several pretenders to their throne. So this running-order accurately reflects the direction in which things were going. Two Mersey Beat groups (The Beatles and The Swinging Blue Jeans) and one from

Manchester (The Hollies) make up the Northern contingent – the other three acts all hailed from the capital.

We can also see a movement towards self-penned songs – those performed include the two Lennon and McCartney compositions and Dave Clark and Mike Smith's 'Glad All Over' – and away from covers of American material – just two here: Chan Romero's 'Hippy Hippy Shake' and Maurice Williams and The Zodiacs' 'Stay'. The only sign of the professional songwriter was 'I Only Want To Be With You', composed for Springfield by Mike Hawker and Ivor Raymonde. The inclusion of two debut records (by The Hollies and The Dave Clark Five) and two second hits (by The Swinging Blue Jeans and The Rolling Stones) illustrates a preoccupation with newcomers, and five of the six records are by groups as opposed to solo singers. 'I Only Want To Be With You' was Springfield's first single, but she was easily the most established performer, having initially entered the charts with The Springfields in August 1961. However even she had to defer to The Beatles who as the closing act were firmly top of the bill on *Top of the Pops*.

All of these factors were significant for the British pop music scene of 1964, but perhaps most interesting of all is that the phrase 'I Want To'/ 'I Wanna' appeared in three of the six selections – a coincidence, perhaps, but indicative of the new self-confidence of native performers. This proved well-founded, since by March every record in the UK Top Ten, for the first time ever, was British.

The Beatles spent the evening of New Year's Day playing the Astoria Cinema, Finsbury Park, London. It was exactly two years since they had failed the audition at Decca and the only song from that day still in their repertoire was – appropriately enough, given what had happened to them since – 'Money'. Of the other eight, five were originals, a ratio which corresponded to the content of their most recent album (*With The Beatles,* released in November 1963), where seven of the fourteen tracks were by Lennon and McCartney and one was by George Harrison.

But while their music was progressing, their career had plateaued at the top of British show business, and this was having unfortunate side-effects for their image. The Astoria gig was part of the *Beatles Christmas Show* run which had begun on Christmas Eve and involved the band in routines and sketches in the pantomime tradition. Moreover they had recently taped an appearance on the *Morecambe and Wise Show* in which they spent a fair amount of time fooling around with the popular comedy double-act. In short, they were heading for a livelihood as all-round entertainers. There is no evidence that the band resisted this direction – they almost certainly enjoyed it, especially John Lennon, whose zany sense of humour was never far below the surface. Compared with unruly new bands like The Rolling Stones, however, they were starting to look old before their time.

Yet to Harold Wilson, leader of the Labour Party and would-be Prime Minister, the widening popularity of The Beatles was absolutely no problem. In fact it was the very thing that attracted him to them in the first place. They had an image that was rebellious but not repugnant. Yes, they wore their hair long and made cheeky remarks about the Establishment, but they also wore smart suits and charmed people of every race, age and social class. For every blazing 'Twist And Shout' or 'Money', there was a lyrical 'Taste Of Honey' or 'Till There Was You' – show tunes, film themes, rock and roll, rhythm and blues, country and western, original compositions, it was all there: as panoramic a repertoire as any popular music act had ever had. Associating himself with The Beatles gave Wilson access to that wide community, but even more importantly the loosening of social mores that they were inspiring suggested his left-wing agenda might find favour with the electorate.

Wilson's relationship with The Beatles is graphically illustrated in the short newsreel film of the Twelfth Annual Luncheon of the Variety Club of Great Britain, at which they received Silver Heart awards as the Show Business Personalities of 1963. The event took place on 19 March 1964 at the Dorchester Hotel, Park Lane, London, with Wilson presenting the awards. His speech is a minor masterpiece, wittily mocking the pretentiousness of music criticism and poking fun at The Beatles and at himself – for using them to gain votes. Thus, subtly, he disarmed his detractors yet at the same time implying a strong bond of familiarity between himself and the band.

> There were attempts recently by a certain leader of a certain party – wild horses wouldn't drag his name from me – to involve our friends The Beatles in politics. And all I could say with great sadness as a Merseyside Member of Parliament, which I am, was that whatever other arguments there may be, I must ask, "Is nothing sacred when this sort of thing can happen?" So to keep out of politics … I'm sure The Times music correspondent spoke for all of us when he said of our friends The Beatles that, "Harmonically it is one of their most intriguing with its changes of pentatonic clusters."

At times he comes close to overplaying his hand, with the repetition of 'our friends The Beatles' and the over-deliberate naming of each member of the band as they come to collect their awards – 'George, there's yours', 'Now Paul', etc. – but he is saved by The Beatles' own one-liners, two of which name-check him:

> [George Harrison]: It's very nice indeed to get one each, because we usually have a bit of trouble cutting them in four!
> [Paul McCartney]: I still think you should have given one to good old Mr Wilson.
> [John Lennon]: Thanks for the purple hearts!★ [Ringo Starr]: Silver, silver! [John]: Sorry about that, Harold!

Anyone present at the award ceremony, or watching it on TV – it was shown by the BBC at 10.30 pm the following day – would be left in no doubt as to the impression of intimacy it created between Wilson and The Beatles. Wilson's leadership was already characterised by, in Ben Pimlott's

---

★Purple hearts, in addition to being a US military decoration, were an anti-depressant, recreational drug (dexamyl)

words, 'an image of possibility and aspiration'; furthermore, his 'lack of any kind of social snobbery had an appeal at a time when social attitudes were going through a period of mutation' (*op. cit.,* p.266). The Beatles had been a primary force in that process and so it was a perfect match.

> The fashion was progressive in the sense of being questioning and irreverent, and against the authority of Church, school, social hierarchy and government. It affected attitudes, not just to sex, censorship and popular music, but also to privilege, social class and opportunity. "You either rode with it or you got out of the way," recalls a former Wilson aide. "It was a time of activity and movement – you just could not hold it back." Partly because of the Beatles, Liverpool was at the heart of it. Wilson, a Liverpool MP, felt it like an avalanche and allowed himself to be swept along ... Yet he sensed (in a way that his far more modish predecessor would never have done) that the tide could be harnessed to his advantage. (*op. cit.,* p. 268)

By the time of the Variety Club luncheon, the harnessing was well under way.

★ ★ ★ ★ ★

The first third of 1964 was arguably the most productive period in The Beatles' whole career. It began with confirmation that they were indeed at the pinnacle of what British entertainment had to offer: the last ten nights of their Christmas show and an appearance on *Sunday Night At The London Palladium* for which they received £1000. After that it was all new ground. First off was a trip to France where they played over 40 shows in eighteen days at the Olympia Theatre, Paris. In spite of a mixed reception from the French public, the trip was memorable, for not only did The Beatles record their second biggest-selling single, 'Can't Buy Me Love', at the Pathé Marconi Studios, but they also learned that what was to become their all-time best seller had reached number one in the USA – 'I Want To Hold Your Hand'.

Back in September 1963, Brian Epstein had encouraged Lennon and McCartney to write a song with America in mind, and this was it. Unlike much of their output it was a genuine 50-50 effort, both in terms of the composition and the vocals, and they went for maximum impact. Driven along by handclaps, it shifts swiftly from phase to phase, with unexpected key changes and textural contrasts. Lyrically, it was simple stuff, but as a piece of music it was all action. As Ian MacDonald has written, 'Apart from ending with the studio exploding, they could hardly have hit their prospective American audience with more in two-and-a-half minutes' (*op. cit.,* p.89).

It was also the antidote for the national depression occasioned by President Kennedy's death, its freshness and energy promising a new start for the new year of 1964. The single provoked a reaction bordering on hysteria: Mark Lewisohn records that

> After just three days, [it] had sold 250,000 copies across the States, by 10 January sales had topped one million, by 13 January it was selling 10,000 copies an hour in New York City alone. (*The Complete Beatles Chronicle*, p.136)

One fourteen-year-old New Yorker caught up in the excitement was Paul Gambaccini, now an eminent music broadcaster and nicknamed 'The Professor of Pop'. We can safely assume he was speaking for a generation when he stated on the documentary *The Beatles Decade* (UK TV), '"I Want To Hold Your Hand" – I heard it and my life was changed.' Indeed, the impact of The Beatles, first appreciated on an international scale with that record and their subsequent American appearances, was such that nearly 50 years later the reverberations are still being felt. Bruce Springsteen, one of the most artistically and commercially successful rock stars of all time, stated recently, 'The first record that I ever learned was a record called "Twist And Shout", and if it wasn't for John Lennon we'd all be in some place very different tonight' (*the soul-shack.blogspot.com*).

The validity of this claim is evident when you consider not only the vast number of bands inspired by The Beatles, either to copy their music or use it as platform for developing their own style, but also the wide cross-section of society in general which continues to enjoy listening to their records, young people included. On 9 September 2009, MTV Games published *The Beatles: Rock Band,* a music video game which simulates playing in the group. At the time of writing it had sold over two million units.

The Beatles' music continues to be popular with those who influence opinion and behaviour: writers, artists from a variety of disciplines, business tycoons, professors, politicians and sports stars. On the long-running British radio show, *Desert Island Discs,* celebrity guests are invited to select the eight records they would wish to take with them to the eponymous island. A sample of those who have recently chosen Beatles recordings includes film director Franco Zeffirelli ('Yesterday'), painter Jack Vettriano ('Twist And Shout'), composers Howard Goodall ('We Can Work It Out') and Peter Maxwell-Davies ('Yesterday'), novelists Stephen King ('She Loves You'), Anthony Horowitz ('Eleanor Rigby') and Paulo Coelho ('Because'), broadcaster Sir David Frost ('The Long And Winding Road'), ballet dancer Darcey Bussell ('Love Me Do'), comedians Billy Connolly ('Across The Universe') and Sanjeev Bhaskar ('A Day In The Life'), academics Kay Davies ('Let It Be') and Baroness Haleh Afshar ('Yellow Submarine'), playwright David Edgar ('Strawberry Fields Forever'), businessmen George Davies ('Do You Want To Know A Secret') and Bill Cullen ('She Loves You'), boxer George Foreman ('All You Need Is Love'!) and UK political heavyweights from the left corner (the first black woman to become an MP, Diane Abbott – 'Things We Said Today'), the right corner (Conservative London Mayor, Boris Johnson – 'Here Comes The Sun') and somewhere in the middle – former Prime Minister, Tony Blair ('In My Life').

It is significant that, of all these records, only two castaways chose the same: 'Yesterday' and 'She Loves You'. This suggests a scale of appeal that transcends the impact, however great, of a few acknowledged classics, and could not be said of any other music act. Traversing the *Desert Island Discs* selections, one finds the same records again and again – David Bowie's 'Space Oddity', The Beach Boys' 'Good Vibrations', 'Nessun Dorma', the Theme from *Schindler's List*. Only Bob Dylan comes anywhere near rivalling The Beatles for ubiquity and variety of choice.

This appeal, while centred on the music, was of a complex nature, relying as much on the attractiveness of The Beatles as people as on their records. Although each member of the band was increasingly seen as a personality in his own right and received individual fan mail, there was something too in the way they presented themselves as a band – for example the indelible image of Harrison and McCartney harmonising behind Lennon's vocals. Other groups had leaders at the forefront – in The Beatles, everyone could take a leading role.

They also exuded a collective sex appeal. In her excellent examination of women and popular culture, *Where The Girls Are*, Susan Douglas distinguishes The Beatles from their predecessors:

> First of all, the Beatles were good – really good – and they took their female audience seriously … they so perfectly fused the "masculine" and "feminine" strains of rock 'n' roll in their music, their appearance and their style of performing. It wasn't just their long hair, or Paul's eyelashes, the heels on their boots, or the puckish way they clowned for the camera. Without ever saying so explicitly, the Beatles acknowledged that there was masculinity and femininity in all of us, and that blurring the artificial boundaries between the two might be a big relief … Electric guitar riffs, driving bass and drums, and John's gravelly voice led into falsetto cries of "ooh" and "yeah", suggesting that male sexuality wasn't so threatening, female sexuality was perfectly normal, and the two could exist together harmoniously … When they recorded their own versions of girl group songs like "Please Mister Postman" and "Chains," they showed that boys could find themselves in exactly the same spot as girls and feel just as trapped and helpless. (p. 116-117)

This analysis goes some way to explaining The Beatles' sway over the young male audience, too. Their songs betokened an easy intimacy between the sexes, accessible to young men in a way that the macho male stereotype embodied by Elvis was not. Suddenly Presley and his ilk were wrong-footed and outmoded and it is tempting to wonder whether – aside from his resentment of their popularity – it was also his revulsion for their relative androgyny that caused him to work secretly for their deportation from the US.

Whatever the case, Douglas's perceptive comments show how The Beatles' music represented a shift in gender relations and a breakdown of the old polarised certainties. It was only a short step from there to thoughts of women's liberation.

★ ★ ★ ★ ★

The Beatles' first visit to the USA lasted from Friday 7 to Saturday 22 February 1964 and was a sensation from the outset. On the ninth they performed live on the *Ed Sullivan Show*, the country's most prestigious entertainment programme, an appearance that had been negotiated by Epstein some months before at a reduced fee, provided The Beatles topped the bill. It is impossible not to admire the band's cool as they swung into the opening number, 'All My Loving', in front of what was then the largest television audience in American history at around 73 million, or 40% of the population. As Harrison related, 'Later they said there was no reported crime – even the criminals had a rest for ten minutes when we were on' (*The Beatles Anthology* – TV series) This was a measure of success that no-one could match, either then or now.

Other footage from the tour is equally enthralling, including a roaring version of 'She Loves You' powered by Starr's supercharged drumming (Washington Coliseum, 11 February – their live concert debut) and 'This Boy' from the Sullivan Show in Miami on the sixteenth, with Lennon, McCartney and Harrison clustered around one microphone. Overall, what comes across is the sheer energy and effervescence of the band without any compromise on musical quality. The reception from the fans was nothing short of ecstatic; when they played Carnegie Hall on the twelfth, 362 additional policemen had to be drafted in to control the crowd.

The impact of this visit was incalculable in musical, sociological and political terms, yet judging from interviews they gave following their arrival back in the UK on 22 February, the whole experience had been, in the band's eyes, not much more than an enjoyable holiday and a good laugh.

Interviewer: What did you most like about the trip, Ringo?

Ringo [other Beatles giggling in the background]: Oh, I just loved all of it. The sun, you know – I didn't know what it meant till I went over there.

Interviewer: Don't you get it up in Liverpool?

Ringo: No, they've finished up there – they've cut it out. [More laughter from the band].

Interviewer: Did you ever have a chance, John, to just get away on your own without anybody recognising you?

John: Yes, we borrowed a couple of millionaire's houses.

Interviewer: You could afford to buy a couple of millionaire's houses, couldn't you?

John: We'd sooner borrow them, it's cheaper.

Interviewer: I hear anyway that the four of you will be millionaires by the end of the year.

George: Oh, that's nice. [More laughter]

The British media, however, saw it differently and the BBC took the unprecedented step of inserting coverage of their touchdown at London Airport and an interview with anchorman David Coleman into the hallowed Saturday afternoon sports programme, *Grandstand*. There was also extensive coverage on the radio and in newspapers. The most indelible images remain those of the screaming crowds of girls against the backdrop of the band emerging from the BEA plane (when flying out to join the others in Paris the previous month, Ringo had held up a sign with the letters TLES next to the airline's logo).

Immediately after their return from the USA, The Beatles started recording the songs to accompany their first feature film, *A Hard Day's Night,* which they began shooting on 2 March 1964.

The history of 20th century popular culture is littered with examples of outstanding songs appearing in lightweight shows and films. The plot of *Anything Goes* (1934) is, for example, entirely insubstantial – not something one can say about the Cole Porter compositions it contains which include 'You're The Top', 'I Get A Kick Out Of You' and the title number. The now barely-remembered *Paris*, from three years earlier, features his immortal 'Let's Do It' while the possibly yet more obscure *Garrick Gaieties* of 1925 includes Richard Rodgers and Lorenz Hart's magnificent 'Manhattan'. In fact, during the early period of the Broadway musical, songs were almost incidental to the plot – apart from isolated examples such as *Show Boat* (1927), by Oscar Hammerstein and Jerome Kern, and the Gershwin brothers' *Of Thee I Sing* (1931), storyline and songs were not fully integrated until 1943's *Oklahoma!,* by Rodgers and Hammerstein.

Their good work was undone by the rock and roll films of the 1950s which represented a return to musicals as promotional vehicles, this time for both songs *and* artists. Crucially important in exporting the music internationally in the era before world tours, they now have period charm, enhanced by the pop stars' risible attempts at acting.

A Hard Day's Night sits firmly in this genre. The effort to portray The Beatles as lovable northern mop-tops, given the intelligence, sophistication and power of their music, now comes over as patronising and dated, though typical of the way in which, in early 1964, adults thought they knew all the answers. The kindest thing one can say of the film is that the innocence of the narrative is to a limited extent matched by the music. 'If I Fell' is an especially interesting example. In effect, the song is a speech by the protagonist to his girlfriend, which so accurately reflects the structure and pattern of everyday language that it could easily be read as a piece of prose. Despite constant, subtle chord changes, there are no great melodic leaps, reinforcing the continuity of the discourse and making for a song – and a record – that, in its style, is no less than perfect.

'If I Fell' was written by John Lennon and recorded on Thursday 27 February 1964. In many ways, the equivalent song by Paul McCartney was 'Things We Said Today', but as this was made for the *Hard Day's Night* album rather than film and not taped until June it will be discussed below. 'Can't Buy Me Love' was used in the film but had been recorded during The Beatles' visit to Paris. Its dramatic opening with unaccompanied vocal, bouncy beat and jazz influence exemplifies what Ian MacDonald (*op. cit.,* p.94) describes as 'The Beatles' ability to be two contradictory things at once – comfortably safe and exhilaratingly strange'. It also includes a fine guitar solo by George Harrison that shows signs of breaking free from the influence of Carl Perkins, the most recent instance of which had been 'All My Loving'.

The eventual 'B' side of 'Can't Buy Me Love', released on 20 March, was 'You Can't Do That', the first song to be recorded after the band's return from the USA. This was another groundbreaking record with an aggression recalling that of 'Money'. This time, however, it was no cover version, but a Lennon original, as worldly-wise and malicious as 'If I Fell' is naive and tender. The searing vocal is matched by an intense, thrilling guitar solo by Lennon himself. It was not included in the film, however – presumably because its naked belligerence did not fit the upbeat mood. Such was the concentrated creativity of the band at this time that at the same session, on 25 February (Harrison's 21st birthday), they recorded two more classics, 'I Should Have Known Better', a medium-paced workout with Dylanesque harmonica, and the much-covered 'And I Love Her' – a poignant acoustic ballad with Harrison on twelve-string guitar and Starr on bongos (though a later version was chosen for issue).

The other three songs written for the film were 'Tell Me Why', 'I'm Happy Just To Dance With You' and the title track. The first is an uninhibited rocker which gives Starr the chance to show off the thunderous drumming of his live performances, the second a showcase for Harrison, whose singing was becoming incrementally more expressive. 'A Hard Day's Night' itself, the very last piece to be recorded for the film, exhibits the confidence of the whole band, and that of their producer,

George Martin. The opening chord hangs in the air, a pregnant moment before the onslaught of another all-out performance with a passionate, blues-influenced vocal from Lennon and more ferocious drumming from Starr. Harrison's jangly guitar sound is said to have inspired The Byrds, yet as we have seen, it was also employed by The Searchers.

Such a collection of songs would grace any film, but there was more quality to come for the tie-in album, *A Hard Day's Night*. 'Things We Said Today' was the standout, and indeed remains among the finest of all Beatles records. Again, the opening is arresting: Lennon's acoustic guitar flourish and Starr's punchy drumming give the song its urgency, despite the reflective lyrics. Like 'If I Fell', it projects beyond the present into the future of a relationship, but is far less tentative. This time, the suggestion is that the lovers will take strength from the words they are now sharing – a more subtle conception indicating McCartney's growing maturity as a songwriter. His singing is also masterly, switching from romantic musing to a more assertive stance in the middle eight and varying his vocal timbre accordingly.

In contrast, Lennon's 'When I Get Home' is hard-hitting but exultant throughout, the protagonist of 'You Can't Do That' in positive mood. 'Any Time At All' is another Lennon *tour de force*: rather like McCartney on 'Things We Said Today', he shows the two sides of his character, restrained and persuasive in the verse and unrestrained, almost desperate, in the chorus. The remaining songs on the album are also by Lennon, making a total of ten of his compositions out of the thirteen tracks. 'I'll Cry Instead' has echoes of Carl Perkins and despite its brevity creates an impact, while 'I'll Be Back' is unusual both in structure and lyrics, signalling a departure from the straightforward conceits of the band's music to date.

* * * * *

Much has been made, justifiably, of George Martin's positive influence on The Beatles, but in reality it was the partnership between him and the band that led to the huge success of their records. From their early days in the studio they were assertive enough to make their opinions known to him. As we have already seen, they vetoed the release of 'How Do You Do It'; they were only interested in their own songs. Martin didn't like the proffered follow-up to 'Love Me Do', 'Please Please Me' – he felt it was too slow and dreary. However on listening to it again he judged it to be worth another try, if it were pepped up a little. In this way the seeds of mutual respect were sown, both parties listening to the other and seeing the good in each other's views. It was a relationship not unlike that between Lennon and McCartney, whereby the one made constructive suggestions about the other's songs and moderated any excesses. To find such an understanding between artist and record producer was rare indeed, and certainly unparalleled in British pop music. One of the main reasons for this was that The Beatles had their own material and therefore something to market, but much credit should also go to Martin who, as an experienced producer, fourteen years senior to the eldest Beatle and several rungs above them in the class hierarchy, could easily have imposed his will with impunity. Certainly there were many precedents in contemporary pop music for the autocratic approach; Phil Spector, for example, was notoriously authoritarian – a fact to which *his* success is frequently attributed.

But in 1964 it was the Beatles-Martin methodology which became the model, signalling a change that was momentous not only for the recording industry but arguably for society as a whole. By listening to the band and letting them have their say, Martin was, albeit unintentionally, sending out a message that young people should be taken seriously. For their part The Beatles were reinforcing what the upward trajectory of their career had been implying all along: that youth was in the ascendancy. In fact this period of pop music reflects the delicate but perfect balance between the producer and the produced, harking back to the time when musicians were tantamount to ciphers but at the same time anticipating an era when artists would have full control over all aspects of their work and its promotion. This meeting of the minds, the blend of raw ideas and wisdom born of experience, resulted in a year of incomparable fecundity for pop music.

The album *A Hard Day's Night*, completed on 23 April and released on 10 July, encapsulated those virtues. Its clean, warm immediacy is a credit to Martin's skills and the more unconventional sounds – Harrison's twelve-string guitar, Starr's percussion and Lennon's harmonica – are integrated imperceptibly. All thirteen tracks are original compositions, a first for The Beatles and consequently for any British group and an inspiration for a new generation of songwriters such as Ray Davies and Pete Townshend.

In the US, following the furore of their first foray, The Beatles' influence was taking root and in time would grow to put almost all American pop music in the shade. The exceptions were to be found in African-American idioms (to be discussed in Chapter 5) and in the efforts of a few independently-minded writers and producers, all of whom had begun operations before The Beatles' arrival on the scene.

Phil Spector's innovations were referred to in Chapter 1 and, although he had peaked the previous year with The Crystals' 'Da Doo Ron Ron' and 'Then He Kissed Me', 'The Boy I'm Gonna Marry' by Darlene Love and The Ronettes' 'Be My Baby' and 'Baby I Love You', 1964 yielded two of his finest productions (and arguably two of the best records of the 1960s). '(Walking) In The Rain' was written by Barry Mann, Cynthia Weil and Spector himself and was as artful a song as ever emerged from the Brill Building. The Ronettes – lead singer Ronnie Bennett, her sister Estelle and their cousin, Nedra Talley – convey its innocent fantasising to perfection:

> I want him and I need him
> And some day, some way, I'll meet him
> He'll be kind of shy, and real good looking too
> And I'll be certain he's my guy by the things he'll like to do,
> Like walking in the rain

The record starts with a clap of thunder, repeated at various junctures, driven along by booming bass and percussion and interspersed with horn riffs and clanging chimes, suggesting the walks through the storm are the prelude to wedding bells.

Even more dramatic was another Mann/Weil/Spector composition, The Righteous Brothers' 'You've Lost That Lovin' Feelin'', released on 6 December 1964. From a gloomy, doom-laden opening, it builds to a frenzied conclusion in front of an intense sonic backdrop, integrating vibraphone and bongo drums with a string section and heavy guitar and bass textures. As Richard Williams puts it,

> It finally created that "wall of sound" that Spector had been looking for. Only two or three years after the record's appearance did fans start hearing the separate instruments: before that, the track existed as an undifferentiated mass of sound, impossible to break down and analyse into separate components. (*op. cit.*, p.71)

Other than his work with Ike and Tina Turner in 1966 and The Beatles in 1970, there were to be few other high spots in Spector's career. By way of compensation, his epic productions inspired The Beach Boys' Brian Wilson to create some of the most innovatory pop music of the late 1960s, including the album *Pet Sounds*.

In 1964, however, The Beach Boys were in transition: having established surf rock as a lightweight but modish genre, heavily indebted to Chuck Berry, they were now in the process of making it more original in concept and execution. *Shut Down Volume Two*, which came out on 2 March, showed only minor progress, despite containing 'Fun, Fun, Fun', their most irresistibly hedonistic recording to date.

The pivotal album was *All Summer Long*; released on 13 July, its opening track, 'I Get Around', was a metaphor for Wilson's impulse to break with the idiom he had created and move into different artistic territory. This 'new place' would admit the influence of Phil Spector and The Beatles but centre on Wilson's unique pop sensibility of which the morose 'In My Room' from the previous year had been a foretaste – essentially a shift from Californian optimism to reflection, doubt and uncertainty. Early signals permeate *All Summer Long*. On 'Wendy', for example, there is incomprehension that a long-term relationship has gone sour and, despite its jolly demeanour, the title track is tinged with melancholy, marking as it does the end of a summer of fun and youthful pursuits. It is almost as if a line is being drawn between innocence and experience, an impression reinforced by the release on 24 August of the single 'When I Grow Up (To Be A Man)': here, the protagonist considers how he will look back on the present and wonders if he will have regrets. Though Wilson wasn't to know it, this group of songs can now be seen to symbolise the pop music of 1964 as a whole, a music beginning to metamorphose from simple entertainment to something akin to an art form.

Over on the East Coast, the old rules were still being applied with great craftsmanship. The output of songwriter Carole King and her partner Gerry Goffin, for instance, continued unabated. Already responsible for a string of hits including 'Will You Love Me Tomorrow' (The Shirelles, 1961), 'Chains' (The Cookies, 1962, covered by The Beatles on *Please Please Me*), 'The Loco-Motion' (Little Eva, 1962), 'It Might As Well Rain Until September' (King herself, 1962) and 'Up On The Roof' (The Drifters, 1963), the duo had a vintage year in 1964.

Among their best songs were three vehicles for female singers: Betty Everett's gospel-inflected 'I Can't Hear You No More', later recorded by both Dusty Springfield and Helen Reddy; Maxine Brown's 'Oh No Not My Baby', a hit the following year for Manfred Mann and covered by Springfield, Aretha Franklin and Linda Ronstadt; and the gently insouciant 'I'm Into Something Good' by Cookies vocalist Earl-Jean McCrea but better known as the first hit by Herman's Hermits. They also provided The Tokens with the plaintive 'He's In Town' which The Rockin' Berries converted into a UK number three.

Goffin and King were archetypical Brill Building composers, part of a tradition of hit songwriting at that New York address that began in the late 1930s. By 1964, the term was being stretched to include other Broadway locations, but the product was still the same: clever, instantly memorable pop songs that captured – and occasionally dictated – the mood of the age. Jerry Leiber and Mike Stoller had worked in and around the building for some time; their CV dated back fifteen years and boasted a portfolio of compositions such as 'Hound Dog', 'Kansas City', 'Jailhouse Rock', 'Yakety Yak' and, in 1963, the sweeping 'On Broadway' by The Drifters, co-written with Barry Mann and Cynthia Weil and featuring a guitar break by Phil Spector. In 1964, their output was less prolific and less commercially successful; it did, however, include the compelling ballad, 'His Kiss', by Betty Harris, and, in collaboration with Bert Russell (real name: Bert Berns, of whom more shortly) and Atlantic Records boss Ahmet Ertegun, Solomon Burke's 'You Can't Love 'Em All' in which Spanish Harlem meets Southern soul.

Leiber and Stoller were, in fact, devoting their energies to Red Bird, the record company they formed with George Goldner in early 1964. They found success immediately with Red Bird 001, The Dixie Cups' 'Chapel Of Love', which entered the *Billboard* chart on 16 May and stayed at number one for three weeks. It was composed by Phil Spector, Jeff Barry and Ellie Greenwich, but presented a contrast to Spector's highly-wrought productions with, for example, the Ronettes, who also recorded it: The Dixie Cups' version has a relaxed, open feel, redolent of the trio's New Orleans origins.

But it was Red Bird 008 that really signalled a new direction for girl-group records. 'Remember (Walking In The Sand)' was written by George Morton, later nicknamed 'Shadow' by Goldner because of his propensity for disappearing from view. Seeking a job in the music business, Morton had visited his former girlfriend Greenwich at the Brill Building and was asked by Barry, her current partner, what he did for a living. Improvising, Morton replied that he was a songwriter. When challenged by Barry to prove it, he went away and composed 'Remember'. Hiring a hitherto unknown female vocal group, The Shangri-Las (two pairs of sisters named Weiss and Ganser), he produced a demo that impressed Barry – and Red Bird – sufficiently to lead to its release: the record made the *Billboard* chart on 5 September, ultimately reaching number five. Despite its brevity it is a conglomeration of arresting and unconventional features which nevertheless cohere to create an utterly convincing whole. After a two-note piano introduction we are straight into the narrative:

Seems like the other day
My baby went away
He went away 'cross the sea

It's been two years ago
Since that's when my baby go [*sic*]
And then this letter came for me

He said that we were through
He'd found somebody new
Oh, let me think, let me think
What can I do?

There the strident, full-on production stops dead while Mary Weiss intones, 'Oh no, Oh no, Oh no, no, no, no, no', and gives way to a new melody, and tempo, in which piano murmurings, handclaps and seagull sound effects provide the only accompaniment:

Remember: walking in the sand
Remember: walking hand in hand
Remember: the night was so exciting
Remember: his lips were so inviting

The dramatic shift in orchestration and atmosphere underline the contrast between the singer's present anguish and past happiness, but it is the repeated, almost whispered 'Remember's by the rest of the group that really twist the knife and give the record its Gothic, almost sinister quality.

The follow-up, 'Leader Of The Pack', this time including Barry and Greenwich alongside Morton in the composer credits, was recorded in

July, hit the *Billboard* chart in October and became US number one in November. With its motorcycle noises, spoken passages and epic sound, it represented a high point for the East Coast girl-group genre. It also marked its end; the epicentre for female vocal groups was now Detroit.

Meanwhile other Brill Building inhabitants continued to resist the tidal wave of Beatlemania. The well-established partnership of Doc Pomus and Mort Shuman, for example, came up with the powerful ballad 'Gonna Cry 'Til My Tears Run Dry' for Irma Thomas (not a hit until the following year) and 'Viva Las Vegas', the latest in a string of compositions for Elvis Presley. But they too, were becoming less productive: Shuman began to spend more time in Europe, co-writing 'Little Children' for Billy J Kramer and The Dakotas, a UK number one in March. In addition to the Spector-produced classics noted above, Barry Mann and Cynthia Weil had success with the jaunty 'Saturday Night At The Movies' by The Drifters and Gene Pitney's 'I'm Gonna Be Strong', a Top Ten hit on both sides of the Atlantic.

The accomplishments of Burt Bacharach and Hal David were as impressive as any. The pair had met in the Brill Building in 1957 and within a year were writing hits like 'The Story Of My Life' (Marty Robbins, and later Michael Holliday) and 'Magic Moments' (Perry Como), back-to-back UK number ones in February-April 1958. In 1964 they exploited the bossa nova craze, sparked off the previous year by albums like *Getz/Gilberto*, to fashion two crucial compositions, 'Always Something There To Remind Me' by Lou Johnson – a UK number one in October for Sandie Shaw who followed it up two months later with another bossa nova, Chris Andrews's 'Girl Don't Come' – and Dionne Warwick's 'Walk On By'. In both, the cool melody contrasts effectively with the simmering heat of the vocals, a formula repeated later in the year for Warwick's 'You'll Never Get To Heaven' and Johnson's 'A Message To Martha', covered in the UK by Adam Faith.

But the biggest hits for Bacharach and David in 1964 all had earlier origins. 'Anyone Who Had A Heart' was written in 1963 and became a US Top Ten hit for Warwick in January. Mersey Beat singer Cilla Black immediately recorded a cover version, produced by George Martin, which reached number one on the UK chart at the end of February, stayed for three weeks and launched her career. Another of their extravagant ballads, 'I Just Don't Know What To Do With Myself', was the 'B' side of Tommy Hunt's 1962 single, 'And I Never Knew', but lay dormant until Dusty Springfield took it to number three on the UK chart in the summer of 1964. While Bacharach and David were to become permanent fixtures on the pop scene for many years to come, it was the work of Bert Berns that was to have greater impact on the development of rock music, and we can date this influence from the year 1964.

Bertrand Russell Berns was born in the Bronx on 8 November 1929. Before working in the Brill Building he had been a dancer in the nightclubs of Havana, and brought his knowledge of Latin American styles to compositions such as The Jarmels' 'A Little Bit Of Soap' and 'Twist And Shout' in 1962 which he wrote with Phil Medley under the name Bert Russell. Although The Isley Brothers had the original US hit, The Beatles' version of 'Twist And Shout' was the one to gain immortality as the climax of the album *Please Please Me* and a fixture in the band's stage act for three years. Also in 1962 he wrote and produced 'Tell Her' for Gil Hamilton (even if later versions by The Exciters and Billie Davis became more successful) and 'Cry To Me' for Solomon Burke, an early example of what was to become known as soul music: it was almost inevitable that Burke should join Atlantic, the premier soul label, the following year.

1964 was a golden year for Berns as both composer and producer Among the many highlights were:

- Writing (with Solomon Burke and Jerry Wexler) Burke's seminal 'Everybody Needs Somebody To Love', a boisterous, gospel-influenced number, covered by The Rolling Stones, Wilson Pickett and The Blues Brothers
- Producing 'Mo Jo Hannah' by Esther Phillips, a much sought-after single among the Northern Soul fraternity

- Writing (with Wes Farrell) The Vibrations' 'My Girl Sloopy' (with a Latin flavour reminiscent of 'Twist And Shout') – as 'Hang On Sloopy' this would be an international hit for the McCoys in 1965
- Producing 'You Can Count On Me' for the veteran Roy Hamilton, a chart-topper in the 1950s with 'You'll Never Walk Alone' and 'Unchained Melody'
- Recording (as 'The Mustangs') 'Baby Let Me Take You Home', covered by The Animals as their first single
- Producing 'Saturday Night At The Movies', 'Under The Boardwalk' and 'I Don't Want To Go On Without You' for The Drifters, co-writing the latter with Wexler
- Writing and – during a visit to London in October – producing Lulu's 'Here Comes The Night'.

In terms of what it led on to, however, his most significant achievement was the record he produced during that same visit to London for the Belfast band, Them: 'Baby Please Don't Go' epitomised the nascent music soon to be known as rock. For the follow-up, they chose 'Here Comes The Night', which reached number two on the UK singles chart in spring 1965.

Together with Jerry Wexler and Ahmet and Nesuhi Ertegun, Berns went on to form Bang Records, releasing material such as 'Hang On Sloopy', Van Morrison's 'Brown Eyed Girl' and his own composition for The Strangeloves, 'I Want Candy', the Bow Wow Wow version of which was used in Sofia Coppola's 2006 film, *Marie Antoinette*. He also founded the Shout label as a vehicle for R&B artists; one of these was Aretha Franklin's elder sister, Erma, for whom he wrote (with Jerry Ragovoy) and produced the classic 'Piece Of My Heart' in 1967. Sadly, it was to be one of his final triumphs, for Bert Berns died of a heart attack on 30 December of that year, aged only 38.

★ ★ ★ ★ ★

Figures such as Berns, Morton and Spector were old-school producers who exercised total control in the studio and often wrote and arranged the material that was recorded. George Martin, as we have seen, was more democratic: his concessions to The Beatles were symbolic of a widening acknowledgement of young people and youth culture.

The Labour Party manifesto for the 1964 General Election, for example, was quite explicit on the subject:

The Youth Service will be developed with grants for youth centres, swimming pools, coffee bars and other facilities.

Most young people, and particularly girls, are still denied adequate training at work or release for further education.
(*Let's Go With Labour For The New Britain*, subsections – *Leisure Services and Modern Social Services*)

As the second extract shows, with its allusion to sex discrimination and the embryonic women's liberation movement, the manifesto took on some of the wider social and political issues directly relevant – and of particular interest – to young people:

[A Labour Government] will legislate against racial discrimination and incitement in public places.

The time is opportune for a new break through in the disarmament negotiations.
(Subsections – *The End Of Colonisation* and *New Prospects For Peace*)

The latter had been a matter of great concern among young adults for some years. The Campaign for Nuclear Disarmament (CND) had been formed in 1958, supported by philosophers, clergy, playwrights and other representatives of the higher echelons of British cultural life. It also attracted increasing numbers of students to its annual marches from

Aldermaston, site of the Atomic Weapons Research Establishment, to London. By 1961, numbers on the march had grown to over 100,000 and co-ordination was becoming difficult. Two years later, the Committee of 100, who believed in non-violent direct action, influenced a large group of marchers to split off and demonstrate at Regional Seat of Government Number 6 (RSG 6). Among them was the feminist writer Sheila Rowbotham:

> The leaders of CND and Committee of 100 were locked in conflict over tactics and strategy. Peggy Duff stood with a loudspeaker as we approached some woods near Reading. "Straight on for lunch", bellowed the portly, grey-haired toughie, who was such an efficient organizer. This time, however, about 1,000 marchers weren't listening … Before long local CND groups were excitedly clambering through the countryside scouting around for their local Regional Seats of Government. Signs were erected announcing their whereabouts and they had become a joke. As for me, this début in political activism was to ruin me for committee meetings and points of order for ever more. It was to be networks and movements which drew me rather than "proper" politics.
>
> (*Promise Of A Dream: Remembering The Sixties*, p. 68-69)

The schism within CND meant that the Aldermaston March of Easter 1964 was a much-reduced event and it never really recovered. But its legacy was unmistakeable: young people – mainly, it must be said from the middle classes – were now becoming actively involved in politics. A further spur was the news from across the Atlantic that President Johnson was expanding the War in Vietnam. Though the creation of the Great Society was his personal priority, Johnson wanted the War, which had begun nine years earlier, drawn to a swift conclusion and escalation seemed to him the best solution (in time it became his *only* solution). This policy had the effect, as we shall see in Chapter 3, of galvanising American students; in the UK, it seemed to be further proof that the world was being put at risk by super-power warmongers. In this context, the disarmament initiatives proposed in the Labour manifesto were readily welcomed.

Wilson himself wanted an end to the war. He had already demonstrated his pacifist credentials in 1951 by resigning from his post as President of the Board of Trade, and hence from the Cabinet, preferring 'to see a cut in defence expenditure rather than a scheme of charges under the National Health Service' (Cabinet Papers CAB 128). Nevertheless he was conscious of Britain's special relationship with the USA. He was to resolve this as Prime Minister by casting himself in the role of international peace-maker; perhaps that was what he was hinting at in the 1964 manifesto with the statement:

[The Labour Government] will work actively to bring Communist China to its proper place in the United Nations.

(Subsection – *New Prospects For Peace*)

Other parts of the manifesto promised a better deal for the arts:

[The Labour Government] will give much more generous support to the Arts Council, the theatre, orchestras, concert halls, museums and art galleries … [it will] encourage and support independent film makers for both the cinema and television.

(Subsection – *Leisure Services*)

Given Wilson's interest in the film industry, as described in Chapter 1, the latter provision was hardly surprising. More significant, however, was the juxtaposition of – and lack of discrimination between – high and popular culture. This caught exactly the mood of a period when the two were coming closer together, whether through the Pop Art of Andy Warhol and David Hockney; the Op Art (a term first used in print by *Time* magazine in October 1964) of Bridget Riley; plays like Shelagh Delaney's *A Taste Of Honey*; novels (and later films) like *Saturday Night*

And Sunday Morning by Alan Sillitoe; and television dramas like *The Wednesday Play* and the soap opera *Coronation Street*, said to be Wilson's favourite programme. While not specifically aimed at young people, this clause in the manifesto nevertheless indicated that Labour, and Wilson, were in tune with the latest trends in art forms that attracted them.

Of course there was a great deal in the manifesto that was not specifically youth orientated – the heavy emphasis on science and technology, for example. Neither did it engage with the moral issues that were the subject of much contemporary debate, in particular, homosexuality, divorce and abortion. Perhaps Wilson felt it was better to avoid controversy at a time when the public was only just recovering from the Profumo scandal of the previous year; there was, in any case, plenty of reforming zeal in the programme as it stood.

On 15 September 1964 the Prime Minister, Sir Alec Douglas-Home, asked the Queen to dissolve Parliament, thus beginning the run-up to Election Day – exactly one month later. The campaign was characterised by some colourful and eccentric speeches from both major parties, notably by Quintin Hogg for the Conservatives and George Brown for Labour. The Tories even made a record, a 45 rpm flexidisc entitled 'Songs For Swinging Voters' – a first for both pop and politics in the UK. Side One consisted of three tracks: 'John Citizen', a brief introduction to the Election; 'Nationalisation Nightmare', delivered in a Peter Sellers-ish mock Cockney accent ; and 'Four Jolly Labourmen' – James Callaghan, Richard Crossman, Brown and Wilson – which satirised their propensity for public spending and disunity on defence policy. Side Two begins with 'One Man Band', a dig at Wilson and his relationship with The Beatles, followed by 'Poor Old Jo' (Grimond, the Leader of the Liberal Party), set to the tune of Stephen Foster's 'Poor Old Joe'/'Old Black Joe' and containing the lines

Whoever wins, sure I'll be down the drain

and

I hear the Gallup pollsters sighing, "Poor old Jo".

Finally, there is a reprise of 'John Citizen', this time exhorting the listener not to vote Labour because

Man alive, in '45, they changed it for the worse.

The whole production had a wit reminiscent of the popular satirical TV show, *That Was The Week That Was,* and so was a welcome addition to the proceedings, but in the end the Conservatives were swimming against the tide. The night before the Election Wilson made his final speech of the campaign at St George's Hall, Liverpool. As Ben Pimlott (*op. cit.,* p. 317) recounts,

Afterwards, a crowd of two thousand accompanied Harold and Mary back to the Adelphi Hotel, where they were staying, chanting "Wilson" and "We love him, Yeah, Yeah, Yeah." It was like a mass celebration of a revolution that had already happened.

Next day that revolution was confirmed: Labour won the 1964 General Election with an overall majority of four seats.

★ ★ ★ ★ ★

On Election Night, 15 October 1964, The Beatles played the Globe Cinema, Stockton-on-Tees, County Durham, their second visit to the North-East town. As related in Chapter 1, their first appearance at this venue was also on an epochal date: 22 November 1963, the day President John F Kennedy was assassinated. Following trips to Europe and Australasia, and a return visit to North America, the show was part of their only British tour of the year. It was to be the last time that audiences in the smaller provincial towns would see the band – their final UK tour the following December was to take in just eight cities – and, increasingly, their lives would be centred on London.

The constant travelling, the need to evade mobs of hysterical fans wherever they went, and the enormous expectations placed on their every word, move and gesture seemed to be having an impact on their music. For when *Beatles For Sale* came out, on 4 December 1964, it was clearly inferior to its predecessor. Granted it was virtually impossible to beat *A Hard Day's Night*, which became one of the most revered albums in pop history, but this one had all the signs of being put together in a hurry in order to cash in quickly on their massive international success: in this context, there is more than a little irony in its title.

A notable consequence of this haste was that the band had reverted to covering other people's material. One of the joys of *A Hard Day's Night* was that it had consisted exclusively of Lennon-McCartney compositions, every one of them a gem. On *Beatles For Sale* no fewer than seven tracks were non-originals. This might not have mattered so much if the songs in question had been by contemporary writers, such as those operating in Greenwich Village, the Brill Building or Detroit; but they were covers of songs by the likes of Buddy Holly, Chuck Berry, Carl Perkins and Little Richard and as such took us straight back to the 1950s. All had been in the band's repertoire for a long time – 'Everybody's Trying To Be My Baby', 'Mr Moonlight' and 'Kansas City' appear on the album *Live At The Star Club, Hamburg, Germany, 1962*. They therefore presented no challenge and needed minimal rehearsal.

It is tempting to conclude that their hectic touring schedule meant that The Beatles were becoming out of touch with current developments in pop and so were unaware of newer songs they could actually cover. Yet this is not borne out by the facts. When Ringo Starr was hospitalised in June, he took with him albums by Bob Dylan, The Supremes and James Brown. Furthermore The Beatles met Dylan himself in New York two months later (when he allegedly introduced them to cannabis). It could be that, conscious of their new-found status, they were reluctant to draw attention to potential rivals by using their material. Perhaps, too, they felt incapable of absorbing into their work the music of the then fashionable protest singers, though they were by no means short of political commitment themselves: on 11 September they had refused to play at the Gator Bowl, Jacksonville, Florida unless the audience was desegregated.

Of the new songs on *Beatles For Sale*, three were outstanding. 'Eight Days A Week' is a catchy, well-constructed number that could easily have been released as a single, while 'I'm A Loser', with its mock self-deprecatory lyrics, is the one piece which does betray the influence of Dylan. But the best of all is 'No Reply' – terse yet touching, without a word, or note, out of place and an excellent illustration of Lennon's ability to fashion a work of art out of everyday language and speech patterns. But the remaining originals were disappointing: 'I'll Follow The Sun' is a good song but was four years old by then – another indication of the haste with which the album was assembled – and the rest were in similar vein to the material on *A Hard Day's Night* but not as strong.

Three exceptional new songs was hardly an impressive haul for a band being hailed as one of the great entertainment phenomena of the 20th century but there was considerable consolation in the single 'I Feel Fine'/ 'She's A Woman' which had come out a week earlier. Both songs display innovations – the use of feedback from an amplifier to open 'I Feel Fine', the lurching off-beat which drives 'She's A Woman' – yet both have an instant and indelible impact. They also serve as a reminder that The Beatles were accomplished musicians; Starr's drumming is excellent on both numbers and the guitar solo (whether by Harrison or McCartney, each has been credited) on the latter is rhythmic and resonant.

Nevertheless, the question must be asked – as 1964 drew to a close, was the gap narrowing between The Beatles and their contemporaries?

Of the British groups that emerged on their coattails, The Searchers, as already noted, were producing singles of consistently high quality and fellow Liverpudlians The Merseybeats were not far behind with the plaintive 'I Think Of You', 'Don't Turn Around' and 'Wishin' And Hopin''.

The Hollies, too, were keeping pace: 'Just One Look' was a respectable cover of Doris Troy's original and the lively follow-up, 'Here I Go Again', also made the Top Five; even better was 'We're Through', an unusual composition for the period with its fast pace, nagging guitar riff and bleak message.

Countless new acts were also arriving on the UK pop scene, including the rhythm and blues-influenced bands to be discussed in Chapter 4. Some, inevitably, were only briefly in the spotlight – The Honeycombs, for example, having made number one with their debut single, the pounding 'Have I The Right', unaccountably failed to make the Top Ten again. Others seemed to have more substance and, as a consequence, more potential staying power. The Zombies, whose gimmick was that they had obtained a prodigious number of GCE 'O' levels between them, made one of the outstanding singles of the year in 'She's Not There'. A haunting, brooding record featuring the cool, but easily heated, vocals of Colin Blunstone, it suggested a long and successful career awaited them. In the event the band had just one further hit, in spite of the fact that their 1968 album, *Odessy And Oracle*, became a cult classic. Voted number 80 in *Rolling Stone*'s 2005 poll for the 500 greatest albums of all time, it yielded 'Time Of The Season', very much of the same calibre as 'She's Not There'.

But none of these artists' output was equal to that of The Beatles in terms of consistent quality, immediate and long-lasting appeal and ineradicable influence – not just on pop music but, increasingly, on a much wider scale. At the end of the year they could look back on their nineteen US hits, six number ones on the UK singles and album charts and sell-out tours across the world; they could also conclude – though they probably did not – that they had contributed to the changes rapidly taking place in society and, more specifically, to the victory in the 1964 General Election of the Labour Party and its leader, James Harold Wilson.

★ ★ ★ ★ ★

Wilson was a Prime Minister of a type that had not been seen since Ramsay MacDonald left office in 1937 – that is, someone who seemed to be quite clearly working class. In fact, as we have seen, he belonged more accurately to the lower middle class, but his pronounced West Yorkshire accent and anti-establishment stance put him, in the public mind at least, in the same bracket as The Beatles. But even if this image of Wilson had been correct, the link was based on a misconception. John Lennon's upbringing, in a detached home in the leafy Liverpool suburb of Woolton, was anything but working class. In fact his education at the selective Quarry Bank High School was very similar to Wilson's, across the Mersey at Wirral Grammar School. Ben Pimlott shows, in a reference to a pre-Election analysis by Perry Anderson, how Wilson's approach to class differed from that of his predecessor as Labour leader, Hugh Gaitskell:

> Where Gaitskell had sought to bury the notion of class difference, Wilson resurrected it – by placing the class divide not between the working class and the upper class, but at the heart of the middle class, appropriating "skilled, scientifically trained specialists" to the Left, replacing the cloth-cap with the white laboratory coat as the symbol of British Labour, and attacking parasitical capitalism (property promotion, the stock market, and so on). On this basis, he could advocate public intervention much more confidently than Gaitskell had been able, or wished, to do. (*op. cit.,* p.273).

Wilson was also young – at 48 years old, the youngest Prime Minister of the 20th century thus far – although his relative youth obscured his long experience in politics, since he had been a Cabinet minister back in 1948.

All this, plus his ability to charm the press, gave him an extremely high profile in the country at large. In retrospect it is surprising that his majority at the Election was not far greater. But as any newly elected party is wont to discover, the problems associated with running a country are rather more difficult than they might appear in opposition. Wilson's immediate concern was the unromantic issue of the balance of payments deficit, and the dilemma of whether or not to devalue the pound would preoccupy him for a long time to come.

Still, the Queen's Speech of 3 November 1964 retained the reforming zeal of the manifesto and the Election campaign. Mention was made of iron and steel nationalisation, the restoration of rent control and increased social security benefits and the acquisition of land for community use, alongside more prosaic matters such as structural measures and economic development.

The new government's first budget, presented eight days later by the Chancellor of the Exchequer, James Callaghan, delivered on two manifesto promises: an increase in the state pension and the abolition of prescription charges, an issue on which, it will be remembered, Wilson had resigned from the Cabinet in 1951. And in time, the reforms did come – laws on race relations and equal pay, the abolition of the death penalty, an expansion in higher education, the decriminalisation of homosexuality, the end of censorship in the theatre, the legalisation of abortion, the relaxation of the divorce laws, the narrowing of the gap between rich and poor – all were addressed before 1970.

That Wilson – together with his Home Secretary, Roy Jenkins, who was responsible for many of these initiatives – was able to carry this programme forward was a direct result of the changing social attitudes that he himself inspired – or perhaps more accurately sensed were in the wind – when he became Labour leader. Jenkins averred that what was often described as the permissive society was in fact the civilised society. Certainly, Britain became a very different place in which to live; the explosion of creativity in the arts, entertainment – and by association marketing and advertising – constituted some of the most tangible and visible evidence. Without making exaggerated claims for them, The Beatles were in at the ground floor of all of this and, having inspired much of the change, took advantage of it themselves in their next period of aesthetic brilliance.

But back in October 1964, their immediate task was to continue their UK tour which by the end of the year was to take them to places far more mundane: Hull, Dundee, Leeds, Kilburn, Walthamstow, Exeter, Plymouth, Bournemouth, Ipswich and Luton. In the last week of December they appeared on a new Radio Luxembourg programme named in their honour.

To prove they still had an affinity with their past, all four Beatles dedicated records to old friends from Liverpool, including Pete Shotton, Ivan Vaughan and Nigel Whalley of The Quarry Men and Al Caldwell, alias Rory Storm, Ringo's former employer in his backing band, The Hurricanes: tragically, Caldwell was to die less than eight years later, at the age of 33.

As for Wilson, he had pressing tasks beyond domestic reforms. There were significant developments in world politics: on the day of the UK General Election, for example, Leonid Brezhnev had taken over from Nikita Khrushchev as the General Secretary of the Central Committee of the Communist Party of the Soviet Union, and hence ruler of this major superpower. Wilson had visited Russia on numerous occasions and was well-known there, so was not apprehensive about relations with Brezhnev. However his pacifist principles promised to make his first summit meeting as Prime Minister more tricky. In December 1964, Wilson flew to Washington, DC to confer with President Lyndon Baines Johnson, who was himself only new elected as his country's leader. High on the agenda was to be a request for Wilson's help in South-East Asia and, more specifically, in the rapidly escalating war in Vietnam.

CHAPTER 3:

The Times They Are A-Changin'

The tradition of protest through song is rooted deep in American history. Like much of the country's folk music it was derived, at least in part, from external sources. For example, 'When Johnny Comes Marching Home', sung by both sides in the American Civil War, is based on 'Johnny I Hardly Knew Ye', a song that originated among Irish soldiers in the early nineteenth century. But there was also something essentially native about the way protest song developed: there was, and is, a clear link with those freedoms that have meant so much to generations of Americans since they were enshrined in the US Constitution of 1787. For this reason, protest song is essentially a white music genre; African-Americans – who, as slaves, had no rights to begin with – have expressed their yearning for freedom through work songs, spirituals, gospel music, blues, soul and, more recently, R&B and rap.

In the first half of the 20th century, most protest songs concerned the plight of the working man, particularly in the farming and mining communities; the poverty brought on by the Great Depression; and the need to unionise in order to combat greedy and oppressive bosses. Very often there was cross-fertilisation between these subjects, creating a strong and vibrant tradition which has endured well beyond their original topicality.

Joe Hill (1879-1915) emigrated to the USA from Sweden and, as an itinerant labourer, wrote political songs and organised union activity. He was executed for murder on very dubious evidence and thus became a martyr among working people. Alfred Hayes wrote a poem in his honour, 'I Dreamed I Saw Joe Hill Last Night', which was set to music in 1936 by Earl Robinson and has been much covered since. Pete Seeger included it on his 1964 album, *Songs Of Struggle And Protest*, and in the early hours of 16 August 1969, Joan Baez sang it at Woodstock as a tribute to her husband, David Harris, who was then in prison for draft evasion.

Blind Alfred Reed (1880-1956) was first recorded at the famous Bristol, Tennessee, sessions of 1927 that also featured Jimmie Rodgers and The Carter Family. He made his last recordings two years later in the aftermath of the Wall Street Crash. One of these was the self-explanatory 'How Can A Poor Man Stand Such Times And Live', revived in 1970 by Ry Cooder for his eponymous debut album.

Other songs, even if not covered by later artists, still have resonance in the present day. Two pieces by Bob Miller reflect the impact of the Crash upon farmers. In 'Bank Failures', he bemoans the loss of hard-earned savings following the Crash:

Something is wrong – the money is gone
What's the use of working if we stay in debt?

while his 'Farmer's Letter To The President', dated 23 October 1929, is a detailed inventory of complaints, along with the request

Now figure out in Washington
Show us in white and black
Why the money we've put on our farms
We never do get back

The songs and stories of Aunt Molly Jackson (1880-1960) describe the privations of the Kentucky coal miners and their families and affirm her own commitment to the union movement. 'I Am A Union Woman' includes a repeated exhortation to 'join the NMU' (the National Miners Union) at the same time making clear the potential ramifications, citing the accusation levelled at her husband that 'your wife's a Russian Red'. In fact Bill Jackson was threatened with dismissal because of Molly's continued membership of the NMU; so strong were her principles that the couple divorced.

Recordings by Jackson and Sarah Ogan Gunning – variously described as her daughter, sister and half-sister – as well as those by Woody Guthrie served as the young Robert Zimmerman's introduction to folk music. This was around 1959, the year that Zimmerman turned eighteen and shortly before he became known as Bob Dylan.

Perhaps the grim tales of the Kentucky miners had a special resonance for him. His home town of Hibbing, Minnesota was itself a mining community; when it was discovered that some of the best ore deposits lay beneath it, Hibbing was physically shifted further south, leaving only its derelict remains behind. It was this area of desolation which he described in the second of the '11 Outlined Epitaphs' accompanying his album *The Times They Are A-Changin'*. As for Guthrie, it is not difficult to understand the appeal of a singer who, to a young man constrained by the conventions and prejudices of a small town, represented the romance of life on the road. However, it was still some time before Dylan's obsession with Guthrie would set in.

At the time Dylan first heard him, Guthrie had not made any new records for nearly ten years. In 1952 he had been diagnosed with Huntington's Disease, a genetic disorder inherited from his mother. By then he had already acquired a national reputation for championing the cause of the oppressed and the disenfranchised, notably in the 'Dust Bowl Ballads' which dealt unflinchingly with the appalling conditions suffered by the Oklahoma migrants seeking a new life in California (a subject tackled by John Steinbeck in his 1939 novel, *The Grapes Of Wrath*). One of Guthrie's most remarkable compositions was 'This Land Is Your Land', which declares that America belongs to all its citizens and not, by implication, to any 'landowner' – a statement which at this point in American history amounted to nothing less than Communism. Guthrie was never a member of the Communist Party (though he had 'This

Machine Kills Fascists' emblazoned on his guitar), but he became a hero to the Left with this and other like-minded songs.

In March 1940 Guthrie played at a farm workers' benefit where he met Pete Seeger; subsequently he joined Seeger's group, The Almanac Singers. The Almanacs were just one of a number of folk groups that proliferated in the 1940s. Some were fairly loose aggregations; others grew out of existing, smaller units, such as the duo of Josh White and Tom Glazer. One African-American, the other Jewish, they expressed their own solidarity and that of the union movement in 'We've Got A Plan', a song that encouraged participation in World War II, without any trace of irony:

> You fight for us and we'll fight for you
> And we'll work together when the fighting's through

Left-wing opinion had initially been opposed to the War; that changed when Germany invaded Russia on 22 June 1941, whereupon the enemy became the Nazi fascists. Here are Josh and Tom again:

> The Union fights my battle every day ...
> I want to send these fascists straight to hell
>> ('Citizen CIO' [Congress of Industrial Organisations] – 1944)

On this number they were joined by The Union Boys, who also made records under their own name. One such is the mournful, anti-racist classic, 'Jim Crow';

> Lincoln set the Negro free
> Why is he still in slavery?
> Why is he still in slavery?
> It's Jim Crow

> When it's time to go to the polls
> Why must the Negro stay at home?

Why must the Negro stay at home?
It's Jim Crow

This is the land of democracy
Put an end to slavery
Put an end to slavery
And Jim Crow

But The Almanac Singers had the highest profile of all the folk groups around at the time, partly because of their line-up of big names – alongside Guthrie and Seeger were, at various times, Burl Ives, Cisco Houston and the African-Americans Josh White, Sonny Terry and Brownie McGhee – and partly due to their commitment and lack of compromise. One early project, inspired by Almanacs co-founder Lee Hays, was to compile a book of protest songs, including those that promoted union activity, with an introduction written by Guthrie to each song. In the event, the compilation was not published until 1964, with folklorist Alan Lomax, who had collected many of the songs in the first place, acting as editor. The Almanacs released six records in all. The first, *Songs For John Doe*, was a set of three 78s that advocated non-intervention in World War II and attacked US companies involved in re-arming Germany. The second was entitled *Talking Union And Other Union Songs,* the highlights of which include the title track –

If you wait for the boss to raise your pay
We'll all be waiting for judgement day

– and the rousing 'Which Side Are You On', written by Florence Reece in 1931 and one of the songs to be included in the aforementioned Guthrie-Seeger book.

It wasn't long before The Almanacs fell foul of the authorities. A sustained campaign of defamation by both the US Government and the right-wing press led to their disbanding and, in 1948, re-forming as The

Weavers. The new group were more overtly commercial, using lush orchestrations to enhance their basic string-band sound and they found huge success in 1950 with their version of Leadbelly's 'Goodnight Irene'. But, as McCarthyism intensified, they were once more under heavy surveillance and in 1935 Seeger and Hays appeared before the House Committee on Un-American Activities. Their popularity was such, however, that The Weavers rode out the storm of anti-Communist paranoia to spearhead the folk music revival of the late 1950s along with The Kingston Trio, whose clean-cut image and relative youth broadened the popularity of the music still further. New York, as for other forms of music, was its epicentre, drawing young hopefuls from all around the country.

One of these was Bob Dylan, who arrived in Greenwich Village at the end of January 1961.

★ ★ ★ ★ ★

Four months later, Vice President Lyndon Johnson visited Saigon and promised its Prime Minister, Ngo Dinh Diem, further US support in his efforts to resist Communist forces: Johnson dubbed Diem the 'Winston Churchill of Asia' for his fortitude. It was a good analogy; at the time the policy of the Kennedy administration was to assist Diem without the direct involvement of American combat troops – Diem should be left to fight the Communists on his own. This suited Diem: his attitude to the US government was, at best, equivocal.

But it would be a matter of considerable concern and embarrassment to Kennedy if the insurgents of the National Liberation Front – the Vietcong – were able to defeat Diem. The consequence would be Communist governments in both North and South Vietnam – a vindication of the widely-held 'Domino Theory' that if one country succumbed to Communism, its neighbours would follow.

So, almost inadvertently, Kennedy began to commit more resources to Vietnam. As Stanley Karnow (*Vietnam: A History*, p. 253) has written,

... Kennedy's restraint was illusory. All the rhetoric now emanating from his administration reiterated its resolve to stop Communism in Southeast Asia, so that he could not backtrack without jeopardizing the American government's prestige – and in time that consideration would become the main motive for the US commitment in Vietnam. The involvement also deepened with the rapid arrival of more and more American advisers and equipment to shore up the Diem regime. The number of advisers had already quadrupled ... from fewer than seven hundred to some three thousand, and the figure climbed to sixteen thousand over the next two years. American pilots began to fly combat sorties out of Bienhoa, an air base north of Saigon, their flights camouflaged as a training exercise for Vietnamese.

Publicly there was a great deal of optimism about the situation in Vietnam. American officials, both military and civilian, were positive in their assessments and the extent of the commitment was minimised. But behind the scenes it was becoming evident that all was not well and that the American investment was not yielding the desired results. The majority leader in the Senate, Mike Mansfield, concluded after a trip to Vietnam in late 1962 that 'substantially the same difficulties remain if, indeed, they have not been compounded' (*ibid.*, p. 268).

Much of the problem lay with Diem himself. An inflexible autocrat, he lacked the guile and political sophistication to deal both with the North Vietnamese and the opposition within his own country. This consisted not only of the Vietcong insurgents but, increasingly, a faction of senior military personnel as well as the so far passive but resolute Buddhist community. A devout Catholic, Diem despised Buddhism but, unlike his ancient predecessors, had refrained from actively persecuting its practitioners. However on 8 May 1963 a crowd celebrating the birthday of the Buddha in Hué was fired on by local troops. Not unnaturally, this led to further confrontations with the authorities and a growing spiral of government repression and Buddhist resistance. In Saigon on 11 June a monk named Quang Duc immolated himself (Malcolm Browne's photograph of the incident became one of the most commonly used images of the 1960s), with others rapidly following suit. Diem made no attempt to conciliate; his response was to blame the Vietcong.

The international outcry at the self-immolations tainted America through its association with Diem. But there were worries, too, about his conduct of the war, particularly his inability to capitalise on all the help the US had provided and marshal a coherent and effective fighting force. Many of his own generals were deeply anxious about his leadership and began to plot his removal. The extent of Kennedy's support for the plot has been a matter of much debate although there is no doubt that their ambassador to Vietnam, Henry Cabot Lodge, encouraged it. In a telegram to Washington on 29 August 1963, he stated,

> We are launched on a course for which there is no respectable turning back: the overthrow of the Diem government. There is no turning back because US prestige is already publicly committed to this end in large measure, and will become more so as the facts leak out. In a more fundamental sense, there is no turning back because there is no possibility, in my view, that the war can be won under a Diem administration.
>
> (Quoted in Karnow, *op.cit.*, p. 289)

On 2 November 1963, the conspiracy of the generals reached fruition: Ngo Dinh Diem and his brother Ngo Dinh Nhu were shot dead at a railway crossing between the suburb of Cholon and the centre of Saigon. 20 days later President Kennedy was assassinated in Dallas, Texas.

★ ★ ★ ★ ★

For the vast majority of Americans, the furore surrounding Kennedy's death meant that Diem's demise went largely unnoticed. The picture in Vietnam was, in any case, obscure and confusing: most of those who took any stance at all were behind their government's policy. However there was significant disaffection among the US student population. This was rooted in the anti-nuclear campaign begun in the late 1950s by SANE (the National Committee for a Sane Nuclear Policy) and the SPU (Student Peace Union). Following the agreement in 1963 of a nuclear test ban treaty, many were looking for a new cause to espouse. Some, like Students for a Democratic Society (the SDS, re-christened by the cartoonist Al Capp as SWINE – Students Wildly Indignant about Nearly Everything), began to advocate for Civil Rights; others focussed on Vietnam. During a conference at Yale University in March 1964, a series of demonstrations against the War was planned for 2 May, when hundreds of students would attend protests in New York, San Francisco, Boston, Seattle, and Madison, Wisconsin. Ten days later, in New York, twelve young men publicly burned their draft cards.

Of course the protest singers had also been tracking developments in Vietnam and by late 1963/early 1964 Bob Dylan was seen as their leading voice. His first album, *Bob Dylan*, released on 19 March 1962, made no references to the war but was nevertheless a startling debut, panoramic thematically, geographically and stylistically and delivered in his soon-to-be familiar nasal intonation that was at once authentic and other-worldly. Though mainly comprised of cover versions, the album demonstrated Dylan's promise as a writer with the Guthrie tribute 'Song To Woody', conceived in the manner of its subject, and the satire on the Greenwich Village folk scene, 'Talkin' New York'.

But the follow-up, *The Freewheelin' Bob Dylan*, which came out on 27 May 1963, contained four anti-war songs. One of them, 'Blowin' In The Wind', was already well-known, having appeared in the sixth edition of *Broadside* – a publication that featured the latest protest (or 'topical') songs – exactly one year earlier. Less specific and broader in its scope than the other three, it became enormously popular, assisted by Peter, Paul and Mary's cover version which reached number two on the US singles chart in July. It was also to prove inspirational among the African-American community and Chapter 5 will examine its influence on, for example, Sam Cooke.

Of the others, 'Masters Of War' condemns those who profit from the manufacture of arms, aircraft and bombs, while in 'Talking World War III Blues' Dylan imagines what life will be like after a nuclear conflagration. 'A Hard Rain's A-Gonna Fall' was presumed to be about fallout, despite Dylan's affirmation that the song refers to the lies perpetrated by the media. A third interpretation proposes that he is predicting divine retribution for the destruction brought about by man. Whatever the case, it was strong stuff, yet in retrospect no more than a prelude to his most harrowing and incisive album, *The Times They Are A-Changin'*, released on 13 January 1964, and one of the most remarkable records of the decade.

The whole presentation of *The Times They Are A-Changin'* is designed to suggest profundity and seriousness of purpose. Its dour, ascetic mood is announced by the front cover: a monochrome photograph of Dylan with short hair, unsmiling, not even facing the camera. He looks like a workman or, perhaps more intentionally, a soldier. On the back cover are '11 Outlined Epitaphs' – dreamlike poems by Dylan in which the imagery, as the title suggests, is of decay, destruction and death. And then there is the music: ten songs performed with the minimalist accompaniment of Dylan's own guitar and harmonica, by this stage acting as extensions to his voice in the manner of the great country blues singers.

The title track has the spirit and anthemic quality of 'Blowin' In The Wind' but is much more assertive: its audacity and authority still stir the emotions today. But the impact in 1964 of the following stanzas on a whole generation of young Americans was at once incalculable and indelible:

Come senators, congressmen
Please heed the call
Don't stand in the doorway
Don't block up the hall
For he that gets hurt
Will be he who has stalled
There's a battle outside ragin'

We'll soon shake your windows
And rattle your walls
For the times they are a-changin'

Come mothers and fathers
Throughout the land
And don't criticise
What you can't understand
Your sons and your daughters
Are beyond your command
Your old road is rapidly agin'
Please get out of the new one
If you can't lend your hand
For the times they are a-changin'

Note Dylan's technique of adding an 'A-' prefix to the word 'changin'': as in 'A Hard Rain's A-Gonna Fall', it anchors the phrasing in colloquial and especially rural speech, thus badging it as a song from the folk music tradition. 'The Ballad Of Hollis Brown' and 'North Country Blues' are both about people beaten down by the system. The first tells of a farmer who kills himself and his family in response to the torment of poverty, and of the indifference that greets their deaths. This piece has a connection to actual folk material, deriving directly from a song-family (which also includes the ballad 'Pretty Polly') with its origins in the Appalachian Mountains. The latter harks back to Aunt Molly Jackson in its account, through female eyes, of the devastation caused by the greed of mining companies. Two songs on the album concern the murder of African-Americans: 'The Lonesome Death Of Hattie Carroll', the Maryland waitress whose killer got off with a light sentence due to the wealth and status of his family; and 'Only A Pawn In Their Game', a more sophisticated composition which, while describing the mindless murder of Civil Rights activist Medgar Evers, concludes that those responsible were only reacting to the racist propaganda fed them by Southern politicians.

'Boots Of Spanish Leather' and 'One Too Many Mornings' are love songs dedicated to Dylan's girlfriend, Suze Rotolo, although musically the former is identical to an earlier composition, 'Girl From The North Country', about Echo Helstrom, his girlfriend in Hibbing. Whether this is a deliberate tie-up on Dylan's part is unclear, but his writing at this period is so skilful that it would be a mistake to rule it out. 'Restless Farewell' again reaches back into folk music, this time to the Irish song 'The Party Glass', and may well be an allusion to his deteriorating relationship with Rotolo. 'With God On Our Side' is another anthem and is of the same calibre as 'The Times They Are A-Changin'' itself. It underlines how God has traditionally been invoked to justify or forgive atrocities from the slaughter of Native Americans to the Nazi Holocaust and the use of nuclear weapons. It does not specifically mention Vietnam but the implications are obvious.

No-one would deny that much of *The Times They Are A-Changin'* is derived from external sources, both thematically and musically. The tune to 'Boots Of Spanish Leather', for example, comes directly from Martin Carthy's arrangement of 'Scarborough Fair', and Dominic Behan called Dylan a 'plagiarist and a thief' for basing 'With God On Our Side' on his song 'The Patriot Game' (though Behan himself took the tune from the Irish folk song, 'The Merry Month Of May'). As indicated above, there are several other instances of links with traditional sources and historical events.

But this is central to Dylan's purpose: to legitimise the protest movement of the present by linking it to a social, political and musical continuum that extends back through the 20th century and beyond. He was never to employ that methodology again, but the album remains a watershed in pop music development, signifying a maturity that would have seemed inconceivable just a couple of years previously.

Immediately after *The Times They Are A-Changin'* came out, Dylan set off on a road trip across the USA. With only a small number of concerts already booked in advance he wanted to turn up and play spontaneously at far-flung and obscure venues and in doing so reconnect with the ordinary people from whom he felt his fame now distanced him. It was only a partial success; their reality distorted by a prodigious intake of drugs, Dylan and his three companions did not always get the warm welcome they had expected. He was also distressed to discover, on making an unscheduled visit to Carl Sandburg, that the triple Pulitzer Prize-winning poet had never heard of him.

They finally arrived in San Francisco, where Dylan gave a memorable concert at the Berkeley Community Theatre before heading home. The whole trip had lasted six weeks. Had they lingered in California for a while longer they may have encountered on the highway, heading to New York, another drug-fuelled group of young people made up of:

- Neal Cassady, on whom the character of Dean Moriarty in Jack Kerouac's novel, *On The Road,* was modelled
- Kenneth Babbs, ex-Marine and helicopter pilot in Vietnam
- Mike Hagen, also known as Mal Function
- Sandy Lehmann-Haupt, a sound engineer and drop-out from New York University
- George Walker, aka Hardly Visible
- John Page Browning, alias the Cadaverous Cowboy
- Ron Bevirt, also known as Hassler
- 'The Beauty Witch'
- Jane Burton, a philosophy professor
- 'Brother John'
- Steve Lambrecht, known as Zonker
- Paula Sundsten, alias Gretchen Fetchin, the Slime Queen
- Dale Kesey
- His cousin, Chuck Kesey
- His brother, Ken Kesey, author of *One Flew Over The Cuckoo's Nest*

Together, this motley crew were known as The Merry Pranksters – a collective formed around the writer at his home in La Honda, California

– and the trip was originally intended to celebrate the completion of his second novel, *Sometimes A Great Notion,* and to visit the World's Fair in New York. But there was more to it than that.

While on a creative writing programme at Stanford University, Kesey had volunteered to take part in a CIA-financed study into psychoactive drugs, including lysergic acid diethylamide (LSD). *One Flew Over The Cuckoo's Nest* was to some extent based on his experience as a medical guinea pig. But LSD had also fascinated him and he began to advertise its hallucinogenic properties to his friends. In time, designs using brightly coloured, fluorescent paint (manufactured by Day-Glo) were used to simulate the effects of LSD and other mind-expanding, or psychedelic, drugs.

The school bus that set out from La Honda on 17 June 1964 with the Merry Pranksters aboard was decorated all over in this way and, with its destination identified as 'Furthur' and the words 'Weird Load' painted on the back, the real purpose of the journey was clear: to test out the reaction of the American people to LSD and the unpredictable actions it inspired. The party headed for Houston and from there to the Deep South, Florida and up through Georgia and Virginia to the North East and New York. Tom Wolfe, in his seminal account of Kesey and the Pranksters, *The Electric Kool-Aid Acid Test,* sums up the atmosphere off and on the bus:

> The trip had started as a great bursting forth out of the forest fastness of La Honda, out into an unsuspecting America. And for Sandy, anyway, that was when the trip went best, when the Pranksters were out among them, and the citizens of the land were gawking and struggling to summon up the proper emotion for this – what in the name of God are the ninnies doing. But the opposite was happening, too. On those long stretches of American superhighway between performances the bus was like a pressure cooker, a crucible … all traces of freakiness or competition or bitterness or whatever were intensified. They were right out front, for sure. (p. 78)

The immediate effects of the project were difficult to evaluate. It is undeniable that the Pranksters introduced many people to LSD but their influence was arguably far less than that of Timothy Leary, Richard Alpert and Ralph Metzner, whose book, *The Psychedelic Experience,* hit the streets in August. No real analysis was made of the results (presumably due to the state of mind of the analysts), but as a statement of the developing counterculture the mission was enormously significant, a fact recognised by the Smithsonian Institution who some time later tried, unsuccessfully, to buy the bus from Kesey.

In a year that was already witness to a musical revolution courtesy of The Beatles, The Rolling Stones and Bob Dylan, here was a hint that broader change was under way: a transformation in attitude, lifestyle and philosophy – and none of it in tune with the Establishment. Yet before too long such developments would not only dominate youth culture entirely, but would start to have an impact on mainstream thinking. Though the Merry Pranksters and their 1964 bus trip to Furthur were motivated by unadulterated hedonism, the alternative society to which they were inadvertently contributing the foundations would become active politically and focus its energies on stopping the Vietnam War.

★ ★ ★ ★ ★

During the early part of 1964, there were clear signs that the war was beginning to escalate. Following Diem's assassination, a military junta ruled South Vietnam with, at its head, General Duong Van Minh, one of the chief plotters against the former Prime Minister. But by the end of January a new regime was in place, led by another general, Nguyen Khanh. This rapid turnover of leadership did little to soothe American fears about the direction the war was taking.

Johnson was caught in a dilemma. With a Presidential Election due in 1964, he did not want to commit US troops to the conflict, yet at the same time he was conscious of the potential threat from the American Right and did not want to appear weak and/or soft on Communism. So he took the course that offered the best of both worlds, pressurising Khanh to deal more effectively with the Vietcong and simultaneously providing him with the support necessary to do the job.

This strategy of beefing up the war effort behind the scenes seemed, on the face of it, to work well. According to a Gallup Poll cited by Dallek (*op. cit.,* p. 162), almost two-thirds of Americans paid little or no attention to the fighting in Vietnam. But in reality, things were going badly. Khanh seemed to be more concerned with the sacking and appointment of military staff and government officials than prosecuting the War, while the Vietcong were scoring notable successes through terrorism and direct combat. Secretary of Defence Robert McNamara visited Vietnam in March and despite his optimistic public proclamations, he informed Johnson that the situation had deteriorated since his previous trip, only four months earlier. The result was an action memorandum from the National Security Council which indicated a shift in its policy towards Vietnam. As Karnow (*op. cit.*, p. 342) relates:

> Until then, the US aim had been limited to helping the Saigon government defeat the Vietcong. Now the administration broadened the objective. More was involved than just South Vietnam or even Asia, the national security document asserted; a Communist victory would damage the reputation of the United States throughout the world. The conflict was a "test case" of America's capacity to cope with a Communist "war of liberation" and the whole of US foreign policy faced a trial.

By May, Johnson was asking Congress for an additional $125 million in aid, the result of a shift in strategy on the North Vietnamese side where there was some anxiety that the efforts of the Vietcong were failing to have the desired effect, or at least not leading quickly enough to the downfall of South Vietnam. Nor were there indications that the South Vietnamese, or the Americans, wished to come to any sort of accommodation with them. President Ho Chi Minh and his advisers therefore resolved to take a more proactive approach than they had in the recent past, not by direct confrontation but by expanding the existing supply route to South Vietnam via neighbouring Laos and Cambodia. Though neither was a Communist country, both were sympathetic to the North Vietnamese. Dubbed the 'Ho Chi Minh Trail' by the Americans, it was in fact a complex system incorporating many roads and pathways. By the end of 1964, the Trail had become a major factor in the North Vietnamese war effort: 20 to 30 tons of materiel were passing through each day and 10,000 troops had used it to move southwards during the course of the year.

The change in attitude of the North Vietnamese coupled with Khanh's continued inability to make inroads against the Vietcong troubled Johnson, as it showed that, try as he might, he could not shift Vietnam from his agenda. Whichever course of action he took was beset with problems:

- *Escalate aggression* – and risk being labelled a warmonger and the Presidential Election being dominated by the war at the expense of the domestic policies and reforms he was keen to pursue
- *Scale down US support and leave Khanh to it* – and so almost certainly allow the Vietcong to triumph, hence enabling a Communist take-over of the whole of Vietnam
- *Do nothing* – and risk being derided as a weak and indecisive leader by his Republican opponent, Barry Goldwater, and possibly the majority of the American public

In the event, the last two options were not really viable; Johnson simply could not bring himself to give up at this critical juncture of the war, and of his career. Instead he chose to step things up, a course of action that led directly to an incident of enormous significance, not just for developments in 1964 but for the history of the entire Vietnam War.

For some time, approval had been in place for covert activity against the North Vietnamese. One type of operation, termed a DeSoto mission, involved raids on its coastline by South Vietnamese commandos, thus bringing the enemy radar transmitters into action and allowing the

American ships in the Tonkin Gulf, east of North Vietnam, to identify their locations and frequencies – vital information for any future plans for bombing and/or invasion.

For a variety of reasons a programme of these raids planned for March 1964 had been cancelled. Still, Johnson extended what had originally been a four-month trial period for a further year, and so it was that the destroyer *Maddox*, under the command of Captain John J Herrick, was assigned to the Tonkin Gulf in July. During the early hours of the 31st, two groups of South Vietnamese commandos got ashore at Vinh and triggered radar signals which were picked up by the *Maddox*. On 2 August the destroyer was approached by three North Vietnamese torpedo boats; interpreting an intercepted message to them as an order to attack the *Maddox*, Herrick made off towards the open sea and fired on the pursuing North Vietnamese vessels. Herrick later claimed that this was a warning shot, but did not record it in his log as such. Whatever the case, the North Vietnamese retaliated, unsuccessfully as it turned out, since by the time the incident was over, one of their boats had been sunk and the other two seriously damaged.

Suspicion that the US provoked the North Vietnamese into attacking them has existed ever since the incident. Certainly Senator J William Fulbright thought so at the time, stating, according to Dallek (*op. cit.,* p. 177), that 'probably the incident was asked for.' Johnson's initial response was to try to play down what had happened; he contacted the Russian Premier Khrushchev to reassure him that this was not a prelude to further US aggression. However he also warned North Vietnam that dire consequences would follow any further attacks on American ships. Johnson's military advisers were, in fact, already planning for those dire consequences; preparations were made for the systematic bombing of strategic targets in North Vietnam while further DeSoto missions by the *Maddox* were authorised. It was during one of these, on 4 August, that intercepted radio signals led Herrick to believe that the North Vietnamese were about to attack, and to order his men to fire in all directions. Though in his report to Admiral Ulysses Grant Sharp Jr, Herrick expressed doubt about the validity of the signals and even of the presence in the area of any enemy ships, the fact that there had been merely the possibility of North Vietnamese attacks was enough for Johnson to act.

He reactivated a congressional resolution to widen US involvement in the conflict that had been sketched out some time earlier by his National Security Adviser, McGeorge Bundy and a retaliatory air strike against enemy torpedo boat bases was scheduled. But before these actions went ahead, Johnson wanted confirmation that hostile acts by the North Vietnamese had definitely taken place. What is not clear is the extent to which he received it. Karnow (*op. cit.*, p. 372) says that,

> At six o'clock in the evening [of 4 August], while Herrick was still struggling to furnish additional evidence, a Pentagon spokesman declared that "a second deliberate attack" had occurred.

Dallek (*op. cit.*, p. 178) states, 'Inquiries to the Joint Chiefs gave Johnson the assurances he demanded'.

It has even been suggested (Gareth Porter, *blacklistednews.com*, 8 July 2009) that McNamara withheld Herrick's doubts from Johnson. Whatever the case, the President made a television broadcast just before midnight to announce that the US would be taking direct action against North Vietnam. He then pressed ahead with the resolution drafted by Bundy.

Not everyone was happy with the way this was playing out. Senator Wayne Morse of Oregon claimed to have received an anonymous tip-off from a Pentagon official that the *Maddox* had, through its part in the DeSoto missions, stimulated whatever aggressive action there may have been, and that the ship's log-book would prove it. But he was one of only two dissenters in the Senate (the other being Senator Ernest Gruening of Alaska) and the Southeast Asia Resolution – often called the Tonkin Gulf Resolution – was passed unanimously by Congress. It meant that Johnson had the power to conduct military operations without declaring war. He was soon to use that power to escalate US operations and, the following March, to send the first US combat troops to Vietnam.

All the evidence suggests that Johnson was so determined to appear decisive that he went ahead with the resolution without knowing the full facts. Arguments have raged for almost 50 years about who knew what, with denials, unaccountable lapses of memory and revised versions of events issuing from those who played a part in the Gulf of Tonkin Incident. What is certain is that Johnson was well aware of the DeSoto missions; whatever evidence there was of North Vietnamese fire, to portray that fire as unprovoked amounted to concealing the truth from the American people.

★ ★ ★ ★ ★

The day after the Tonkin Gulf Resolution saw the release of *Another Side Of Bob Dylan.* At the very time that he could have hit the jackpot with a killer album of protest songs, here was, as the title clearly stated, a departure from everything he had come to represent. This was not to be the last time that Dylan confounded expectations and, as we shall see, it was in any case a forerunner to yet another transition. But there were many other singers willing and able to fill the vacuum created by Dylan's change of direction.

One of the leaders in the field was Phil Ochs, born on 19 December 1940 in El Paso, Texas. He came to New York the year after Dylan, with the same ambition and a similar writing technique, picking up his subjects from articles he read in the newspapers or in magazines such as *Newsweek.* Not surprisingly, they became friendly rivals; Dylan was quick to praise Ochs's work while Ochs returned the compliment with substantial interest:

> The first time I heard him sing his first few songs, at some party or at the Broadside offices, I thought, "This guy is it. He's the best writer, the best singer that anyone has ever heard." And I wondered what the future had in store for him. He was just so extraordinary. (Quoted in Scaduto, *Bob Dylan,* p. 119)

Ochs's comment on Dylan's voice is interesting and perhaps

underlines the major difference between the two men. Dylan sounded as if he were from another time and place, his rural, unsophisticated whine giving no hint of the age or origin of the singer. Ochs, meanwhile, like almost all of the other contemporary folk singers, had a smooth, white middle-class vocal style, limited in range but with clear enunciation. Yet his songs – succinct, perceptive and emotionally-charged – were anything but ordinary. He became sufficiently well-known in the clubs of Greenwich Village to merit a set at the 1963 Newport Folk Festival, where he received a standing ovation for his song 'Power And The Glory', which was subsequently included on his first album, *All The News That's Fit To Sing*, recorded in February 1964.

The title of the record was typical of his wit; it parodied the strapline of *The New York Times*, 'All the news that's fit to print', while indirectly alluding to the fact that it was founded by his namesake (but no relation) Adolph Ochs. The album opens with 'One More Parade', co-written with his mentor, Bob Gibson, which depicts the eternal continuum of war and the lot of the soldier,

> So young, so strong, so ready for the war,
> So willing to go and die upon a foreign shore,
> All march together, everybody looks the same,
> So there is no one you can blame,
> Don't be ashamed, light the flame,
> One more parade.

The heavy irony of the first two lines suggests that Ochs stops short of blaming soldiers for their actions during wartime, intimating instead that those who orchestrate wars are the guilty parties. But it is a fine dividing line which he approaches again later in the song ('ten thousand ears need only one command') and symptomatic of the ambivalence felt by many protest singers on this issue. Anyone who had the temerity to attach guilt to the soldier was also likely to attract opprobrium from outside the folk music world.

'The Thresher' is about the sinking of a US nuclear submarine during deep-diving tests in 1963. Without stating it outright, Ochs attributes the disaster to those who would have nuclear weapons in the first place. 'Talking Vietnam' is in the now-familiar medium of satire via a talking blues: with unremitting sarcasm, Ochs excoriates the American military support that masqueraded as training:

> Sailing over to Vietnam,
> Southeast Asian Birmingham.
> Well training is the word we use
> Nice word to have in case we lose
> Training a million Vietnamese
> To fight for the wrong government and the American Way

> Well the sergeant said it's time to train
> So I climbed aboard my helicopter plane.
> We flew above the battle ground
> A sniper tried to shoot us down
> He must have forgotten we're only trainees
> Them Commies never fight fair

> Friends, the very next day we trained some more
> We burned some villages down to the floor.
> Yes we burned out the jungles far and wide
> Made sure those red apes had no place left to hide
> Threw all the people in relocation camps
> Under lock and key, made damn sure they're free.

'Talking Cuban Crisis' is in similar vein.

Other songs deal with personal tragedy: 'Lou Marsh', killed when trying to break up a fight in New York; the imprisoned immigrant 'Celia', parted from her American husband; the 'Ballad Of William Worthy', a journalist prosecuted by the US authorities for travelling to China and

Cuba; and 'Bullets Of Mexico', its subject the Mexican revolutionary Rubén Jaramillo Méndez, who was gunned down in May 1962. 'Too Many Martyrs' commemorates Medgar Evers, the Civil Rights leader whose death Dylan had written about in 'Only A Pawn In Their Game'.

Just to show that oppression by the state is not unique to the US, 'Knock On The Door' alludes to the unannounced visits made by the secret police in totalitarian regimes. 'Automation Song' bemoans the loss of jobs caused by the introduction of new technology and 'What's That I Hear' celebrates the historic struggle of the African-American people.

Finally two compositions honour Woody Guthrie in different ways: 'Bound For Glory' is a touching tribute that features the harmonica of John Sebastian, later of The Lovin' Spoonful; but 'Power And The Glory', the song that electrified Newport is, in many ways, the more impressive achievement. Effectively a contemporary take on Guthrie's 'This Land Is Your Land', it gives the listener a tour of the wonders of the US and asks, 'Who could ask for more?' while reminding us that,

> She's only as rich as the poorest of her poor
> Only as free as the padlocked prison door
> Only as strong as our love for this land
> Only as tall as we stand
>
> But our land is still troubled by men who have to hate
> They twist away our freedom and they twist away our fate
> Fear is their weapon and treason is their cry
> We can stop them if we try.

As an appraisal of world politics, and their impact on individuals, *All The News That's Fit To Sing* would take some beating in any era of music. In 1964, it climbed to heights only previously scaled by Bob Dylan, making Phil Ochs, for a while at least, the leading pretender to Dylan's crown.

Not far behind was Tom Paxton, who had by that time been

performing in Greenwich Village for four years. He had made one album in 1962, *I'm The Man That Built The Bridges,* recorded live at the Gaslight Folk Club. His appearance at the 1963 Newport Folk Festival was followed by gigs all around the country – including in Hazard, Kentucky, where he lent his support to striking miners. On his return to New York, he signed to Elektra Records and recorded the album *Ramblin' Boy* in 1964.

Paxton's brand of folk music was, unlike Dylan's, very much a product of the New York scene: that is, pure both in intention and delivery. As previously noted, there existed in the Village a strong impulse to codify and collect folk songs, particularly those written in response to capitalist oppression – a practice which often translated into a musical and political conformism that bordered on pedantry. Paxton was in many ways the acceptable face of that culture and, although he wrote all but one of the songs on *Ramblin' Boy*, almost all of them sound like traditional pieces. Moreover, many have choruses that are easy to sing along with, a feature which enhanced their appeal at the increasingly popular hootenannies where audience participation was important since it reinforced the sense of community, shared experience and collective response. His voice was clear, his enunciation excellent, and he had an extremely personable stage manner. Yet Paxton was by no means as bland as those attributes suggest. His compositions were often surprisingly hard-hitting and the traces of emotion that were at times evident in his voice implied repressed vulnerability.

His accompanists on *Ramblin' Boy* are Barry Kornfeld, on guitar, banjo and harmonica; and Felix Pappalardi, later to find fame as the producer of the rock band Cream, on guitarrón, a six-string acoustic bass guitar of Mexican origin. Both musicians play an unobtrusive, supporting role.

The album is more wide-ranging thematically than the contemporary work of either Dylan or Ochs. Three pieces are on the familiar subject of employment, or the lack of it: 'A Job Of Work' ('Lord, gimme a job of work to do'); 'Standing On The Edge Of Town', about the consequences of automation; and 'High Sheriff Of Hazard', a corrupt official who condoned the use of unregulated labour in the mines. 'When The Morning

Breaks' is a soldier's song, 'Harper' a pacy murder ballad, and 'Fare Thee Well, Cisco' a tribute to the late Cisco Houston, confrere of Woody Guthrie. There are two love songs, 'The Last Thing On My Mind', of which there have been nearly 50 subsequent cover versions, and 'My Lady's A Wild, Flying Dove', dedicated to his wife, Midge, and one of his more sentimental compositions. 'Goin' To The Zoo' scarcely requires any introduction as it has been a childhood favourite for half a century.

As for protest songs, the highlights are 'Daily News', which mocks people who are gullible enough to believe what they read in the right-wing press, and 'What Did You Learn In School Today?', an attack on the propaganda fed to children:

> I learned that war is not so bad …
> I learned our government must be strong
> It's always right and never wrong

In addition, 'A Rumblin' In The Land' is a lively piece in the narrative tradition that alludes to the mobilisation of downtrodden working people ('A great flood is a-risin' fast').

Finally there are three wistful ballads, the kind of song that came to define Paxton's art: 'I Can't Help But Wonder Where I'm Bound' finds its answer in 'I'm Bound For The Mountains And The Sea'; while the gentle cadences and sing-along potential of 'Ramblin' Boy' make it the standout track on the album to which it gives its name. Written between sets at the Gaslight, it had been recorded by The Weavers in 1963 so was already established as a folk classic, and it is hard to imagine a more succinct eulogy for a travelling companion:

> He was a man and a friend always
> He stuck with me in the hard old days
> He never cared if I had no dough
> We rambled 'round in the rain and snow
> And here's to you, my ramblin' boy

May all your ramblin' bring you joy
And here's to you, my ramblin' boy
May all your ramblin' bring you joy.

Paxton's commercial success was a crucial factor in bringing protest songs to a wider audience and his personal popularity inspired confidence in the message they conveyed.

By mixing them in with more immediately accessible, and acceptable, material, he subtly extended the emotional response evoked in the listener by the likes of 'The Last Thing On My Mind' and 'Ramblin' Boy' to encompass 'Daily News' and 'What Did You Learn In School Today?'. At this stage, Dylan could be easily dismissed by all but his devoted following as an outlaw – a one-dimensional artist with only one string to his bow – as he himself was quick to recognise. But Paxton, with his smoother style and more amiable personality seemed to have one foot in the Establishment. Who is to say which of them had the greater impact in 1964?

★ ★ ★ ★ ★

Born on the Piapot Cree Indian Reserve in the Qu'Appelle Valley, Saskatchewan, Canada, Buffy Sainte-Marie was brought up in Maine by adoptive parents. Her debut album, *It's My Way!*, came out in 1964 and contained two of the most memorable protest songs of the year. 'The Universal Soldier' seemed on the face of it to lay the blame for war squarely on the shoulders of the fighting man and was seized upon by Jan Berry of Jan and Dean who released an 'answer' record called 'The Universal Coward' the following year. But the song was about the impetus to fight that exists in all of us: as Sainte-Marie herself put it, 'It's about individual responsibility for war and how the old feudal thinking kills us all.'

He's five foot-two, and he's six feet-four
He fights with missiles and with spears.

The Times They Are A-Changin'

He's all of thirty-one, and he's only seventeen
Been a soldier for a thousand years

He's a Catholic, a Hindu, an Atheist, a Jain
A Buddhist and a Baptist and a Jew
And he knows he shouldn't kill
And he knows he always will
Kill you for me my friend and me for you

And he's fighting for Canada
He's fighting for France
He's fighting for the USA
And he's fighting for the Russians
And he's fighting for Japan
And he thinks we'll put an end to war this way

And he's fighting for Democracy
He's fighting for the Reds
He says it's for the peace of all
He's the one who must decide
Who's to live and who's to die
And he never sees the writing on the wall

But without him
How would Hitler have condemned him at Dachau?
Without him Caesar would have stood alone
He's the one who gives his body
As a weapon of the war,
And without him all this killing can't go on

He's the Universal Soldier and he really is to blame
His orders come from far away no more
They come from here and there and you and me

And brothers can't you see

This is not the way we put the end to war

'Now That The Buffalo's Gone' is a withering portrayal of the destruction and deceit wrought upon Native Americans. Ever since the General Allotment Act of 1887 – also known as the Dawes Act – the profile of the Native American was much diminished. Its effect had been to parcel up land into reservations and give each family between 80 and 160 acres. Unmarried adults got between 40 and 60 acres, reminiscent of the '40 acres and a mule' given to freed slaves after the Civil War. This dramatically reduced the amount of the territory available to Native Americans: within 30 years they had lost over two-thirds of their land and seen the rest sold to white settlers.

Even defeated Nazi Germany, Sainte-Marie reports acerbically, was treated better: at least 'You left them their pride and you left them their land'. The song specifically refers to the recent breaking of 'a treaty forever George Washington signed' in order to build the Kinzua Dam in Pennsylvania. The 1794 Treaty of Canandaigua gave the Seneca, part of the Iroquois Tribe, permission to occupy 10,000 acres of land on the Allegheny River. Despite their protests, President Kennedy had pressed ahead with the project and 600 Seneca were forced to move to Salamanca on the northern shore of the newly-created Allegheny Dam, which was dubbed Lake Perfidy by the dispossessed tribe members.

Sainte–Marie wasn't the only folk singer to draw attention to this incident. Peter La Farge, whose five Folkways albums between 1962 and his death in 1965 all contained songs on Native American themes, wrote about it in 'As Long As The Grass Shall Grow' – a composition which appeared as the first track on one of the most remarkable protest albums of 1964, Johnny Cash's *Bitter Tears*.

Cash had emerged almost ten years previously on the quintessential rock and roll label, Sun; his first single was 'Hey Porter' / 'Cry, Cry, Cry', released on 21 June 1955 and an immediate hit on the country and western chart. It was followed up by 'Folsom Prison Blues' and 'I Walk

The Line', establishing the tough-guy sound and image that characterised the whole of his career. But Cash had a reflective, tender side, too – the emotionally-charged timbre of his voice held the potential to bark or cry.

Like Sainte-Marie and La Farge, Cash was of Native American descent and *Bitter Tears* was concerned exclusively with that heritage, as indicated by its subtitle, *Ballads Of The American Indian*. Five of the eight tracks, including the aforementioned 'As Long As The Grass Shall Grow', were written by La Farge. 'Custer' is a comic piece which canters along over a country and western beat, declaring in its refrain that, 'The general, he don't ride well any more'; Custer's Last Stand is seen not as a massacre but as a victory over someone who had broken a promise. 'Drums' describes how a young man is taught to be ashamed of being a Native American but remains proud of his culture and its history:

> There are drums beyond the mountain, Indian drums that you can't hear
> There are drums beyond the mountain, and they're getting mighty near

'White Girl' is about a young woman who will not marry her lover because he is a Native American, while 'The Ballad Of Ira Hayes' is the story of a Pima Indian who joined the Marines and participated in the celebrated flag-raising at Iwo Jima, Japan in 1945; despite returning a hero, Hayes lapsed into alcoholism and died prematurely and in poverty on the Gila River Reservation where he was born.

Cash's own compositions are both striking. 'Apache Tears' deals with the mass and individual oppression perpetrated by the white invaders:

> Who saw
> The young squaw
> Tried by their whisky law
> Tortured till she died of pain and fear

'The Talking Leaves' is a spoken narrative in which the young Sequoia asks his father about the white leaves (paper) left on the battleground. Told that these are used to communicate with people far away, Sequoia responds by cutting the Cherokee alphabet into stone, demonstrating that Native Americans can record their thoughts in writing, too.

The final track on the album is 'The Vanishing Race', written by Johnny Horton, who graduated from smouldering rockabilly classics like 'I'm Coming Home' to so-called saga songs like 'The Battle Of New Orleans', a US number one in the summer of 1959. His death in a car accident on 5 November 1960 hit Cash, a close friend of his, very hard. 'The Vanishing Race' unfolds over solemn Indian drumming and its vivid images graphically convey the decline of a culture and its people.

Bitter Tears was released on 1 October 1964, reaching number 47 on the album chart, Cash's best result to date. It confirmed his credentials as a supporter of campaigns and causes and in a year where Vietnam was starting to become the focus of most protest singers' ire, it was a timely reminder that the genre could and should encompass a wider range of issues.

Of course this fact was already well known to the previous generation of folk musicians. Pete Seeger, who by 1964 had been involved in protest music for a quarter of a century, was certainly not diverted by the war. Although a noted composer himself – among the best-known pieces he wrote/adapted are 'Where Have All The Flowers Gone?', 'If I Had A Hammer', 'Turn! Turn! Turn!' and 'We Shall Overcome' – Seeger was also a folk music archivist. As noted earlier in the Chapter, an anthology of the songs he and Woody Guthrie had collected was published in 1964 by *Sing Out!* magazine, under the editorship of Alan Lomax.

All aspects of Seeger's methodology were reflected in his 1964 album, *Songs Of Struggle And Protest 1930-1950*. Inevitably, a number of songs cover the subjects of unionisation and employment/unemployment. 'Joe Hill' and 'Talking Union' have already been described; 'Harry Simms' is a brisk piece about the 'bravest union man that I've ever seen', a 19 year-old NMU organiser murdered in 1932; and the sing-along 'I Don't Want

Your Millions, Mister' declares,

> All I want is the right to live, mister
> Give me back my job again

We also hear about the consequences of industrialisation in 'Pittsburgh':

> All I do is cough and choke
> From iron filings and sulphur smoke

Seeger's mordant wit comes to the fore in three songs. In 'Aimee McPherson' he lampoons the preacher who duped her congregation to make herself rich, while 'What A Friend We Have In Congress' (set to the tune of 'What A Friend We Have in Jesus') describes how the government 'spends three-quarters of our taxes getting ready for a war':

> Modern bombs are sure to carry loads of glory, joy and thrills
> What a privilege to bury all the dead our money kills

'The D-Day Dodgers', another audience participation piece, is equally heavy with irony:

> We landed at Salerno – a holiday without pay
> On the way to Florence we had a lovely time
> The artful D-Day Dodgers in sunny Italy

Finally there are the adaptations: Leadbelly's 'Bourgeois Blues' –

> The home of the brave, the land of the free,
> I don't want to be mistreated by no bourgeoisie

– and Beethoven's 'Ode To Joy', recast as 'Hymn to Nations ("Brother Sing Your Country's Anthem")':

105

Then in your final glory
Brother, lift your flag with mine.

In its way, Seeger's vision was as broad as that of any of his fellow protest singers. He drew on a rich fund of material, from the rural black and poor white communities, from international sources, from the great folk artists of the past, and from the impressive catalogue of his own compositions. He was, however, to prove completely out of step with the direction in which folk music was destined to go next.

★ ★ ★ ★ ★

The 'difficult second album' has become a cliché of rock music criticism, but has a good deal of truth in it. The overwhelming majority of acts who produce an artistically successful first record have been unable, mainly because of their limited talent, to sustain their creativity for long. Perhaps it is an indication of the distance between Bob Dylan and the rest that it took him four albums to run into a crisis. As we saw in Chapter 2, The Beatles also experienced problems at this juncture, in their case because the album in question, *Beatles For Sale*, was rushed. But the problems with *Another Side Of Bob Dylan* were of a different nature.

Dylan was going through a number of changes in the spring of 1964. His journey through the US had taught him a number of things, not all of them palatable. For one, his fame was not as widespread as he had been led to believe; for another, protest music had not been espoused universally and most young people were into The Beatles. Dylan says he became aware of their music when they came to New York, though his road trip began on 2 February 1964, five days before their arrival there. Whatever the case, he was drawn to their work very soon after, as he told Anthony Scaduto (*op. cit.,* p.175),

'When we were driving through Colorado we had the radio on and eight of the top ten songs were Beatles songs. In Colorado! "I Wanna Hold Your Hand", all those early ones.

'They were doing things nobody was doing. Their chords were outrageous, just outrageous, and their harmonies made it all valid …

'But I just kept it to myself that I really dug them. Everybody else thought they were for the teenyboppers, that they were gonna pass right away. But it was obvious to me that they had staying power. I knew they were pointing in the direction of where music had to go … You see, there was a lot of hypocrisy all around, people saying it had to be either folk or rock. But I knew it didn't have to be like that. I dug what the Beatles were doing, and I always kept it in my mind from back then.'

On Dylan's return to New York, his relationship with Suze Rotolo deteriorated still further and he began to take out his frustration and unhappiness on others; her sister, Carla, became a frequent butt of his anger and he blamed her for engineering their final break-up. In May he left for a tour of England which served to confirm to him that rock music was the way forward. He was astounded by, in particular, The Animals' version of 'The House Of The Rising Sun', a traditional number he had included on his debut album.

On 9 June 1964, he went into the studio to record *Another Side Of Bob Dylan*. It wasn't rock – Dylan had yet to work out a way of adjusting to that medium – but neither was it folk. Entirely shorn of protest music, the album consisted of love songs. Of a sort. In some instances 'hate songs' would be a better description. (In time, Dylan would perfect the genre; 'Like A Rolling Stone', from the following year, is a masterpiece.) The eight-minute 'Ballad In Plain D' is the most vituperative: a self-pitying, clumsily written rant against Carla Rotolo which occupies over 15% of the album. There is bitterness too in 'I Don't Believe You (She Acts Like We Have Never Met)', a metaphor for the souring of his relationship with Suze. At the opposite extreme, Dylan attempts humour but, possibly because of his state of mind, this comes over as forced and unfunny. 'Motorpsycho Nitemare' is a parody of Alfred Hitchcock's 1960 film *Psycho* but displays neither wit nor insight, and much the same can be said of 'I Shall Be Free – No. 10', a talking blues much inferior to its predecessors. The latter does, however, contain a clever reference to Lyndon Johnson's opponent in the 1964 Presidential Election that turns his potential appeal to uneducated, rural people on its head.

Such lapses in Dylan's accustomed standard can be explained by his turbulent personal life and the first, sometimes faltering, steps towards a new style for himself and for contemporary American music as a whole. And these factors led to success as well as failure. 'Chimes Of Freedom' is a heady combination of narrative and poetic techniques, and 'Black Crow Blues' is similarly adventurous; a ramshackle number with Dylan on piano which, with its use of antithesis (albeit derived from Richard 'Rabbit' Brown's terrifying 'James Alley Blues' of 1927), provides evidence of Dylan's new, more literary writing style.

And in spite of the disasters cited above, the best three tracks on the album are all autobiographical. 'My Back Pages' is a confession that his work to date has been immature and that his protest songs have betrayed a certainty about the world which in retrospect appears misguided and simplistic: in reality things are not so straightforward. Dylan contrasts the palpable seriousness and weight of experience that characterised his earlier work with his re-birth as an artist who has the innocence of youth.

'All I Really Want To Do' and 'It Ain't Me Babe', while ostensibly addressed to individuals (possibly Suze Rotolo again), also convey the rejection of his previous artistic existence, along the lines of 'I'm not the man you thought I was'. Unlike the examples cited earlier, in 'All I Really Want To Do' the comedy works well: the yodelling à la Jimmie Rodgers and the high and low voices supply an insouciance which helps reinforce its message. This song is usually interpreted as a cheerful farewell to Suze Rotolo, but it is tempting to see Dylan himself as the person who is being simplified and classified (and, anticipating the events of the following year, crucified) by critics and the public. In contrast, some observers have seen the above stanzas as an indication of Dylan's support for the women's liberation movement, then in its early stages of development in the US.

Despite its inconsistent quality *Another Side Of Bob Dylan* is an important record. Though Dylan was absorbing The Beatles' music at this time, compositions like Lennon's 'I'm A Loser', included on 1964's *Beatles For Sale,* show that the band were in turn influenced by the Dylan album. And, as we shall see, it had a considerable impact on one of the most important British songwriters of the mid-1960s, Pete Townshend of The Who.

Above all, it represents the crucial bridge between protest music and folk-rock. Perhaps the connection may have been still clearer had another song recorded by Dylan that day been included on the album. Instead it was The Byrds' version of 'Mr Tambourine Man', released on 12 April 1965, that became recognised as the first record of a new genre: folk-rock. Three months and one day later, producer Tom Wilson went straight from recording Dylan's' 'Like A Rolling Stone' to overdubbing electric guitar, bass and drums on to an otherwise acoustic track from the previous year. The artists, Simon and Garfunkel, were not even consulted – but 'The Sound Of Silence' became another landmark for folk-rock.

The song had been written by Paul Simon on 19 February 1964 and was included on the duo's debut album, *Wednesday Morning, 3 A.M.*, which came out nearly eight months later. Art Garfunkel describes it as follows:

> "The Sound Of Silence" is a major work. We were looking for a song on a larger scale, but this was more than either of us expected ... Its theme is man's inability to communicate with man. The author sees the extent of communication as it is on only its superficial and "commercial" level (of which the "neon sign" is representative). There is no serious understanding because there is no serious communication ... The words tell us that when meaningful communication fails, the only sound is silence.

These comments are part of a 'listener's guide to the songs' attached to a jocular open letter to Simon that accompanies the record. The intention is to parody the conventional sleeve note but Garfunkel's observations are so perceptive as to qualify as some of the earliest meaningful rock criticism, a genre yet to establish itself.

The rest of the album does much to justify its subtitle, *Exciting New Songs In The Folk Tradition*, although some tracks are neither exciting nor new. The gospel numbers 'You Can Tell The World' and 'Go Tell It On The Mountain' are incongruous and uninspiring while the cover version of 'The Times They Are A-Changin'', taken much faster than the original, lacks its intensity. The traditional 'Peggy-O' also seems twee when set next to Dylan's lusty rendition on his debut album. The most satisfying tracks are the Paul Simon compositions: 'Sparrow' is a clever allegory, again on the theme of communication, and 'Bleecker Street' an atmospheric song with the memorable couplet

> Voices leaking from a sad café
> Smiling faces try to understand

'He Was My Brother' takes us nearer to conventional protest song:

> Freedom rider
> They cursed my brother to his face
> Go home, outsider
> This town's gonna be your burying place
> He was singing on his knees
> An angry mob trailed along
> They shot my brother dead
> Because he hated what was wrong
> He was my brother
> Tears can't bring him back to me
> He was my brother
> And he died so his brothers could be free

But best of all, alongside 'The Sound Of Silence', is the title track, the story of a liquor store robber about to go on the run, later re-made as

'Somewhere They Can't Find Me'. 'Wednesday Morning 3 A.M.' may not have the pace and urgency of the later version, but its understated, gentle delivery makes its effect all the more touching.

In the albums *Another Side Of Bob Dylan* and *Wednesday Morning 3 A.M.*, we see the transition from traditional folk music to folk-rock nearing its fulfilment, an evolutionary process in which the year 1964 is critical – as demonstrated by the following diagram:

<   _____Protest Song_____   >

Traditional Folk > 'Old' Folk (traditional + originals) > 'New' Folk (all original) > Folk-Rock

1900 (and earlier)   > 1920s >   early 1960s   >>   1964   >>   1965

Largely through the efforts of Bob Dylan, although many others played an important part, 1964 saw folk music propelled from the outer fringes of popular culture to the cutting edge of contemporary rock. The emphasis on archiving and preservation gave way to a burgeoning creativity which endured for the remainder of the decade and was to have an indelible impact both on youth culture and national politics.

★ ★ ★ ★ ★

None of this was dreamed of by Lyndon Johnson as he contemplated the Presidential Election to be held on 3 November 1964. Certainly he was aware of the unrest on campuses across the country, especially at the University of California, Berkeley, where students had defied university regulations that prohibited political activity by participating in the Freedom Summer project and raising money for Civil Rights causes. A subsequent sit-in (at which Joan Baez performed) resulted in the arrest of 800 demonstrators, marked the birth of what became known as the Free Speech Movement and led to escalating militancy among students – but it was no more significant to Johnson in November 1964 than a variety of other issues he had to face.

111

It had, for example, been a year of freak weather events. March had seen an earthquake in Alaska that killed 100 people, as well as extensive fires in California; while in September Hurricanes Dora and Hilda had hit Florida and Louisiana respectively. Johnson had involved himself on every occasion, declaring those locations worst affected to be disaster areas and promising help with the re-building of communities.

Abroad, there had been a variety of challenges. Rioting had occurred in Panama when Canal Zone Police tore up the Panamanian flag during clashes with local students, an episode symptomatic of tensions regarding sovereignty of the Canal. The US Army was despatched to quell the trouble and, after three days of conflict, 21 Panamanians and four US soldiers were dead. More positive news came in April when Johnson and the Russian Premier, Nikita Khrushchev, concluded an agreement on nuclear disarmament, whereby the US cut the production of enriched uranium and Russia discontinued the construction of two plutonium reactors. And then there was Vietnam, where 35,000 troops were being drafted every month in the wake of the Gulf of Tonkin Incident.

Johnson was frustrated that such matters were diverting him from what he saw as his main duty as President: the creation of 'the Great Society', a Utopian vision that encompassed the end of social injustice, racial prejudice and discrimination, improved educational opportunities and rural and urban regeneration. Concerned that his opponent, Barry Goldwater, would destroy all of these ambitions if he won, Johnson approached the Election with some pessimism and took even the smallest setback or negative poll rating as a harbinger of defeat.

He needn't have worried: the margin of his victory – 43 million votes to Goldwater's 27 million – was the highest in US history.

CHAPTER 4:

A Shot Of Rhythm And Blues

By the beginning of 1964 the standard of living in the UK had reached a new peak. Gross National Product (GNP), the value of products and services in the economy, had reached £30.49 billion compared with £29.98 billion in 1960 and a mere £13.31 billion in 1950. Arguably, economic advancement was to be expected as the country got back on its feet after the restrictions of war, but in a changing world that presented such new challenges as a diminishing Empire and the need to fund a Welfare State it was still impressive progress.

Back in 1957 Prime Minister Harold Macmillan said:

> … let us be frank about it – most of our people have never had it so good. Go around the country, go to the industrial towns, go to the farms and you will see a state of prosperity such as we have never had in my lifetime – nor indeed in the history of this country.

Seven years on, there seemed little reason to doubt this assessment, the invective of the Labour Manifesto notwithstanding.

In reality things were not as bright as they seemed. In 1965 Professors Peter Townsend and Brian Abel-Smith demonstrated in their *Child Poverty Memorandum* that hardship continued to lurk under this surface of affluence. There had also been a rejuvenation of countries hardest hit by the War, notably West Germany and Japan, and they were beginning to threaten Britain's pre-eminence in world trade.

Overall, however, for the majority of British citizens things were looking up in a number of vital areas. The years between 1951 and 1961 saw an increase in life-expectancy for both men and women and a decline in infant mortality. During the same period levels of unemployment were comparatively low, fluctuating year by year, but never amounting to more than 3% of the workforce. The quality of the UK's housing stock was rising and the post war years witnessed a boom in the construction of semi-detached houses *

The picture was especially encouraging for young people who benefited from all of these improvements, and from a series of government measures which awarded them a better education and more independence. The National Assistance Act of 1948 allowed under-sixteens to be assessed on their own income, rather than that of their parents, and the Family Allowances Act of 1945 introduced a new source of income for families with fifteen to eighteen year olds either in education or unemployed. In 1956 family allowance was made available for young people in apprenticeships and finally, in 1964, extended family allowance was introduced for dependants up to nineteen years of age who were in full-time education. Meanwhile the earliest date for leaving school was brought forward from Christmas to Easter.

Needless to say, such measures brought a dramatic increase in the proportion of young people going to college – particularly from families with no history of further or higher education – and between 1948 and 1964 the number of UK full-time students achieving first degrees almost doubled. A favoured destination for the creatively-minded – and a fertile breeding-ground for 1960s pop stars – was the Art School.

The net result was that teenagers in the early 1960s, whatever their status and family background, were far better off than their parents' generation. The unemployed could claim benefits in their own right, there was work for those who wanted it and a fast-growing student population, funded by the State.

---

* The statistics quoted in this and the subsequent two paragraphs are derived from Joe Hicks and Grahame Allen, *A Century Of Change: Trends In UK Statistics Since 1900* (House of Commons Research Paper 99/111, 21 December 1999)

Nevertheless clear dividing-lines existed in matters of culture and sub-culture. Among the working classes the teddy boys had reigned supreme for a decade, a sign of how the rise in young people's disposable income had driven developments in fashion and – never far behind – pop music. With their drape jackets, drainpipe trousers and slicked-back hairstyle, the teds were visually arresting and it was their radical appearance as much as anything that symbolised the threat to the Establishment posed by post-war youth culture.

Closely related to the teds were the rockers, whose image and values (or lack of them) derived from Marlon Brando's film *The Wild One* and its motorcycle-riding, leather-clad nihilists. Centred on the rather less romantic British institution of the transport café, rockers were less fastidious than the teds when it came to dress, opting for a uniform of grubby leather jackets and jeans and unkempt hair. They rode their motorbikes from one 'caf' to another, frequently hitting speeds of 100 miles per hour and thus earning them a second sobriquet: the 'ton-up boys'.

Both the teds and the rockers were into American youth culture and, specifically, rock and roll. However their marginal variations in musical taste – the teds leaning more towards Elvis Presley and Bill Haley, the rockers to Eddie Cochran and Gene Vincent – were indicative of a slight age differential. By 1964, the teds were beginning to fade while the rockers were moving into the spotlight; they were even the subject of a feature film released in January, *The Leather Boys*, directed by Sidney J Furie and starring Rita Tushingham.

The rockers were scruffy, unsophisticated and suspicious of anything they considered to have effeminate undertones including the use of recreational drugs, all of which placed them in diametric opposition to the other major working-class youth faction of the era, the mods.

The term 'mod' and the fashion sense that went with it came from the young supporters of modern jazz who throughout the 1950s and early 1960s had clashed both ideologically and, ultimately, physically with adherents of traditional jazz. It had begun peacefully enough, despite an incident at a 1953 concert by the Humphrey Lyttelton Band at Birmingham Town Hall. Trad fans had displayed a banner bearing the words 'Go Home, Dirty Bopper!' aimed at the group's new alto saxophonist, Bruce Turner, who had a background in bebop (or 'bop') and had studied with one of its most advanced practitioners, Lee Konitz. In 1960 the Beaulieu Jazz Festival was interrupted by fights between the rival factions and when the violence was repeated the following year the owner of the site, Lord Montagu of Beaulieu, discontinued the festival.

The devotees of modern jazz were, inevitably, dubbed 'modernists'. The cadre based in the East End of London opted for a radical style of tailoring with sharply cut suits and jackets, and when the trend crossed to the West of the capital, the emphasis on sartorial detail went with it. While musical tastes began to change as the modernists became known as mods, their dress sense and the fine tuning that would render the wearer either cutting-edge or hopelessly outmoded was always at least as crucial as the music. Teds and rockers maintained a greater equilibrium in their interests. For the former, the opposite sex, American cars and rock and roll were just as important as what they wore. Substitute motorbikes for cars and the same can be said of the rockers, though a studied untidiness was *de rigueur*. Minor lapses in trend awareness were tolerated in both cases, but for mods the tiniest variations in outfit were hugely significant. As the writer Dave, chronicler of the mod scene in Manchester, recalls,

> ... fashion and style had changed weekly and frantically – like going from "see through" plastic macs and bell-bottom jeans, to ice cream van salesman's jackets dyed ice-blue with button down shirts and paisley ties, almost in the blink of an eye. These things changed rapidly in 64 and 65. The size of your suit vents, your top handkerchief positioning, or the way you buttoned your suit, these things would show to those who knew if you were really in or out. It was a secret code. (*The Manchester Wheelers: A Northern Quadrophenia*, p. 39)

The obsessive nature of mod made it different from many of the cults that both preceded and followed it – it was intense to the point of being a religion. What made it especially remarkable, however, was that it was located within the routine of day-to-day life and not outside it, as the hippies and punks, for instance, aspired to be. Mods needed to work, if only to fund their clothes-buying habit, and indeed their smart appearance and short hair, meant they were often looked on favourably by employers.

There were other mod trademarks apart from clothing: the motor scooter, the drugs (principally amphetamines) and the propensity for cool anonymity. Music was also of some significance in that it provided the backcloth – whether in the caf, the pub or the dance hall – for social gatherings. But attributing to them the exclusive ownership of any one style is tricky. Indeed Dave Marsh (*Before I Get Old – The Story Of The Who*) states that,

> There was no mod music, just music that mods liked. Unlike the British style cults of a decade later, mod fashion didn't build itself up around bands. Instead a group of rock bands did its best to play music that would appeal to mods. (p.6)

In the main, rhythm and blues (or 'R&B') would encompass most of what mods were into. At the time it was a catch-all term, encompassing a wide spectrum from the raw urban blues of Chicago via the music emanating from the Southern United States and becoming known as 'soul', right through to the softer sounds of Detroit and Philadelphia. It was therefore African-American music and could only be accessed directly through records or, from August 1963, the occasional appearance of an R&B singer on Rediffusion's youth-oriented music programme, *Ready Steady Go!* Of the British bands, The Rolling Stones were consistently popular.

But lots of other people liked these artists, too: at the beginning of 1964, what the mods needed was their own band. This they found in an outfit variously known as The Detours, The High Numbers and The Who.

★ ★ ★ ★ ★

The first that the mass of the British public got to hear about the mods were the riots in the seaside town of Clacton over the Easter weekend (26 and 27 March) of 1964. Hundreds of mods and rockers clashed in the streets and on the beach, terrifying the local populace and what few holidaymakers were braving the bitterly cold weather. With hindsight it is easy to see how a pent-up, introspective culture like mod was likely to erupt and ignite the predisposition to violence of the rockers who, as noted above, were vehemently opposed to just about everything the mods stood for.

But the national press was in no mood for such analysis – their first instinct then, as now, was to make moral pronouncements of the most stentorian kind. From the vantage point of the early 21st century, when the media is obsessed with youth but all too ready to demonise the young, this reaction is easily recognisable. The most extreme of the tabloids, *The Sun*, was not yet in existence (it was launched on 15 September 1964) but there was still sufficient outrage throughout the media to spark off what sociologist Stanley Cohen described as a 'moral panic'. Not that this worried the mods – or the rockers. On the contrary, during Whitsun there were further clashes in Margate, Brighton and Bournemouth and in August police had to be flown in to deal with a contemporary battle of Hastings. Unsurprisingly the enormous publicity given to the mods by the newspapers had the opposite effect to that which was intended: it acted as a clarion call to young people to join them. By the end of 1964, mod had become *the* fashionable teenage cult, supported and encouraged by high street retailers, record companies and broadcasters.

Crucially, at a time when politicians like Harold Wilson were becoming interested in pop music for its potential to further their careers, mod had forged an independent existence: it would be hard to imagine MPs fraternising with The Who, for example, in the way that Wilson had with The Beatles. What the rise of the mods – and their middle-class cousins, the R&B fans – demonstrated was that youth culture was a force to be reckoned with on its own terms and had the potential to dictate social, political and even economic developments. Thus 1964 was a pivotal year for the teenager: the year the 1950s' perception (no doubt fostered by the

War when young people had no choice but to grow up fast) that teenage tastes and behaviours were merely a short-lived diversion on the road to 'maturity' gave way to an acknowledgement of the centrality of youth within both popular culture and the wider Western world.

As noted above, The Who were the quintessential mod band, but it was typical of the mod movement that this was as much to do with the way they dressed and behaved as it was with the music they played which, up until guitarist Pete Townshend began to take over the leadership and song writing duties in late 1964/early 1965, consisted almost exclusively of R&B.

As regards their image, the crucial figure was Peter Meaden, who had begun to promote them at the end of 1963. Dave Marsh (*op. cit.,* p. 74) reports his advice to the band:

> "Look, you know, there's a million groups looking like the Rolling Stones. Cut your hair, get their [i.e. the mods'] gear, be what they want, be how they are."

Meaden's makeover also included a new name, The High Numbers, another tactic to make them stand out from their peers.

By spring 1964, the band had a strong reputation for hard-hitting R&B and a devoted following, built up at venues like the Goldhawk in Shepherd's Bush. At an audition for Fontana Records the band created a favourable impression with their version of American R&B giant Bo Diddley's 'Here 'Tis'. But their drummer, Doug Sandom, was considered inadequate, so the search commenced for replacement, culminating, one Thursday in April, with the recruitment of sixteen year-old Keith Moon.

On their return to Fontana, The High Numbers recorded their first single, 'I'm The Face', released on 3 July 1964. It was written by Meaden, as was the flipside, 'Zoot Suit', and while both had melodies derived directly from R&B their lyrics were pure mod. The 'face' was mod parlance for the leader, or trendsetter, and the song is an affirmation of that dominance; 'Zoot Suit' is a paean to the sharp-dressed man. They are confident performances with neat guitar solos, dynamic drums and authoritative vocals from Roger Daltrey, whom Meaden was consciously developing as the 'face' of the band. Bright and breezy in atmosphere and tempo, they make an interesting contrast to The High Numbers' live sound, a glimpse of which can be caught on recordings made at the Marquee the month before 'I'm The Face' came out.

The most noticeable differences are in Daltrey's voice, which on stage is gruff and guttural in the manner of blues artist Howlin' Wolf, and the leaden, thumping rhythm that pervades 'Long Tall Shorty' and Wolf's 'Smokestack Lightning'. Their version of the Janie Bradford and Berry Gordy composition, 'Money', converted by The Beatles into primal heavy metal the previous year, is a chaotic epic – in effect, a blues medley incorporating a reprise of 'Smokestack Lightning' ,Tommy Johnson's 'Big Road Blues' and improvised instrumental interludes involving a bass guitar solo by John Entwistle and drum fills by Moon. 'Here 'Tis' and another Bo Diddley number, 'Pretty Thing', are more animated but still rendered gloomy by Daltrey's rasping vocals.

Insufficiently promoted, 'I'm The Face' didn't make the chart but it gave Meaden and The High Numbers an insight into the possibilities beyond those available to a run-of-the-mill R&B band. Though these were not fully realised until 1965, The High Numbers were now on a trajectory towards originality and an audience far wider than a loyal band of mods.

As a first step, the heavier urban blues numbers by the likes of Howlin' Wolf and Muddy Waters were gradually dropped; they had only been included in the first place to copy The Rolling Stones, under whose influence the band had fallen since opening for them the previous year at St Mary's Ballroom, Putney.

They were also, almost without realising it, developing their visual impact. Daltrey was being groomed as the front man, but the recruitment of the manic Moon added a new dimension. In most British beat and R&B groups, drummers tended to be anonymous, shadowy figures – only Ringo Starr and Dave Clark, who led his own band, were personalities in their own right. Moon, with his flailing arms and transfixing stare, seemed to be from a different world and drew attention like a magnet; at the same time his thrilling fills and flourishes became an essential element in the band's sound.

And then there was Pete Townshend, who claims to have come upon his guitar-smashing routine accidentally during a gig at the Railway Tavern, Wealdstone. Trying to eliminate a whistling noise, he knocked the instrument into the pub's low ceiling – pleased with the effect, he repeated it and when encouraged to do it once more inadvertently ruptured the neck of the guitar: wanting to look as if he had done so deliberately, he broke the whole thing up. Perhaps he was also subconsciously recalling the lectures he had heard at Ealing Art School by Gustav Metzger who, assisted by Yoko Ono, smashed up pianos to reflect the damage being done to the planet by man, and by Malcolm Cecil who had sawed up a double bass in class. As well as his onstage antics, Townshend was beginning to focus on his song writing, deriving inspiration from, in particular, *Another Side Of Bob Dylan*.

In late summer 1964, The High Numbers were filmed at the Railway Tavern by Kit Lambert who, with his business partner Chris Stamp, took over the band's management a short time later. The result, now documented on the DVD *Six Quick Ones*, is a useful barometer of the band's progress. To begin with, the material is rather lighter than that heard at the Marquee in June: Jessie Hill's 1960 number, 'Oo Poo Pah Doo', was a bouncy, infectious slice of New Orleans R&B, while 'I Gotta Dance To Keep From Crying', written by Eddie Holland, Lamont Dozier and Brian Holland and recorded by The Miracles the previous year, was emblematic of early 1960s Motown. Daltrey, with short hair, shades and wielding maracas, is very much in foreground and sings with vigour and assurance, though there is an energy and attitude about the entire band, with Moon at this stage more prominent than Townshend and Entwistle. In short they were about halfway to where they would end up as The Who, one of the most exciting rock bands of all.

At Lambert's insistence they soon reverted to their former name and thanks to his persistence obtained a Tuesday residency at the Marquee. He also coined their (not entirely accurate) slogan 'Maximum R&B' and had it printed on a poster he commissioned that featured a photograph of Townshend in profile, with his arm raised and ready to bear down on his guitar. All of this won the band new legions of fans, but there was more to it than marketing.

Each member of the band was now making his own distinctive and essential contribution: Daltrey's powerful, assertive vocals; Moon's all-action drumming; Entwistle's prodigious bass; and more latterly Townshend's crashing guitar chords that provided a contemporary, electrified take on flamenco. What's more, they frequently made these contributions *all at the same time,* conjuring up a collective improvisation entirely new to pop music. As Noel Gallagher has said,

They're all playing lead, all of them … it's insane. (*Six Quick Ones*)

In January 1965 The Who released 'I Can't Explain', a punchy Townshend composition that merged influences ranging from fellow mod favourites The Kinks to surf music (brought into the mix by Moon)to create an unforgettable gem of a record, and set them on the first rung of the ladder to national and international success.

★ ★ ★ ★ ★

So perfectly did The Who seem to encapsulate the mod ethos that it is tempting to forget that other music was of interest, too. The sound of Jamaica, for example, was beginning to filter through in 1964, with vocalist Derrick Morgan among the first to appeal to the mods. Especially popular were his 'Housewife's Choice' (1962), recorded with Millicent Todd and released as by Derrick and Patsy, and 'Blazing Fire' from the following year.

The Mersey Beat groups still held some sway, and it was characteristic of mod that some of the more obscure bands were as fashionable as the star performers. For example, The Undertakers – who acquired their name after a local newspaper had printed the wrong caption under their photograph – made an impression in summer 1964 with the strutting R&B staple, 'Just A Little Bit', the original of which was a hit in 1959 for Rosco Gordon. (The Undertakers' vocalist, Jackie Lomax, went on to make one of the outstanding singles of the late 1960s, 'Sour Milk Sea', written and produced by George Harrison and bearing the catalogue number APPLE 3.) Bass player Tony Jackson had recently left The Searchers to form his own outfit, Tony Jackson and The Vibrations, and enjoyed some success in September with 'Bye Bye Baby', a lively cover of (but not a patch on)Mary Wells's self-composed debut single from 1960.

Then there were the bands formed at the time of mod's ascendancy and reflecting mod culture. Some of these, inevitably, were ephemeral. Take, for example, Peter's Faces – their name changed from the more prosaic Peter Nelson and The Travellers to be on trend – who made just three singles, including the ingenuous 'Just Like Romeo And Juliet', released in October 1964, four months after the original version, by Detroit blue-eyed soul quartet The Reflections, had made the US Top Ten. Others transcended mod to become long-term contributors to rock music. Among these were The Kinks, whose first single, their interpretation of 'Long Tall Sally', came out on 7 February 1964. As this was at least the eighth version of the Little Richard number – including recordings by Elvis Presley and Pat Boone – it predictably failed to chart. 'You Still Want Me', this time an original by band-member Ray Davies, fared no better in April.

Their contract with Pye Records under threat, The Kinks brought out a third single, 'You Really Got Me', on 4 August; it turned out to be one of the most explosive records of the year, if not the decade. A stark, unaccompanied, and unforgettable, guitar riff is the opening salvo, whereupon the rest of the band break in; Davies's vocal – which could so easily, given the force of piece, have been laden with hysteria – is by contrast calm and measured, only intensifying as the title-phrase chorus approaches. Two walloping drum breaks by Mick Avory and a wild guitar solo by Ray's brother, Dave, pile on the aggression until the tension is finally resolved by four climactic chords. 'You Really Got Me' entered the UK singles chart on 13 August, reaching number one on 10 September.

The formula was repeated for the follow-up, 'All Day And All Of The Night'. Released on 23 October and possibly even better, it only reached number two, perhaps because of the close resemblance to its predecessor. Another elemental riff kicks things off, with Davies's singing – as befits the overtly sexual lyrics – laced with a menacing leer; we get more belting drums, another crazed guitar solo and an almost identical coda. Both singles were produced by the American, Shel Talmy (as indeed was The Who's 'I Can't Explain', modelled to some extent on the two Kinks records), and they owe much of their success to the taut atmosphere he creates. However, Dave Davies also deserves some credit for coming up with the harsh, distorted guitar sound – achieved by applying a razor blade to the speaker cone in his amplifier.

Whether or not The Kinks qualify as 100% mod remains a topic of debate. Certainly in their early days they displayed a sense of sartorial style – though they came to ridicule this two years later with their single 'Dedicated Follower Of Fashion'. There is no question either that they appealed to mods: they are often bracketed with The Who and The Small Faces (who were formed in 1965) as the quintessential mod bands. But they wore their hair long which, alongside their R&B roots, allied them to the more middle-class and bohemian Rolling Stones – indeed Mick Avory had played with The Stones at their first-ever live appearance, which took place at the Marquee on 12 July 1962.

★ ★ ★ ★ ★

At the time of that auspicious occasion, the Marquee was located at 165 Oxford Street, London. A former ballroom, it had been under the successful management of Harold Pendleton for four years. Like many other venues in the capital it was tracing a transition of musical taste which spanned the decade 1954-1964 as follows:

TRAD JAZZ > SKIFFLE > R&B > ROCK

Trad had developed shortly after the Second World War as a consequence of a renewed interest in New Orleans Jazz among young white West Coast-based musicians such as Lu Watters and the publication in 1939 of *Jazzmen*, edited by Frederic Ramsey Jr and Charles Edward Smith, which lionised the pioneers of the music. One such was trumpeter Bunk Johnson who was in his fifties when he came out of retirement to work with Watters and make his first recordings in 1942. In this environment New Orleans jazz was considered the real McCoy, a sharp contrast to both swing, which was seen as overblown and commercial, and bebop, which was derided as incomprehensible and barely music at all. This search for the Holy Grail of authenticity was, as we shall see, to recur constantly up to 1964 – and well beyond.

Trad jazz was, in essence, the response outside the US to these developments. The bands of Graeme Bell, in Australia, Claude Luter, in France, and George Webb, in the UK, were among its first exponents. The Webb ensemble introduced a number of individuals destined to achieve the fame that he did not, including clarinettist Wally Fawkes, later well known as the cartoonist 'Trog', and trumpeter Humphrey Lyttelton, whose career as a bandleader led on to a successful sideline in broadcasting.

The key figure in trad jazz was, however, trombonist Chris Barber. His first band was formed in 1953 with clarinettist Monty Sunshine, and included trumpeter Ken Colyer, who had acquired celebrity in the jazz world after being imprisoned in Louisiana for playing alongside African-American musicians, drummer Ron Bowden and guitarist Tony – later Lonnie – Donegan. For the interval between sets, Barber took to featuring a slimmed-down version of the full band, with himself on bass, Donegan on guitar and vocalist Beryl Bryden on washboard. The repertoire was American folk music, including work songs, ballads and original compositions like 'Rock Island Line', first recorded in 1934 for the Library of Congress, under the supervision of John A Lomax, by a group of convicts (Kelly Pace, who wrote it, Charlie Porter, LT Edwards, Willie

Hubbard, Luther Williams, Napoleon Cooper, Albert Pate and Willie Lee Jones) at Cummins State Farm, Gould, Arkansas. Three years later, it was popularised through a recording by the singer and guitarist, Leadbelly, a former convict himself, and it was this rendition that the Barber group used as basis for their recording of the song in 1954.

A hit on both sides of the Atlantic under Donegan's name, 'Rock Island Line' marked the beginning of skiffle, the lively, light-swinging style that combined DIY with music and inspired the formation of groups up and down the country – among them The Quarry Men who on their calling-card billed themselves as 'Country-Western-Rock 'n' Roll-Skiffle'. If that were not a big enough contribution to the history of rock music, Barber was also instrumental in bringing a host of US blues and gospel stars to the UK, such as Big Bill Broonzy, Sonny Terry and Brownie McGhee, Muddy Waters and Sister Rosetta Tharpe.

The Marquee was heavily involved in all of this, providing gigs both for British jazz and skiffle groups and the American visitors. One artist who frequently appeared at the Marquee was former Barber guitarist Alexis Korner. In 1962 he recorded a live album there, *R&B From The Marquee,* with his band Blues Incorporated, the line-up of which contained the likes of saxophonist Dick Heckstall-Smith, singer Long John Baldry and the co-leader of the group, harmonica player Cyril Davies. Davies had come to blues from trad jazz and his full-blooded approach to music, and to life, endeared him to fans and colleagues alike; he died of acute leukaemia on 7 January 1964, aged 31.

Korner acted as host to visiting American artists and as mentor to many budding British ones, including guitarist Brian Jones who had introduced himself to Korner at a Blues Incorporated gig in his native Cheltenham in late 1961. Korner also took under his wing a young vocalist from Dartford named Mick Jagger, whose first public appearance, in March 1962, was sitting in with Blues Incorporated at the Ealing blues club Korner had founded with Davies less than two weeks earlier.

As well as the Marquee, there were numerous London venues for both mods and R&B enthusiasts to choose from in 1964. Many were run by men like Harold Pendleton: independently-minded, larger-than-life entrepreneurs who played as big a part in the development of the music as some of the performers.

One such was Jeffrey Kruger, who started the Flamingo Club in 1952. Originally in Coventry Street, it moved in April 1957 to 35-37 Wardour Street where, five years later, it acquired notoriety as the scene of a fight between two of Christine Keeler's lovers, Johnny Edgecombe and Aloysius Gordon, an incident which sparked the investigations leading ultimately to the Profumo scandal. At that time, the Flamingo was a jazz club, though Kruger had already begun to diversify by going into music publishing and founding the pop label, Ember.

1964 was an especially strong year for Ember. John Barry had joined the company the previous year as a producer, having already made a name for himself for his work on the soundtracks of the first two James Bond films, *Dr No* and *From Russia With Love,* orchestrating the first and composing the second. Barry made a series of pounding instrumentals for the label including the offshoots from his soundtrack for the film *Zulu* (released on 22 January 1964) 'Zulu Stamp', 'Monkey Feathers', 'High Grass' and 'Big Shield'. He also continued to produce the rather insipid duo Chad Stuart and Jeremy Clyde, with whom he had success in 1963 with 'Yesterday's Gone'; but despite his imaginative arrangement featuring flute, strings and an acoustic guitar solo, the follow-up, 'Like I Love You Today', failed to chart on its release in January. Chad and Jeremy were to find greater fame in the US than at home, with seven Top 40 hits between 1964 and 1966 – their image in America was not hindered by the fact that Clyde was the great-great-great grandson of Arthur Wellesley, the first Duke of Wellington – and something of their soft-centred approach can be perceived in the work of Simon and Garfunkel. Other notable Ember releases in 1964 included The Washington DCs' 'Kisses Sweeter Than Wine', a rocking version of the 1957 hit by Jimmie Rodgers; 'She'll Never Be You'/ 'Gonna Make A Woman' by A Band Of Angels (the latter written by the band's vocalist, Mike D'Abo, later to become famous with Manfred Mann and as the composer of 'Handbags And Gladrags'); and Marcus

Tro's cover version of 'Tell Me', the only Mick Jagger and Keith Richard composition on The Rolling Stones' debut album.

Meanwhile the Flamingo was establishing itself as a haunt for mods, R&B fans, London's Caribbean community and GIs in town for a good time. One of the outfits able to appeal to this eclectic mix was Georgie Fame and The Blue Flames. Fame, whose real name was Clive Powell, was ersatz in almost all respects: the title of his band was a cheeky take on Chris Powell and his Blue Flames, the group with which the immortal jazz trumpeter, Clifford Brown, made his recording debut, and his vocal style was directly derived from the American master of vocalese (the application of lyrics to jazz instrumental solos), Jon Hendricks. He was, however, an extremely able imitator and a skilful alchemist of genres. His fourth single of 1964, 'Yeah, Yeah', was also one of the year's best , a cool but funky version of the piece written as an instrumental by Pat Patrick and Rodgers Grant, popularised by Mongo Santamaria, and to which Hendricks had added the words. On 21 February 1964 he released his debut album, recorded live at the club, the rather noisy *Rhythm And Blues At The Flamingo.*

Another club frequented by mods was The Scene, owned by Ronan O'Rahilly, the grandson of one of the heroes of the Irish Easter Rising of 1916, and the manager of Blues Incorporated. O'Rahilly also began to manage Georgie Fame, but soon became frustrated at his inability to get any air time for his records. Radio Luxembourg would only feature releases from their sponsors, while the BBC were simply indifferent. Enraged at what he saw as a closed shop, O'Rahilly vowed to start his own radio station in protest, and this he did: Radio Caroline (named after John F Kennedy's daughter) began operations over Easter 1964 – the same weekend that mods and rockers were clashing in Clacton. By transmitting from a boat five kilometres off the coast of Felixstowe, Suffolk, Caroline circumvented British broadcasting laws; it also departed, in some style, from British broadcasting traditions. Commercials, jingles, fast-talking disc-jockeys and the very latest records combined in an intoxicating mixture – this was pop music radio American-style, and UK teenagers adored it. Soon other 'pirate' radio stations opened for business, each of them introducing new DJs as well as new music. It all seemed too good to be true – and indeed it was.

Pressurised by the BBC and other Establishment interests, Postmaster General Anthony Wedgwood-Benn constructed the Marine Offences Act, effectively rendering unlicensed offshore broadcasting illegal. The Act took effect on 14 August 1967; the following month, the BBC began its own national pop music station, Radio One, employing many former DJs from Caroline and the other pirates, but before long they became stale and predictable. As for Wedgwood-Benn, he later changed his name to Tony Benn, and became known as one of Britain's most famous socialists.

O'Rahilly's impulse to create Radio Caroline was no doubt also fuelled by the power that records could exercise over young people, something he had witnessed first-hand at The Scene. There the DJ, Guy Stevens, who specialised in R&B or – as its more contemporary incarnation was starting to be called – 'soul', was a huge attraction for the mods, and many other young people. As O'Rahilly recalls in Bill Brewster and Frank Broughton's book, *Last Night A DJ Saved My Life*:

"Everybody would come to hear Guy ... The Stones, The Beatles, Eric Clapton – all the major stars. People would come from all over the country on Monday nights, and from France and Holland too; it was that good." (p. 67)

Stevens was a pioneer in two crucial respects: he was the first British club DJ to emerge as a personality in his own right, and probably the first also to set trends, rather than follow them. His subsequent career in music was distinguished but brief: he ran the Sue division of Island Records (and so introducing UK fans to a whole new crop of quality R&B artists), brought Chuck Berry to this country for his debut tour and, in 1979, produced the classic Clash album, *London Calling*. Two years later, at the age of 38, he died of a drug overdose.

When he was just getting established in London, O'Rahilly took a class in Konstantin Stanislavski's 'method' acting where he met another budding R&B entrepreneur, Giorgio Gomelsky. Born in Russia, Gomelsky had lived in Switzerland, Italy and Germany before he discovered blues and R&B during a spell working for Chris Barber. His first venture into club management was the West End Jazz Club, followed by the Piccadilly, where he first presented The Rolling Stones. In 1963, he set up shop on Sunday nights at the Station Hotel, Kew Road, Richmond, calling his new venue the Crawdaddy after a Bo Diddley song. The Crawdaddy, both at the Station and its subsequent relocation at Richmond Athletic Club, hosted acts that were to become some of the biggest names in rock music history – The Stones, Rod Stewart, Elton John, and The Yardbirds, who featured, at various times, Eric Clapton, Jeff Beck and Jimmy Page. Gomelsky managed The Yardbirds, securing them a contract with EMI and organising the recording of an album at the Marquee in March 1964. Though the band had backed Sonny Boy Williamson for an LP made at the Crawdaddy the previous autumn, this was in effect the first live album by a major British band of the 1960s.

Of all the notable characters involved in R&B club management in 1964, perhaps the most unconventional was Arthur Chisnall, who organised events on Eel Pie Island (or Eelpiland, as it became known), just a short distance down the River Thames from Richmond. Chisnall, unlike Kruger, O'Rahilly and Gomelsky, was not a creature of the music business. Rather, he was interested in young people for their own sake and took pleasure in providing them with a space in which they could relax and be themselves. As Michele Whitby has written (Dave van der Vat and Michele Whitby, *Eel Pie Island*, p. 54-5),

> Arthur Chisnall's strengths lay in guiding and empowering others. The desire to facilitate was the real inspiration behind Eelpiland, the music scene being almost secondary. By and large, he viewed the musical acts he booked as the means of attracting the needful youngsters whom he wanted to reach out to and inspire … Here was a man who had booked the Rolling Stones, hung out with Rod

Stewart, shared a beer with Eric Clapton, Jeff Beck and countless others, yet he preferred to talk about politics rather than partying, and was almost cross at my suggestion that he had seen a gap in the market for youth entertainment: "No, no, you have to realise, I was a researcher, I was interested in why this generation of youngsters was different and how they could be helped. I wasn't looking at it commercially."

Chisnall became involved in presenting bands at the Eel Pie Hotel in the late 1950s – at the time, these were almost exclusively trad outfits, led by the likes of Barber, Lyttelton and Colyer. Almost immediately he injected an element of fun into the proceedings, devising mock passports for entry to the Island and jokey rules and decrees – for instance, 'This number is unimportant and should not be remembered', 'This is to certify the person herein named has passed all tests for jiving and skiving' – thus sending up the rigid conformity that dominated young people's lives. In this respect, as in many others, he was ahead of his time, anticipating the irreverent humour of *Beyond The Fringe, I'm Sorry I'll Read That Again* and, ultimately, *Monty Python's Flying Circus*.

His interest in the personal and social development of young people was also radical for the period; it was certainly well beyond the scope of professional youth work which operated on very traditional lines until the new Labour Government of 1964 began the drive towards improved provision and practice.

It was a matter of principle with Chisnall that all young people were welcome at Eelpiland, irrespective of their background, although mods went there (and the Crawdaddy, for that matter) only grudgingly – and would never have ventured there at all had not a favoured band been playing. The problem was not that they weren't welcome, but that they had an antipathy to the middle-class teenagers who populated these clubs, and their affluent surroundings. Despite the fact that they were only a short distance from Shepherd's Bush and Acton, Richmond and Twickenham were a world away economically and socially.

Chisnall encouraged the bohemian, free-thinking, anything-goes approach and it is clear to see in retrospect how vital this was in the development of what became the British hippy sub-culture – indeed Chisnall put on several bands who would become associated with the hippies, such as Pink Floyd. But in 1964 it was R&B that ruled the roost, with a mixture of leading names and rock stars-in-waiting that included Long John Baldry and The Hoochie-Coochie Men, featuring Rod Stewart; The Artwoods (led by Ron Wood's brother, Art, and including Jon Lord, later of Deep Purple); The Alex Harvey Band; and Davie Jones and The Manish Boys whose leader later became more famous as David Bowie.

However, the most popular band that Chisnall ever put on ('Never mind the hotel, the bloody island was overflowing') did not play there after September 1963. By then, The Rolling Stones were moving on to bigger and better things.

★ ★ ★ ★ ★

Alongside The Beatles, The Rolling Stones tower over pop music: almost every major development during the last 50 years can be traced back to either, or both, bands. It now seems almost inconceivable that they emerged within a year of each other and indeed – despite their alleged, and much publicised, rivalry – formed a close friendship. When The Stones were seeking a follow-up to their first single, the Chuck Berry composition, 'Come On', John Lennon and Paul McCartney presented them with 'I Wanna Be Your Man', which entered the UK Top 40 on 14 November 1963 and reached number twelve, nine places higher than its predecessor. In later years, Mick Jagger was seen at the recording of The Beatles' 'All You Need Is Love' (1967), part of the first live global TV broadcast in history, while Lennon featured in the film *The Rolling Stones' Rock And Roll Circus*, made in 1968 and released in 1996. Arguably there was some reciprocal influence; The Stones looked up to The Beatles and wanted to emulate their fame and fortune, but they also pushed them – by presenting an alternative, rebellious image – a few degrees away from the safe, comfortable family- friendly act they were threatening to become at the end of 1963.

The two bands came from similar origins – a mixture of lower middle class (Jagger, Lennon) and working class (McCartney, Ringo Starr, Keith Richard). They also shared a common musical orientation, American rhythm and blues. But whereas The Beatles came from the Rhythm direction, that is, the rock and roll/pop of Little Richard, Larry Williams and early Motown, The Stones were into the Blues of artists like Howlin' Wolf and Muddy Waters.

There was, however, substantial middle ground: The Coasters, Arthur Alexander, whose early 1960s blend of country music and soul was years ahead of its time, and – especially – Chuck Berry.

1964 was a critical year for both bands. As recounted in Chapter 2, it saw The Beatles achieve worldwide acceptance with an epoch-making visit to the USA in February, their feature film debut, and a series of peerless, almost perfect, recordings. The Stones, meanwhile, had their first number one single, 'It's All Over Now', their first album release, *The Rolling Stones*, which also made number one on the UK album chart, and made their first foray into America.

As noted above, The Rolling Stones' live debut was at the Marquee on 12 July 1962. Mentored by Alexis Korner, they had been trained to cherish authenticity above all else, and this meant the music of the blues giants: the harsh, hardcore sound of the Mississippi Delta and its electrified counterpart in Memphis and Chicago, to which many of the artists had migrated. Korner had a reputation as a blues purist, so valuing the earliest incarnations of the blues that he had, allegedly, threatened to blacklist the US guitarist and singer Brownie McGhee if he played electric guitar on stage. By this point, he had relented somewhat and was playing in an electric band himself, though this was only because he had revised his own parameters as to what was authentic.

Korner's attitude was by no means unique. Earlier in this chapter we saw how trad jazz was a reaction against what was seen as the debased and/or commercial forms of the music; British R&B or more correctly,

British blues, was symptomatic of that same response, this time, to the teenage-oriented pop that dominated the chart (and for some, this included even The Beatles). In the 1940s there had been a political dimension to this, also, with the impulse to celebrate the authentic voice of the African-American linked to the idealisation of the working man and left-wing politics. The writer, record producer and impresario John Hammond, who discovered, among others, Billie Holiday, Count Basie and, much later, Bob Dylan and Bruce Springsteen, was, while not actually a Communist, often accused of socialist leanings for his pioneering work in promoting African-American and Jewish musicians.

In 1964, the politics were, as yet, under-developed but the yearning for authenticity was present in abundance, hence both Jagger's comments in *Jazz News* (cited in Chapter 1) prior to their Marquee debut and the scepticism that greeted it – mainly because of the band's name. This had been chosen by Brian Jones, at that stage their self-appointed leader, in honour – ironically – of the Muddy Waters record, 'Rollin' Stone'. But some in the band, including pianist Ian Stewart, were not enthusiastic:

"The Rolling Stones – I said it was terrible! It sounded like the name of an Irish show band, or something that ought to be playing at the Savoy." Mick Avory, the drummer they had recruited, felt equally dubious. (Philip Norman, *The Stones, op. cit.*, p. 62)

The Marquee line-up comprised Stewart (piano), Avory, Jones (who styled himself 'Elmo Lewis'), Jagger, Richards and, on bass, Dick Taylor. Eighteen months, and two hit singles later, Avory and Taylor had been replaced by Charlie Watts and Bill Wyman (né Perks), Stewart had been rowed out for not looking the part, Keith Richards had become 'Keith Richard', and The Rolling Stones were on the verge of international stardom. The last three developments were all attributable to their manager, Andrew Loog Oldham.

Oldham was only nineteen when he started to manage The Stones but was already a seasoned operator, having worked for Mary Quant,

Brian Epstein and Phil Spector. The latter became his role model, in matters of appearance, attitude and technique. Hugely ambitious, he was fortunate to have a music business veteran, Eric Easton, as his business partner. It was through Easton that Decca A&R man Dick Rowe came to sign up The Stones – but it was Oldham's chutzpah that led to their first record for the company being made at the independent Olympic Sound rather than Decca's own studios in West Hampstead. This was a trick learned from Spector and meant that Oldham, rather than Decca, would retain the copyright. Such an arrangement was new to the UK and an astonishing coup for a new band. Oldham also declared, despite having no previous experience, he would produce the record himself, though in the event the issued version of the single, 'Come On', was that recorded at IBC a couple of months previously.

Under Oldham's direction and with Easton shrewdly taking care of the business detail, the band's career began to take off. Oldham, however, was keen to ensure that they would not perceived as just another version of The Beatles. He developed their image as reprobates and rebels who grew their hair long and eschewed pasted-on smiles and chirpy banter. Immediate evidence was to be found on the cover photograph of their first EP, *The Rolling Stones*, released on 17 January 1964. Only three of the band are even facing the camera; none of them are smiling; and Richard, while sporting a flat cap, has no tie. (The Beatles had departed from convention on the cover of their second album, *With The Beatles*, by not wearing ties, but they at least were dressed in the uniform of a black roll-neck sweater.) Other than the straight but affecting rendition of Arthur Alexander's ' You Better Move On', the music has a vigorous, punkish feel to it which suits 'Poison Ivy' (a Jerry Leiber/Mike Stoller composition and a big hit for The Coasters in 1959) and Chuck Berry's 'Bye Bye Johnny', but not 'Money' where the rather forced excitement makes it fall woefully short of The Beatles' titanic version, discussed in Chapter 1.

Much better was The Rolling Stones' third single, 'Not Fade Away', which entered the UK chart on 27 February and reached number three, their best result yet. Few who saw the band perform the song on *Top Of*

The Pops will forget Jagger, brandishing an enormous pair of maracas, swinging and swaying to the Bo Diddley 'hambone' beat to which they subjected the Buddy Holly song. This exercise in re-composition was described by Oldham as 'the first song the Stones ever wrote' (quoted in Norman, *op. cit.,* p. 114-5).

Their first album, released on 16 April, moved the band's image up a gear. Like the EP, it was given the no-frills title, *The Rolling Stones*, but the name did not appear on the front cover. In fact, other than record label logo, it bore no writing of any kind, a move which would have been surprising for an established act; for a new band it was nothing short of revolutionary. Then there was the cover photograph itself. The Stones were stretched out in a line in a shadowy half-light, again unsmiling, this time two without jackets and two without ties. Oldham himself wrote the sleeve notes, commencing in characteristic style,

The Rolling Stones are more than just a group – they are a way of life.

As to the music, the album represents the spectrum of R&B, from the urban blues of Muddy Waters to the contemporary sound of Motown. Those who have come to know The Stones through timeless self-composed classics like 'Paint It, Black', 'Gimmie Shelter' and 'Miss You' will be astonished to find that by far and away the worst track on the album is the one Jagger-Richard piece, the dreary ballad, 'Tell Me'. Two others were written by the whole band under the pseudonym 'Phelge'. 'Now I've Got A Witness', featuring Ian Stewart on organ, is a lively instrumental account of 'Can I Get A Witness' (written by Eddie Holland, Brian Holland and Lamont Dozier for Marvin Gaye) which elsewhere on the album; the medium paced 'Little By Little', the 'B' side of 'Not Fade Away', includes Phil Spector, credited as co-composer, and Gene Pitney as backing musicians, and brims with belligerence and raunch.

The cover versions, too, are of mixed quality. The opener, Bobby Troup's 'Route 66', is an energetic workout on a song previously recorded by Nat 'King' Cole, Chuck Berry and the composer himself . Much the same can be said of Berry's 'Carol' and 'Walking The Dog', on which Jagger contrives to replicate the good-humoured swagger of the Rufus Thomas original. He does a similarly excellent job on Slim Harpo's 'I'm A King Bee', investing it with a menace underlined by buzzing bass and stinging guitar, and 'Honest I Do', where he accurately apes the languor of its composer, Jimmy Reed. Less successful are 'I Need You Baby' where Jagger entirely lacks Bo Diddley's gravitas and 'You Can Make It If You Try', by Nashville R&B pioneer Ted Jarrett, in which his vocals verge on the anaemic. The Stones take Willie Dixon's 'I Just Want To Make Love To You' at a breakneck tempo completely at odds with the brooding, threatening atmosphere of the Muddy Waters original. Here The Stones make the mistake common to British bands of the time (for example, The Hollies' version of Maurice Williams and The Zodiacs' 'Stay') of speeding up their source material in the hope of making it more exciting. Contrast The Beatles' approach to songs like 'You Really Gotta Hold On Me' where they *slow down* the original tempo to enhance the effect (see Chapter 1).

Nevertheless it was a creditable debut album with a great deal of promise. The production, by Oldham and Easton – though one wonders if Spector also had a hand in it – is tight and immediate, and the whole presentation, including more moody photos of the band on the back cover, is utterly convincing.

In the USA, the album was re-titled *England's Newest Hitmakers* and its release on 30 May heralded their first tour there, which began one week later. Still reeling from the impact of The Beatles' visit in February, America was not quite sure what to make of The Stones. A lot was made of the length of their hair and the myth that they seldom washed, and they were ridiculed by Dean Martin, then a pillar of the US entertainment Establishment. On the principle that no publicity is bad publicity, this would not have displeased Oldham, especially since he was consciously peddling The Stones' 'bad boy' image. And, while the tour was considered disastrous by the band, his instincts were correct.

For during 1964 there was a change in the role that pop music played in young people's lives. Always of central importance as a form of recreation, it now started to become a vehicle for their dissatisfaction too. Whereas the teds, rockers and mods also rebelled against society, they were considered to be 'from the wrong side of the tracks': being working class and/or dispossessed, they had something to be dissatisfied *about*. But in 1964 young people of all economic and social backgrounds were caught up in the mania for pop music; the fact that those from the middle and upper classes were into The Rolling Stones and their ilk was viewed as a much more dangerous prospect for society. What makes the transition remarkable was that it happened swiftly and that it occurred within the consciousness of the same young people – where once you were pleased if your parents liked The Beatles, *now* you were pleased if they hated The Stones.

When the band were in Chicago they went to Chess Studios, scene of so many of the blues and R&B recordings they admired, including those by Chuck Berry, Muddy Waters and Bo Diddley. Here they made 'It's All Over Now' which was released on 25 June and became their first UK number one, though it reached only 26 in the US. Written by Bobby and Shirley Womack and produced by Sam Cooke, The Valentinos' original was a tough act to follow, and in truth The Stones do not attempt to change it too much, but turn out a bouncy, confident version, decorated by an inspired guitar solo from Keith Richard. Jagger's vocals are relaxed and distinctive, even if it is possible to trace in his clipped delivery the influence of Southern soul singer Don Covay. The 'B' side, 'Good Times, Bad Times', is the second Jagger-Richard composition to be recorded, again a slow piece but a marked improvement on 'Tell Me'.

Acceptance was slow in the States, but there was no stopping The Stones in the UK, where they supplanted The Beatles as Top British Group in *Record Mirror*'s popularity poll. In Europe levels of hysteria were such that the Belgian government tried – unsuccessfully – to cancel their appearance at the Brussels World's Fair arena, and indeed riots did occur two days later when the band played the Olympia Theatre in Paris. This

was a far cry from the muted reception accorded The Beatles at the same
venue eight months earlier and must have bemused the support act,
veteran British rock and roller Vince Taylor, who had jumped on the R&B
bandwagon himself earlier in the year with a single that coupled Berry's
'Memphis, Tennessee' with Arthur Alexander's much-covered 'A Shot Of
Rhythm And Blues'.

In November, they upped the musical ante with the release of 'Little
Red Rooster'. Written by Willie Dixon, it had been recorded by Howlin'
Wolf in 1961 and converted into a hit by Sam Cooke two years later. The
Stones' version is closer to Wolf's and despite its slow tempo is imbued
with an urgency that is fuelled by brisk brushwork from Charlie Watts.
Brian Jones also makes a major contribution to the record with his incisive
slide guitar and wailing harmonica solo which accompanies the fade-out.
'Little Red Rooster' was, and remains, the only blues number ever to top
the UK singles chart; it was also the last occasion for nearly 20 years that
The Rolling Stones would use someone else's material for a UK single
release.

★ ★ ★ ★ ★

Philip Norman (*op. cit.,* p. 153) provides a graphic description of The
Stones' performance of 'Little Red Rooster' on *Ready Steady Go!* :

> [It] had an avant-garde audacity which would have done credit to
> Samuel Beckett. At first, all the viewer saw was a mouth, unmistakable
> for its sullen and insolent, overstuffed lips … The mouth on its own
> sang a full chorus before the camera pulled back to show Jagger's face
> and, at length, the other Stones behind him, misty and subservient.

By then *Ready Steady Go!* had been on the air for over a year and was
well used to presenting cutting-edge pop music appropriately and
sympathetically, a task perhaps made easier by the fact that, at least when
the programme was being transmitted from the Kingsway studio, the

artists mimed to their records (sometimes with amusing results – Van Morrison completely lost the plot during Them's rendition of 'Baby Please Don't Go' while Jagger had to pretend to play Brian Jones's harmonica part on 'Little Red Rooster). With its strap line 'The Weekend Starts Here', it became compulsory, and compulsive, viewing for Britain's teenagers. Mods were especially attracted to it – as Dave (*op. cit.,* p. 77) recounts, 'London mods tried to get into *Ready Steady Go!*, to be seen dancing on TV'.

Behind the euphoria there was some clever, premeditated thinking: in order to span both the new generation and to the (very) slightly older body of pop fans, the show featured two presenters, the amiable, straight-looking Keith Fordyce and Cathy McGowan, who had come to the show after answering an advertisement for 'a typical teenager'. McGowan was unprofessional in her approach, often forgetting her lines and singing along with the bands, but this added immeasurably to the live, spontaneous feel of the show as well as portraying her as someone not interested in the boring old adult way of doing things. She also set fashion trends, her long hair and heavy fringe being much copied.

In effect, *Ready Steady Go!* was the TV counterpart to Radio Caroline – between them they encapsulated what UK teenagers wanted, and needed: a rich diet of everything that was up-to-date in pop music. It was mainly down to their activities that sales of singles in the UK soared from 61 million in 1963 to nearly 73 million in 1964. But there was something especially exciting about being able to *see* acts you had previously heard only on record or on the radio, including semi-mythical American artists like Martha and The Vandellas, Marvin Gaye, and Otis Redding.

One band, however, that *Ready Steady Go!* was slow to pick up on was The Yardbirds, probably because they had no hit singles until 1965. But in many ways they were the heirs to The Rolling Stones, following, often literally, in their footsteps as The Stones' fortunes improved. Originally called The Metropolitan Blues Quartet, The Yardbirds had formed at Kingston Art School, but it was not until they brought in a past student of the college, Eric Clapton, that they started to go places. Although he was one of the Kingston crowd, Clapton was different in two important respects. Firstly his attention to clothing set him apart as a mod, and thus something of a loner, in the otherwise bohemian college set, and secondly he had experience as a professional musician, having played guitar for The Roosters and, latterly, Casey Jones and The Engineers. Casey Jones was the latest stage-name of Brian Casser, the former leader of Mersey Beat outfit Cass and The Cassanovas, and described by John Pidgeon as a 'cocky, diminutive Liverpudlian' (*Eric Clapton,* p.26). Tom McGuinness, later of Manfred Mann, was with Clapton in both The Roosters and The Engineers and recalled for Pidgeon their antipathy to Jones/Casser:

> He tended to sing sharp most of the time, so it wasn't much pleasure accompanying him. And he was a bit of a showbiz figure: he liked leaping around and the adulation of the crowd – all twenty of them who turned up. I turned up for a gig somewhere in town and Eric didn't turn up for that one. I think I saw him later that night wandering the streets of Soho and he said, "No, no, I couldn't do it any more." So I said, "I know what you mean, but he's still got my amplifier." (*ibid.,* p. 27)

So it was that Clapton came to be looking for another band and, on joining The Yardbirds, initiated a rock music dynasty that went on to include Cream, Blind Faith and Led Zeppelin.

The Yardbirds had been asked by Giorgio Gomelsky to take The Rolling Stones' place at the Crawdaddy and it was Clapton's playing as much as anything else that won them approval there– and, increasingly, at venues across London, culminating in a Marquee appearance in January 1964. On 20 March, before they had even released a single, Gomelsky had them recording a live album at the Marquee, and the result, *Five Live Yardbirds,* sums up the excitement – and the naivety – of the British blues scene of 1964. In contrast with the rather polite playing on their previous live recording, made at the Crawdaddy with Sonny Boy Williamson, the band are wild and uninhibited. Most contemporary Chicago blues artists avoided fast tempos as, indeed, had Williamson. Yet The Yardbirds revel in them and despite leading to mistakes and ragged edges, it is hard to resist the band's sheer enthusiasm. Though deriving their material from the same sources as The Rolling Stones, they were careful to select different songs – thus, while The Stones played Chuck Berry's 'Carol', The Yardbirds chose his 'Too Much Monkey Business'; Slim Harpo's 'I'm A King Bee' and Bo Diddley's 'I Need You Baby' were replaced by 'I Got Love If You Want It' and 'I'm A Man' respectively.

In the main Keith Relf's vocals are unconvincing, a common problem in British blues bands, but Clapton is electrifying and injects supercharged solos into 'Monkey Business', The Isley Brothers' 'Respectable', 'John Lee Hooker's 'Louise' and 'Five Long Years', written by Eddie Boyd and one of the few slow numbers in the set. It may seem strange that he doesn't get to feature more, but these were the very early days of the guitar hero, a position to which Clapton himself would be elevated in the not-too-distant future. Relf's harmonica is showcased on 'I'm A Man', which is taken too quickly to retain any of Bo Diddley's assertiveness, and on Howlin' Wolf's 'Smokestack Lightning', which anticipates Cream in the way its theme becomes the framework for an instrumental workout. The album concludes with another Bo Diddley number, 'Here 'Tis', which degenerates into an unashamed thrash.

Unfortunately *Five Live Yardbirds* did not trouble the chart-compilers and neither did the band's debut single, Billy Boy Arnold's 'I Wish You Would', but the follow-up, 'Good Morning Little Schoolgirl', a blues standard, usually attributed to Sonny Boy Williamson I – confusingly, not the artist The Yardbirds had accompanied, who was Rice Miller, aka Sonny Boy Williamson II – reached number 44 in November. They had, nevertheless, helped to establish the British blues movement of the mid-1960s, building on what The Rolling Stones had achieved, but taking it to a more intense level. Chart success was, in any case, of little consequence to Clapton: when The Yardbirds began to head in a more commercial direction the following year, he left them to join John Mayall.

At the time, Mayall was regarded as the epitome of authenticity within the British blues community and it was this which, paradoxically, led to his success as an album artist in the mid-1960s and well beyond. He also became a mentor to young talent, especially guitarists, possibly because he himself had been encouraged by Alexis Korner to move from Manchester to London and become a professional musician in January 1963. Mayall was a versatile, capable instrumentalist, but not an especially strong singer, a fact that slightly blunted the impact of his otherwise bright and attractive debut single, the autobiographical 'Crawling Up A Hill', which was recorded on 20 April 1964 at Decca's West Hampstead studio. Of equal interest was the 'B' side, 'Mr James', a tribute to the major blues singer and guitarist, Elmore James, who had died the previous year and the first of Mayall's unselfish efforts to celebrate the often neglected giants of the music.

'Crawling Up A Hill' sold only 500 copies, and Mayall might have been dropped by Decca had it not been for his strong reputation as a live performer, and it was therefore in this setting that they decided to record him next – at the Railway Hotel, West Hampstead, conveniently located next door to the Decca studio. On music nights the venue was known as 'Klook's Kleek', and the soul club there was especially popular with mods. The album recorded that night, 7 December 1964, was entitled *John Mayall Plays John Mayall*, for the disarmingly simple reason that all the tracks bar a medley of Jimmy Forrest's 'Night Train' and Little Richard's 'Lucille' were his own compositions. This was highly unusual at a time when everyone else was plundering the catalogues of US blues labels for material.

The announcements are gauche, the attempts at humour in some of the songs unfunny, and Mayall's voice is characteristically strained. But there are many good moments, too, including a storming version of 'Crawling Up A Hill', with rollicking harmonica from the leader; the lengthy, hard-driving guitar solo by Roger Dean on the slow burner, 'I Need Your Love'; and the duet between the two on the instrumental set to the 'hambone' beat, 'Chicago Line'. Best of all is the moody 'Heartache', to which Mayall contributes atmospheric organ and full-blooded harmonica. All in all, *John Mayall Plays John Mayall* represented another new stage in the evolution of British blues: indeed Mayall's commitment is so clear and unwavering that it is tempting to view the album as the movement's first major milestone.

The Rolling Stones, The Yardbirds and John Mayall were at the centre of a musical maelstrom that sucked in all manner of artists. The Scottish guitarist and singer, Bert Jansch, though primarily a folk musician, was one such, as tapes of his early live performances show. Thus, at the sessions he recorded at Clive Palmer's Incredible Folk Club in Glasgow in 1964, we find, alongside traditional material like 'Pretty Polly' and striking originals such as 'I Am Lonely, I Am Lost', versions of songs by country blues artists Furry Lewis ('Dry Land Blues'), Walter Davis ('Come Back Baby') and Tommy McClennan ('Bottle It Up And Go') plus a compelling account of singer/songwriter Jackson C Frank's 'Blues Run The Game'. Even then, a year before his debut album, Jansch had a reputation as a sublime acoustic guitarist and there is ample evidence in these recordings, notably the bluesy instrumental he composed with John Renbourn, 'Tic-Tocative'. But equally impressive are his strong, expressive vocals, particularly on the blues numbers; in fact Jansch should be considered one of the better British blues singers, precisely because he doesn't attempt to sound like an African-American.

The same is true of Eric Burdon, lead singer with The Animals. Certainly Burdon borrows the timing and phrasing prevalent in genuine blues singing but his Geordie origins are unmistakeable. The Animals made their recording debut in 1964 with a cover version of The Mustangs' 'Baby Let Me Take You Home'. As noted in Chapter 2, The Mustangs were in reality writer and producer Bert Berns, who credits himself, together with Wes Farrell, with the song's composition. However it actually dates back at least to 1957, as 'Baby Let Me Hold Your Hand', by Professor Longhair, with subsequent variants by Snooks Eaglin in 1958 and Bob Dylan three years later. The Animals are more circumspect, attributing it to 'Trad. arr. Price' (their keyboard player, Alan Price) – as they did their next single, 'The House Of The Rising

Sun'. This was another song with a tangled history, but coincidentally (or perhaps not) it had also appeared on Dylan's first album in 1961. A complete contrast to the bouncy 'Baby Let Me Take You Home', it is rightly considered one of the great singles of the 1960s. Following an arresting guitar introduction, Burdon's soulful vocals build gradually to a mighty crescendo, capped by a chilling organ finale by Price. At four minutes in length, it exceeded the standard playing time by a minute, yet such was its primeval power that it leapt to number one on 9 July. Following up such a record was an impossible task but The Animals responded as well as they could with the rumbling original, 'I'm Crying', which entered the chart in September.

With Mickie Most as their producer, The Animals were at the commercial end of the British blues/R&B spectrum; more hardcore were The Pretty Things, named after a Bo Diddley number, and including Dick Taylor, formerly of The Rolling Stones, in their ranks. We saw earlier in the chapter how the length of The Stones' hair caused a stir in the entertainment business, but ultimately worked to their advantage: exploiting their deliberately tongue-in-cheek name, The Pretty Things went still further, with several band members, especially lead singer Phil May, courting opprobrium for their shoulder-length locks. But their music was too harsh and uncompromising to elevate them beyond tenth place in the UK chart, which they achieved in November 1964 with the brutal 'Don't Bring Me Down'.

★ ★ ★ ★ ★

In the three years since The Beatles had auditioned unsuccessfully for Decca the UK music business had changed radically from a paternalistic set-up in which the record companies, producers and A & R men -and they *were* always men – controlled artists to the point of manipulation to a recognition that the bands and singers, and their representatives like Andrew Loog Oldham, should have a say in the recording and promotion of their music. Back in January 1962 no-one could have foreseen an urban blues record at number one, a four-minute single or a band that looked like The Pretty Things.

Decca, and Dick Rowe in particular, rectified their error in rejecting The Beatles (though, as we saw in Chapter 1, he wasn't wholly without justification in doing so) by not only signing The Rolling Stones but also releasing a series of singles, many by new bands, which were unprecedented in terms of quality and innovation. In this batch of records it is possible to trace the shift in the industry from traditional formulas to new ideas. Granted much of the material was still largely imported from the US, but the significance lay in what was being done *with* that material. By then bands were well past using sheet music as a guide – in the case of many R&B and blues songs this was unavailable/non-existent anyway – they learned instead by listening to records. A process, reinforced by the geographical and cultural separation from the source, that inevitably meant an imperfect copy, even if there was no conscious desire to interpret. More often than not, however, there was a genuine desire to refashion and reshape.

The table opposite lists the twenty outstanding singles released by Decca during 1964. All are by UK acts, except the PJ Proby, which was recorded in London. # indicates an attempt merely to copy the original; + indicates where the act concerned transforms the original; and ★ indicates an original recording/composition.

It will be readily apparent that only four (20%) of these records closely resemble the originals. As noted above, The Stones' version of 'It's All Over Now' is similar to The Valentinos, but adds a fine guitar solo by Keith Richard, while Lulu's 'Shout' certainly has the drive and spirit of The Isley Brothers, a remarkable achievement for a fifteen year-old. Brian Poole and The Tremeloes were chosen by Decca instead of The Beatles at the audition of 1 January 1962 and did at least repay them with several hits, the best of which were the cover versions of The Contours' 'Do You Love Me' (1963) and Roy Orbison's 'Candy Man', listed above. Though inferior to the originals, they were creditable efforts and the latter boasts an especially fierce guitar solo. The same can be said of The Moody Blues'

Cat No.	Artist	Title	Composer	Producer	Mus. Director
F11801	Tony Meehan	Song Of Mexico	Jerry Lordan ★	Tony Meehan	Tony Meehan
F11823	Brian Poole and The Tremeloes	Candy Man	Beverly Ross, Fred Neil #	Mike Smith	
F11833	The Applejacks	Tell Me When	Les Reed, Geoff Stephens ★	Mike Smith	
F11845	The Rolling Stones	Not Fade Away	Norman Petty, Charles Hardin (Buddy Holly) +	Impact Sound	
F11853	The Mojos	Everything's Al'right	The Mojos ★		Earl Guest
F11884	Lulu and The Luvers	Shout	O, R & R Isley #	Peter Sullivan	Earl Guest
F11900	John Mayall	Crawling Up A Hill	John Mayall ★		Earl Guest
F11904	PJ Proby	Hold Me	Jack Little, David Oppenheim, Earl Shuster +	Jack Good	Charles Blackwell
F11918	The Mojos	Why Not Tonight	Stu James, Terry O'Toole ★	Belinda Recordings	
F11923	Marianne Faithfull	As Tears Go By	Mick Jagger, Keith Richard, Andrew Loog Oldham ★	Andrew Loog Oldham	Mike Leander
F11930	The Nashville Teens	Tobacco Road	John D Loudermilk +	Mickie Most	
F11934	The Rolling Stones	It's All Over Now	Bobby & Shirley Womack #	Impact Sound	
F11937	Dave Berry	The Crying Game	Geoff Stephens ★	Mike Smith	Earl Guest
F11940	The Zombies	She's Not There	Rod Argent ★	Marquis Enterprises	
F12000	The Nashville Teens	Google Eye	John D Loudermilk +	Mickie Most	
F12013	Twinkle	Terry	Twinkle ★	Tommy Scott	Phil Coulter
F12014	The Rolling Stones	Little Red Rooster	Willie Dixon +	Impact Sound	
F12017	Lulu	Here Comes The Night	Bert Russell (Bert Berns) ★	Bert Berns	Mike Leander
F12018	Them	Baby Please Don't Go 'B' side – Gloria	Big Joe Williams + Van Morrison ★	Bert Berns	Arthur Greenslade
F12022	The Moody Blues	Go Now!	Bessie Banks #	Alex Murray	

147

'Go Now!', a treatment well short of Bessie Banks's gut-wrenching original but with a strangely alluring vocal by Denny Laine.

All of the self-composed pieces are exceptional. 'Song Of Mexico' combines a lavish arrangement with former Shadow Meehan's crisp and propulsive drumming, hinting at a bright future as a hit-maker that was never fulfilled. The records by The Zombies and John Mayall have been referred to already as has 'Here Comes The Night' but the latter record deserves a little more attention. Lulu begins it with a murmur, scarcely audible, immediately establishing an intense atmosphere which continues throughout; her emotionally-engaged, soulful vocal soars to a climax, followed by a dramatic, pulsating instrumental crescendo. Full marks to writer and producer Bert Berns, musical director Mike Leander and of course to Lulu – still only fifteen – for a performance of great maturity; but no marks to British pop fans who could only manage to buy sufficient copies to get it to number 50 on the chart.

The Applejacks' 'Tell Me When' is a fast-paced, swirling number with an irresistible melody, rebuffing all the accusations of gimmickry laid at their door for employing a female bass-player, Megan Davies. The other Geoff Stephens number, 'The Crying Game', is a complete contrast, mournful, melancholic and a key element in the success of the 1992 film of the same name, directed by Neil Jordan. 'Terry' is a classic death-disc in the same mould as 'Leader Of The Pack', and The Mojos' records are thick, satisfying slabs of Mersey Beat which promised more than the band could subsequently deliver, despite the acquisition in late 1964 of the gifted rock drummer Aynsley Dunbar and the bassist Lewis Collins (later of the TV series *The Professionals*). The seventeen-year-old Marianne Faithfull's 'As Tears Go By' establishes the blueprint for The Stones' own version recorded the following year, and Faithfull warbles the touching lyrics effectively, but the most impressive feature is the lush arrangement by Mike Leander who, along with fellow musical director Earl Guest, is one of the unsung heroes of these superb Decca releases. 'Gloria', by Them, is justifiably regarded as one of the highlights of Van Morrison's career: he barks out the vocal over a brooding backdrop which builds up the tension until the piece explodes into a rip-roaring finale.

Now to the records that re-worked their source material. 'Not Fade Away' and 'Little Red Rooster' have been discussed above; the PJ Proby can be swiftly dealt with as an exuberant account of a well-worn standard, featuring an incisive guitar solo by Jimmy Page. The Nashville Teens were in fact from Weybridge, Surrey, but this didn't stop them turning in two commendable versions of numbers by the idiosyncratic American singer/songwriter John D Loudermilk: 'Tobacco Road' is by far the better, its hefty beat, harsh guitar sound and booming bass prefiguring aspects of late 1960s heavy metal. But the outstanding track of the bunch, and one of the great records of the decade, is Them's 'Baby Please Don't Go'. Opening with a ringing guitar intro, it clicks into gear with driving drums, wailing harmonica, and insistent organ. Then Morrison enters with his rasping vocals tearing into Big Joe Williams's hard-hitting and, at times, almost surreal, lyrics. Note, for example, how he veers between contempt and desperation in the lines

Well, your mind done gone
Well, your mind done gone
Well, your mind done gone
Left the county farm
You had your shackles on
Baby please don't go

and how his barely-concealed anger threatens to rise to the surface on

Before I be your dog
Before I be your dog
Before I be your dog
To get you way down here
I'll make you walk alone
Baby, please don't go

The production, by Bert Berns, is vibrant, imaginative – the latter verse, for instance, is a duet between Morrison and Alan Henderson's bass – and laden with menace, propelling the record to the only conclusion possible: a repeat of the guitar intro and a sudden, abrupt stop.

Following the success of The Beatles, the 'British Invasion' of the US began in earnest: more than a dozen different UK acts reached the Top 40 there in 1964 alone. Alas, they did not include Them: 'Baby Please Don't Go' did not even make the Top 100. It was left to others to reintroduce America to its own music.

CHAPTER 5:

Keep On Pushing

Despite the increasing demands made on his attention by the Vietnam War, President Lyndon Johnson was determined not to be deflected from the domestic agenda. Foreign affairs had never been his strong point and although, as Vice President, he had enjoyed his trips abroad as America's goodwill ambassador, he had made a fool of himself on a number of occasions by his glad-handing enthusiasm and inappropriate comments. What motivated him most about his encounters overseas were, in fact, the very issues that preoccupied him at home: the desire to extend democracy, improve education and end poverty. Johnson was an odd mix: unscrupulous, at times dishonest, and certainly guilty of poor judgement, but beneath his bluff, bullying exterior, he genuinely cared about improving the life chances of the disenfranchised.

Immediately upon taking office in November 1963, Johnson made it his business to build upon what Kennedy had been planning in terms of Civil Rights and anti-poverty programs. As we saw in Chapter 1, Johnson's record on Civil Rights had not always been unblemished and he could only be considered a convert from the late 1950s onwards. But his interest in economic and social regeneration dated back to 1928 when, as a teacher in Cotulla, Texas, he observed the destitution among the local Mexican community. Seven years later, he became Texas Director of the National Youth Administration and was able to put many of his principles into practice, resulting in a substantial decrease in unemployment among the

State's young people. Now Johnson declared an 'unconditional war on poverty' and as a first move, on 16 March, introduced the Economic Opportunity Act of 1964. There were distinct echoes in the Act of his NYA work: it contained provisions for the creation of an Office of Economic Opportunity (OEO) to co-ordinate employment, education and training initiatives but also placed emphasis on the need for the economically-disadvantaged to participate in the designing of suitable programs.

The Economic Opportunity Act was extensive in its scope, but to Johnson it was just part of a much more wide-ranging vision – what Robert Dallek (*op.cit.,* p. 325) has described as his 'passion for grand designs, for history-making deeds.' At the suggestion of his speech-writer, Richard Goodwin, Johnson adopted the term 'The Great Society', first as a slogan to characterise his general aspirations as President, and then as an umbrella term for the series of programs he wanted to introduce in relation to Civil Rights, education, health, consumer and environmental protection, the arts, transport and his war on poverty. Johnson launched his ideas for The Great Society at University of Michigan, Ann Arbor, on 22 May 1964. In his speech he promised that a comprehensive plan would be formulated by drawing on expert knowledge from all round the world and organising conferences on the major issues and challenges. Cities would be rebuilt, the countryside preserved, pollution eliminated and Americans would become 'more concerned with the quality of their goals than the quantity of their goods.'

In the end, The Great Society was undermined by the Vietnam War which drained away both resources and motivation. In 1965, with more than a hint of sarcasm, San Francisco singer Grace Slick named her first band after Johnson's initiative. But despite such scepticism, it actually accomplished a good deal, in legislative terms at least, commencing with the Civil Rights Act of 1964. While this Act is often thought of as a measure to ensure racial equality, it also included provisions – albeit added at the last minute – to outlaw discrimination based on gender and as such it represented the latest in a sequence of measures begun by the previous

Administration. In 1961, Kennedy had set up the President's Commission on the Status of Women, chaired by Eleanor Roosevelt and charged with 'the responsibility for developing recommendations for overcoming discriminations in government and private employment on the basis of sex and for developing recommendations for services which will enable women to continue their role as wives and mothers while making a maximum contribution to the world around them.' Two years later, the Equal Pay Act 1963 addressed the question of wage disparity, yet certain sectors – domestic work, agriculture, executive and professional occupations – were excluded, thus only partially satisfying what became known as the second-wave feminists (the first wave being concerned principally with women's suffrage). There was also lingering discomfort at the emphasis on women's 'role as wives and mothers', a topic tackled that year by Alice S Rossi in a paper for the American Academy of Arts and Sciences entitled *Equality Between The Sexes: An Immodest Proposal* (published in 1964) and by Betty Friedan in her groundbreaking book *The Feminine Mystique*.

Friedan bemoaned the fact that large numbers of American young women were negating their potential in education and career terms by their aspiration to marry early, have children and settle down to a domesticated existence. She demonstrated by using a variety of research methods that once immersed in this lifestyle many of them became frustrated, unfulfilled and unhappy but, plagued by a sense of guilt and failure, were unable to take the requisite corrective action. Admittedly academic in some respects – she evaluated, disparagingly, the work of both Sigmund Freud and the anthropologist Margaret Mead – the book was written in such a way as to be accessible to any reader, for example using surveys conducted by women's magazines as part of her evidence base.

The Feminine Mystique created a sensation and the aftershock was still being felt in 1964. Predictable criticism followed: that the book went too far, and that women could easily change if they wanted to (Lucy Freeman, *The New York Times*); or that it did not go far enough and a wider social revolution was required (Evelyn Reed, *International Socialist Review,* Winter

1964) but surprisingly neither Friedan nor anyone else made any immediate attempts to follow it up, possibly because the book was so far-reaching in its implications that it needed some time to digest. Dale Spender offers the following summary:

> It is very seductive to try to plot the course of events after the publication of Betty Friedan's *The Feminine Mystique*, but I suspect that it is impossible at present, even for those who were involved … the most satisfactory explanation I can find for the development from a single voice to a chorus, for the emergence of a contemporary women's liberation movement, is the "virus theory": women's liberation was in the air and scores of women on different continents caught it. (*For The Record*, p.20)

Spender goes on to show how other factors ('student protests, black protests, anti-war protests'), many of them described elsewhere in this book, helped to spread the virus. What was particularly notable was the progress made by women, though sometimes slow, within the previously male-dominated left-wing or revolutionary organisations, such as trade unions, political parties and radical newspapers. On 18 October 1964, for instance, Barbara Castle was appointed by Prime Minister Harold Wilson to the post of Minister for Overseas Development – the first female UK Cabinet Minister since Ellen Wilkinson almost 40 years before. Another contemporary example, however, cited by Spender (*ibid.*, p. 22) was that of Ruby Doris Smith Robinson who in 1964 wrote a paper on the position of women in the organisation she had helped found, The Student Non-Violent Co-ordinating Committee (SNCC). Given the prominence of women within the SNCC, it seems remarkable that her efforts were ignored, but all attention that year was focussed on what the Civil Rights Act was saying about race equality.

The Act was the culmination of almost ten years of struggle, protest and lobbying, commencing in Montgomery, Alabama, on 1 December 1955 when Rosa Parks refused to give up her seat for a white passenger on a city bus. Her arrest led to a boycott of the buses by Montgomery's African-American community, led by NAACP activist Ed Nixon and the pastor of the Dexter Avenue Baptist Church, Martin Luther King Jr. King had been a church minister for just eighteen months, but even at that stage he espoused the doctrine of non-violence. Though his father was also a minister, he had taken some time to decide that the Church was to become his career and, unlike the older generation of African-American preachers, saw its role as challenging the racial discrimination endemic to the South. While the bus boycott was only partially successful, the fact that it had made any headway at all was a stimulus to further action, both by African-American protestors and their racist opponents. King, an eloquent and persuasive speaker, was seen as the leader of the movement and appeared on the cover of the February 1957 edition of *Time* magazine; shortly afterwards he was elected President of the Southern Christian Leadership Conference (SCLC). Despite his own pacifism he continued to attract acts of violence: in the earliest days of the boycott his home had been firebombed and in September 1958 he was stabbed in the chest at a book-signing in New York.

In early 1960 the Civil Rights movement moved up a gear when a group of African-American students, refused service at the lunch counter of FW Woolworth's store in Greensboro, North Carolina, initiated a sit-in, which set a pattern of similar protests throughout the South. By April 1960 SCLC secretary, Ella Baker, had organised a conference for 200 sit-in delegates at which King, the keynote speaker, proposed the establishment of an organisation that would unite the various student groups and in response to this the SNCC was created. The following year saw the first of the Freedom Rides where protestors used various forms of transport, mainly buses, to challenge the racist laws and practices that governed interstate travel. In December 1961 King was there to welcome the Freedom Ride to Albany, Georgia, where he was working to combat segregation, and was subsequently imprisoned. The same fate befell him in Birmingham, Alabama, a city even more notorious for its virulent racism, and the mass protests there became a cause célèbre in the summer of 1963. They were followed on 28 August by the March on Washington, the culmination of which was the assembly of over 250,000 people at the

Lincoln Memorial where King made his immortal 'I have a dream' speech.

But as 1964 began, King's status as a spokesman for his race was by no means unrivalled and, as he was the first to admit, any success he had achieved was dependent on the contributions of a variety of individuals including church leaders, campaigners, activists, key political figures and, increasingly, musicians and singers.

★ ★ ★ ★ ★

At 52, Mahalia Jackson was one of the foremost gospel artists in America. In fact, it was probably no exaggeration to describe her, as did the title of her debut album for Columbia, as the world's greatest gospel singer. Fame had come to her relatively late, for she was in her mid-thirties when she recorded the eight-million-selling 'Move On Up A Little Higher' in 1948, after which she became a popular attraction around the world with her authoritative presence and resonant contralto voice. In 1961 she performed at President Kennedy's inaugural ball and two years later shared the stage with Martin Luther King at the March on Washington. Then in 1964 she put her weight behind Lyndon Johnson. In *President Johnson's Blues* (p. 18-20) Guido van Rijn relates that not only did she compose a song specially for his presidential campaign – 'Onward, President Johnson', set to the tune of 'Onward, Christian Soldiers' – but wrote to him on 2 October declining an invitation to attend a ceremonial dinner on the basis that

> I think it is best that I stay in Chicago to keep the voters in line. We are working hard on [voter] registration this year. I think I will enjoy the dinner better when the victory is won.

Following his victory Johnson sent her a telegram stating:

> I pray that we may work together in the months ahead to keep our country safe, strong and successful as we continue our responsible efforts to assure freedom's victory in a world of peace.

Note Johnson's use of the word 'responsible', contrasting the Jackson/King strategy of working alongside the authorities to bring about change with the more radical stances being taken by Stokely Carmichael and Malcolm X.

In terms of her music, other than the example cited above, Jackson recorded few overtly political songs: it was part of her methodology to avoid open challenges to government unless strictly necessary. However in all probability she felt she didn't need to; gospel music is laden with references to the emancipation of enslaved people, ostensibly derived from the Bible, but clearly reflecting the aspirations of the African-American community. Much the same is true of blues, which may be taken at face value or seen as conveying more profound observations and emotions: it also had the capacity to be appropriated by other forms of music, particularly jazz and rock. One is left marvelling at the flexibility and multi-dimensional nature of these two idioms, so often dismissed as basic and unsophisticated.

Harry Belafonte was another high-profile black singer who assisted in the struggle for Civil Rights. Like Jackson he was an established star by the early 1960s and his 1956 album *Calypso*, which contained 'Day-O', later known as 'The Banana Boat Song', was the first LP to sell a million copies. Belafonte's support came in the form of much-needed financial help, via donations to the SCLC and SNCC and in standing the bail to get activists and protestors, including Martin Luther King, out of prison. 1964 represented a peak in both his financial and artistic efforts for the cause. His album *Ballads, Blues And Boasters*, for example, featured Woody Guthrie's 'Pastures Of Plenty' and his own composition, 'Back Of The Bus', made direct reference to the protests led by King:

If you miss me at the back of the bus
You can't find me nowhere
Oh come on over to the front of the bus
Because I'll be riding up there
I'll be riding up there, I'll be riding up there

Come on over to the front of the bus
Because I'll be riding up there.

If you miss me on the picket line
You can't find me nowhere
Come on over to the city jail
Because I'll be rooming over there
I'll be rooming over there
I'll be rooming over there oh
Come on over to the city jail
Because I'll be rooming over there.

Belafonte also provided funding for the 'Freedom Summer' project which commenced in June 1964 and aimed to boost voter registration in the state of Mississippi where the percentage of African-Americans on roll was the lowest in the country. Freedom Summer, organised by a coalition comprising the Mississippi branches of the SNCC, SCLC, NAACP and CORE (Congress of Racial Equality), caught the imagination not only of black activists like Belafonte, who flew to Mississippi with $60,000 in cash and performed for project workers in the city of Greenwood, but also over a thousand young white volunteers, mainly from the Northern states. Among them were Tom Paxton and Marshall Ganz, who played a leading role in training staff for Barack Obama's presidential campaign of 2008.

Nina Simone was six years younger than Harry Belafonte and though not quite as big a star, was beginning her ascendancy in 1964. Desperately keen to train as a classical pianist, she had been rejected by the prestigious Curtis Institute in Philadelphia very possibly on the grounds of her race, an experience which scarred her emotionally for the rest of her life. However it was the murder of Medgar Evers and the bombing in September 1963 of the Sixteenth Avenue Baptist Church in Birmingham, Alabama, in which four girls were killed, that galvanised her. In response she composed 'Mississippi Goddam' which, in protest song terms, took her a stage beyond the achievements of Jackson and Belafonte.

Keep On Pushing

Picket lines, school boycotts
They try to say it's a communist plot
All I want is equality
For my sister, my brother, my people and me

Yes, you lied to me all these years
You told me to wash and clean my ears
And talk real fine just like a lady
And you'd stop calling me Sister Sadie

Oh, but this whole country is full of lies
You're all gonna die and die like flies
I don't trust you any more
You keep on saying "Go slow!"
"Go slow!"

But that's just the trouble – too slow
Desegregation – too slow
Mass participation – too slow
Reunification-too slow

"Do things gradually!"– too slow

But bring more tragedy – too slow
Why don't you see it?
Why don't you feel it?
I don't know
I don't know

You don't have to live next to me
Just give me my equality
Everybody knows about Mississippi
Everybody knows about Alabama
Everybody knows about Mississippi Goddam.

'Mississippi Goddam' first appeared on *Nina Simone In Concert,* which was recorded live at Carnegie Hall, New York City, during March and April 1964. In its anger and impatience it locates Simone closer to Malcolm X and Stokely Carmichael than Martin Luther King, and indeed Simone became a staunch supporter of the SNCC, which Carmichael was to chair in 1966. According to her biographer, David Brun-Lambert, she

> ... turned her concerts into a veritable platform for the movement. On stage she appeared as an African queen ... a warrior calling people forward to the armed fight, interrupting her performance to ask how many members of the SNCC were present. She aimed to incite her audience, to convince them of the validity of taking up the fight. (*Nina Simone: The Biography*, p. 114)

Just before the recording of 'Mississippi Goddam,' the Civil Rights landscape had changed with the departure of Malcolm X from the Nation of Islam. For almost twelve years he had been the organisation's most effective spokesman and to all intents and purposes he was deputy to its founder and leader, Elijah Muhammad.

Malcolm's early life had been characterised by violence and disaffection. Born in Omaha, Nebraska, his family had been hounded out of town by the Ku Klux Klan, partly because his father, Earl Little, was a prominent member of the United Negro Improvement Association (UNIA) and espoused the pan-African ideology of its founder, Marcus Garvey Jr. Their house in Lansing, Michigan, was set on fire and two years later his father was run over by a streetcar, an incident that Malcolm and many others attribute to the Black Legion who, despite their name, was a white supremacist group. His mother Louise was certified insane in 1938 when Malcolm was thirteen after which he lived in a number of foster homes before going to join his half-sister in Boston. A succession of temporary jobs ensued; he relocated to New York in 1943 where he became increasingly involved in criminal activities such as drug dealing, prostitution and burglary, for which he was arrested and incarcerated in January 1946.

It was while he was in prison that he became interested in the Nation of Islam, a group whose message of black unification accorded with that of the UNIA with which he was already familiar. The Nation of Islam taught him discipline and self-respect and gave him a purpose in life and for the rest of his time in prison he was in regular contact with Elijah Muhammad. On his release in 1952, he abandoned his surname:

> The Muslim's "X" symbolized the true African family name that he never could know. For me, my "X" replaced the white slavemaster name of "Little" which some blue-eyed devil named Little had imposed upon my paternal forebears. (*The Autobiography Of Malcolm X*, p. 229)

Malcolm's maternal grandfather was apparently Scottish and though the light skin and reddish hair he inherited was a source of pride when he was a small child, this in time became something to be ashamed of.

Ostensibly Malcolm X and Martin Luther King were polar opposites in terms of their background, attitude and approach to Civil Rights. Malcolm X resisted the notion that black and white people could integrate with each other and, despairing of King's non-violent solutions to interracial conflict, mocked the language and aspirations of his 'I have a dream' address. One of his own most famous speeches was *The Ballot Or The Bullet,* delivered for the first time at the Cory Methodist Church, Cleveland, Ohio, on 3 April 1964, just three weeks after leaving the Nation of Islam:

> No, I'm not an American. I'm one of the 22 million black people who are the victims of Americanism. One of the 22 million black people who are the victims of democracy, nothing but disguised hypocrisy. So, I'm not standing here speaking to you as an American, or a patriot, or a flag-saluter, or a flag-waver – no, not I. I'm speaking as a victim of this American system. And I see America through the eyes of the victim. I don't see any American dream; I see an American nightmare …

So it's time in 1964 to wake up. And when you see them coming up with that kind of conspiracy, let them know your eyes are open. And let them know you – something else that's wide open too. It's got to be the ballot or the bullet. The ballot or the bullet. If you're afraid to use an expression like that, you should get on out of the country; you should get back in the cotton patch; you should get back in the alley.

While King had wanted to work alongside Kennedy and Johnson, Malcolm X was dismissive, calling the latter a 'Southern cracker' and describing JFK's assassination as 'chickens coming home to roost', a statement which led to his suspension and eventual departure from the Nation of Islam. In some ways Malcolm was more politically astute than King, courting and exploiting publicity effectively, inventing slogans such as the 'farce on Washington' to describe the March on Washington and convincing many African-Americans that he was better able to express their dissatisfactions than King. In July 1964, for example, the chant 'We want Malcolm X' was heard throughout the three-day riots in Harlem that followed the killing by police of fifteen-year-old James Powell.

However, as James H Cone illustrates in his book *Martin & Malcolm & America,* the two men complemented each other and during 1964 came closer to each other's point of view. As early as 1903 the visionary writer WEB Du Bois had noted in his essay *Of Our Spiritual Strivings* that African-Americans inhabited two 'worlds', leading to what we might today describe as an 'identity crisis' or in Du Bois's terms 'double consciousness':

The history of the American Negro is the history of this strife, — this longing to attain self-conscious manhood, to merge his double self into a better and truer self. In this merging he wishes neither of the older selves to be lost. He does not wish to Africanize America, for America has too much to teach the world and Africa. He would not bleach his Negro blood in a flood of white Americanism, for he knows that Negro blood has a message for the world. He simply wishes to make it possible for a man to be both a Negro and an American without being cursed and spit upon by his fellows, without having the doors of Opportunity closed roughly in his face. (*The Souls Of Black Folk*, p. 11)

Pursuing the theme, Cone argues that Malcolm X and Martin Luther King represented

... the two warring ideas struggling to make sense out of the involuntary presence of Africans in North America. During the early part of their participation in the black freedom movement, their answers to Du Bois's question, "What am I?" were clear, emphatic and opposite: "American" was Martin's answer and "African" was Malcolm's. The battle between them, to a large extent, was fought in the white media, which portrayed them as adversaries. But they were not. On the contrary, they were like two soldiers fighting their enemies from different directions ... they represented – and continue to represent – the "yin and yang" deep in the soul of black America. (*Martin & Malcolm & America*, p. 270-271)

The two men met only once, on 26 March 1964 when they attended the debate in the US Senate on the Civil Rights Bill and by all accounts the encounter was cordial. During the remainder of the year, both achieved a growing degree of international attention. King was awarded the Nobel Peace Prize and went to the University of Oslo to pick it up, stopping off en route in London where, in St Paul's Cathedral, he gave his sermon *Three Dimensions Of A Complete Life*, which he had preached at his first service as pastor of Dexter Avenue Baptist Church, Montgomery, back in January 1954. During the course of the year he also visited West Berlin, partitioned just three years previously, and went to the Vatican, where he met the Pope. In April 1964, Malcolm X made a pilgrimage to Mecca, an experience that led him to adjust his thinking: he came to see Islam as the unifying force to which Muslims of all races would contribute. He travelled to Nigeria, where he was given the honorary name Omowale -'the son who has come home' – by the Nigerian Muslim Students Association, and to Egypt, where he attended a meeting of the Organisation of African Unity (OAU) as a representative of the Organisation of African-American Unity (OAAU), the group he had founded on leaving the Nation of Islam. He was thus seen as an international statesman by many heads of state on the continent of Africa.

In November 1964 he spoke in France and afterwards came to Britain, where he participated in a filmed debate at the Oxford Union, of which Tariq Ali had become President that year. By then, as Sheila Rowbotham (*Promise Of A Dream*, p. 98) has related, 'he was in the process of breaking with the Black Muslims to develop a left-wing black politics which combined race, class and anti-colonialism.' Amiri Baraka, in his essay *Malcolm As Ideology*, writes that:

> The ideological struggle and development of Black Self-Determination begins with Malcolm's OAAU and proceeds past the general United Front to a political party. A Party created to struggle for total US social transformation, based on the call and mobilization for Black Self-Determination. An independent US party, probably formed and, in the main, led by Afro-Americans, but open to the whole of the US people. (*Malcolm In Our Own Image,* edited by Joe Wood, p. 30)

So as the year 1964 came to a close, Malcolm X was maturing as a thinker and a politician. The successive transitions he had made on the way had all the characteristics of a parable – from traumatic childhood to crime and imprisonment; from religious conversion to black nationalist rhetoric, and now to a fully-formed philosophy which was both coherent and challenging. No wonder he was idolised by significant numbers of African-Americans: he was, as Amiri Baraka puts it (*ibid.*, p. 18), 'a figure of ideological development and change.' Unfortunately, he also had many enemies, and not just among white racists. Toward the end of the year, the Nation of Islam minister Louis Farrakhan (formerly violinist The Charmer who recorded 'Trinidad Road March' accompanied by Johnny McCleverty's Calypso Boys) stated that he deserved to die, and on 21 February 1965 three fellow Nation members took him at his word and shot Malcolm X dead at an OAAU meeting in the Audubon Ballroom, New York.

Keep On Pushing

★ ★ ★ ★ ★

The Civil Rights Act became law on 2 July 1964. Among those present to see President Johnson sign it was Martin Luther King. Though the Act was broadly welcomed, African-American leaders knew there was more to do, a feeling succinctly expressed by The Impressions' 'Keep On Pushing' which entered the US singles chart five days previously:

I've got to keep on pushing
I can't stop now
Move up a little higher
Some way, somehow
'Cause I've got my strength
And it don't make sense
Not to keep on pushing.

Hallelujah, hallelujah
Keep on pushing.

Now maybe someday
I'll reach that higher goal
I know that I can make it
With just a little bit of soul
'Cause I've got my strength
And it don't make sense
Not to keep on pushing.

'Keep On Pushing' was written by the group's lead singer, Curtis Mayfield, and was his most overt statement to date on the struggle for Civil Rights. Like his 'It's All Right' from the previous autumn, it had an uplifting, positive message, reinforced by the group's silky sound and sweet harmonies. Shortly after it hit the charts, The Impressions released an album of the same name that featured the old gospel song 'Amen', but with the phrase 'keep on pushing' squeezed in.

All of these records were big national hits: the singles 'It's All Right', 'Keep On Pushing' and 'Amen' made numbers four, ten and seven respectively, while the album reached number eight. 'Amen', as Guido van Rijn notes (*op. cit.*, p. 39-40), was the basis for 'Everybody Wants Freedom', a protest anthem with lyrics that could be adapted to any occasion. The Impressions were consequently an important force in engaging in Civil Rights not just the 'converted' audience of African-Americans but a wider demographic that included white young people.

There was also evidence that white protest singers were influencing African-American artists, of whom Sam Cooke was among the most popular. In terms of numbers of hits, 1964 was his most successful year to date; of his four entries in the Top 40, the best were the effervescent 'Good News' and 'Good Times', a gospel-drenched relative of Shirley and Lee's 'Let The Good Times Roll'.

But as early as 1963 Cooke was showing signs of sympathy with the protest movement. He was moved by the fact that someone who was not black could come up with such an anti-racist song as 'Blowin' In The Wind', and he covered the Dylan number on his live album *At The Copa*, recorded at the Copacabana, New York City, on 7 and 8 July 1964. Omitted from the record when it was first issued, this rather tame, chug-along account is far outstripped by another live version, this time captured on film. Despite the rather incongruous presence of go-go dancers and an audience clapping on the wrong beat, he injects real emotion into his performance, capped in the most extraordinary way when the all-white front row leaps to its feet joyously and, still clapping, surrounds him for the finale – a reception unlikely to have been accorded even a Dylan rendition of the song. The impact, both racially and politically, of this footage on the US viewing audience is incalculable.

His own, entirely successful, attempt at writing a song of comparable significance was 'A Change Is Gonna Come'. Partly about the accidental death of his son Vincent and partly about his own experience of racial discrimination, it was recorded on 21 December 1963 for the album *Ain't That Good News*, released in January 1964 and the first manifestation of

Tracey Limited, Allen Klein's production company. Klein saw great potential in the song and persuaded Cooke to sing it on *The Tonight Show* on 7 February. But since this was the day that The Beatles hit America for the first time, it failed to achieve the impact it might otherwise have made. It was agreed to issue the recording on a single, and it duly came out as the 'B' side of the rocker 'Shake' on 22 December 1964, eleven days after Cooke was shot dead in a Los Angeles motel. Rene Hall's beautiful orchestration and Cooke's controlled passion are remarkable but what made the song into a Civil Rights anthem were the lyrics: ostensibly based on Cooke's life, the song was also a metaphor for the African-American experience as a whole and preached fortitude and optimism in the face of adversity.

' A Change Is Gonna Come' featured to telling effect in Spike Lee's 1992 biopic, *Malcolm X*, and on 5 November 2008, newly-elected President Barack Obama paraphrased its chorus when he stated, 'It's been a long time coming, but tonight change has come to America.'

★ ★ ★ ★ ★

Sam Cooke, like Ray Charles and Nat 'King' Cole before him, had achieved his national success by creating music and developing an image acceptable to the white population, at the same time retaining the support of his original African-American audience. It was a tightrope that was impossible to walk without being pelted with abuse by the (initially exclusively white) purist critics. Back in 1946, for example, Rudi Blesh complained in *Shining Trumpets* (p. 134) that Duke Ellington's music was 'ridiculous and pretentious hybridizing' while Louis Armstrong was also taken to task for the arrant commercialism of his band the All Stars, formed the following year. Such accusations were also levelled at Berry Gordy Jr, but by then he was far too well-established for them to damage his career.

In 1964 Gordy had already been in the music business for seven years, having first come to notice as the composer – with his sister Gwen and the producer Billy Davis – of Jackie Wilson's 'Reet Petite', which entered the UK chart on 15 November 1957, reaching number seven (reissued 29 years later, it made number one). From 1959 onwards he formed a succession of record labels in his native Detroit, starting with Tamla and including Gordy, Rayber and Motown, on which The Miracles' 'Bad Girl' was the first release. Gordy wrote some exceptional material during this time, including 'Do You Love Me' for The Contours; 'You Got What It Takes' with Gwen Fuqua, Tyran Carlo and Marv Johnson who recorded it; and 'Money' (with Janie Bradford) for Barrett Strong and subsequently covered by The Beatles (see Chapter 1). He also co-wrote 'Bad Girl' with The Miracles' lead singer, Smokey Robinson, and was responsible for the astonishing production in which the first quarter of the record consists of the six-piece vocal group, fronted by Robinson's soaring falsetto, accompanied only by flute.

Gordy collaborated with Robinson again for The Miracles' 'Shop Around', which in early 1961 became the first million-seller for the Motown Record Corporation, the umbrella name for all his labels, which he created in April 1960. In subsequent years, however, he concentrated on the business aspects of Motown, increasingly leaving the compositional duties to Robinson and the song writing team of Brian Holland, Eddie Holland and Lamont Dozier. Holland, Dozier and Holland (or HDH, as they are often known) wrote 25 number one singles for Motown between 1962 and 1967. Even by the standards of this extraordinary song-writing team, 1964 was a vintage year, when their hits included:

'How Sweet It Is To Be Loved By You' by Marvin Gaye (number six on the US singles chart, number 49 in the UK)

'Baby I Need Your Loving' by The Four Tops (number eleven US)

'Where Did Our Love Go', 'Baby Love' and 'Come See About Me' by The Supremes (number one US/number three UK, number one US/number one UK and number one US/number 27 UK, respectively)

Marvin Gaye was Berry Gordy 's brother-in-law, having married his sister Anna (also a label-owner and seventeen years Gaye's senior) in late

1963. He had been a Motown mainstay since 1960, first as a drummer and then as a recording artist with hits such as 'Hitch Hike' and 'Can I Get A Witness', which was covered by The Rolling Stones on their first album. 'How Sweet It Is' was his biggest hit to date, selling 900,000 copies in the US alone. Easy-paced, yet dynamic, its most conspicuous features are Gaye's relaxed, sinuous singing and the insistent tambourine that was invariably prominent in the Motown mix during this period.

Unlike most of the Motown acts, The Four Tops were an established outfit before they joined the company, but were yet to break through nationally. 'Baby I Need Your Loving' was a well crafted song which gave lead singer Levi Stubbs ample opportunity to show off his impassioned vocal style. It was the first of their 22 American hits – nine of the first eleven were written and produced by Holland, Dozier and Holland before their departure from Motown in 1967.

But the leading Motown group of the period, and one of the most successful female vocal groups in history, were The Supremes. Originally a Detroit quartet called The Primettes, the line-up that joined Motown in 1961 comprised founder members Diane (later Diana) Ross, Florence Ballard and Mary Wilson. Their first two years on the label were devoid of chart success, which came only when they recorded their first Holland-Dozier-Holland composition, 'When The Lovelight Starts Shining Through His Eyes', which got to number 23 at the beginning of 1964. HDH also wrote the 'B'-side, 'Standing At The Crossroads Of Love', which they would later remodel for The Four Tops as 'Standing In The Shadows Of Love'. Unfortunately, the follow-up, 'Run Run Run', allegedly an attempt to present The Supremes as a girl-group in the Phil Spector mould, was a failure and made only number 93 on the US singles chart.

Although Ross had sung lead on both of these records, The Supremes still saw themselves as having three lead singers: Ballard for the hard-hitting R&B material, Wilson for the ballads, and Ross for the pop tunes. Berry Gordy, however, decided that Ross had the most commercial voice and should therefore become the sole lead singer. As Wilson recalls in her book *Dreamgirl*,

Of course Flo and I were disappointed, but we never thought that the arrangement would be permanent. Certainly, when a song came along that either of us could do very well, we'd get our chance ... One day in March 1964 Eddie Holland wanted us to record "Where Did Our Love Go" which needed a subtle lead. Since that was my forte and I'd been doing the ballads for as long as we'd been singing together, I was certain it would be given to me ... It was too smooth, and I couldn't imagine anyone liking it. Still, this was probably going to be my lead, so I decided to make the best of it. But it was soon clear just what Berry had meant by his announcement. (p. 142-143)

In the event, the recorded version of 'Where Did Our Love Go' is anything but a smooth ballad. The tough, edgy HDH arrangement is set against the plaintive pleading of the lyrics, a tension symbolic of the relationship between R&B and pop and thus appealing to both camps. Following a hand-clapping, foot-stomping introduction, Ross's sensuous vocals wrap themselves around the pounding, repetitive beat, with timely interjections from the backing duo of Ballard and Wilson. A brief saxophone solo lightens the mood, before Ross returns, unhurried yet somehow retaining the urgency befitting the piece, and the fade-out comes all too soon.

Gordy's instincts had been right (but not those of The Marvelettes, who had turned down the song) – 'Where Did Our Love Go' hit number one on the American chart on 22 August 1964 and, in a summer dominated by the Civil Rights debate, offered celebration, release and relief.

The follow-up, 'Baby Love', did even better, topping the charts on both sides of the Atlantic, though it was markedly inferior and the cloying, repetitive title phrase placed it firmly in teenybop territory. The balance was restored with 'Come See About Me', which gave the group their third consecutive US number one on 19 December 1964. The song, again by HDH, is cleverly constructed to allow for an effective dialogue between Ross, at her most alluring, and Ballard and Wilson, while the simple naivety of the lyrics reflects the trio's rapidly developing sweet, feminine image.

The Supremes went on to be the third most successful chart act in America, after The Beatles and Elvis Presley, during the 1960s. It therefore goes without saying that they attracted enormous numbers of white as well as black record buyers. But Wilson resists the notion that the lessons in etiquette, deportment and grooming they received were designed purely to court the white audience:

> The truth is that Berry never signed anyone to Motown who needed to be "remade". The uncouth, boisterous, and slovenly couldn't get a foot in the door anyway. Almost everyone who came to Motown wanted to move up in the world. None of us came from homes that didn't teach manners. We were all trying to get ahead, and it always bothered me that some people have assumed that by accepting what some consider "white" values, we sold out. It's just not true. (*ibid.*, p. 150)

That urge to 'move up in the world', if in itself apolitical, was much more in tune with Martin Luther King than Malcolm X. Gordy himself was the quintessential self-made African-American entrepreneur and a positive role model who consciously avoided controversy. In spite of the fact that he appeared to sidestep the Civil Rights movement, in a strange way he embraced it through a personal, and business, philosophy that was centred on universality; when he dubbed Motown 'The Sound of Young America', it was not just a marketing slogan (though it also happened to be a good one). In all the years that he was based in Detroit, only once did this modus operandi threaten to come unstuck.

Martha and The Vandellas' 'Dancing In The Street' came out on 31 July 1964, the same month that the Civil Rights Act was signed by President Johnson and that the Harlem riots took place. Written by Marvin Gaye, Ivy Jo Hunter and Mickey Stevenson, it seemed to many observers to capture the revolutionary implications of these events:

> Calling out around the world
> Are you ready for a brand new beat

Summer's here and the time is right
For dancing in the street

They're dancing in Chicago
Down in New Orleans
In New York City ...

This is an invitation, across the nation
A chance for folks to meet
There'll be laughing, singing
And music swinging
Dancing in the street
Philadelphia, PA
Baltimore and DC
Can't forget the Motor City ...

Way down in LA, every day
They're dancing in the street
Let's form a big strong line
Get in time
We're dancing in the street.

Both Gordy and Martha Reeves hotly denied any such intention, but it is hard to escape the provocative nature, conscious or otherwise, of phrases like 'Summer's here and the time is right', 'This is an invitation across the nation' and 'Let's form a big strong line'. At the very least it must be classed with 'Sweet Little Sixteen', Chuck Berry's pan-American exhortation to rock and roll – 'They're really rocking in Boston, Philadelphia, PA, deep in the heart of Texas, around the Frisco Bay, all over St Louis, way down in New Orleans' – which mobilised the class of '58.

★ ★ ★ ★ ★

Berry himself was one of the few rock and roll stars who still shone brightly in 1964. With the exception of 'Viva Las Vegas', Elvis Presley produced nothing worthwhile and was mired in a sequence of lightweight films; Jerry Lee Lewis had left Sun the previous year and seemed lacking in direction; and Little Richard, despite recruiting an unknown guitarist called Jimi Hendrix to his band, was reduced to covering classic R&B numbers and re-hashing his old hits. Not that Berry did not continue to rely on the style that had proved so successful for him in the late 1950s but – perhaps because The Beatles and The Rolling Stones continued to champion his music – he underwent something of a renaissance during the course of the year.

First there was 'Nadine', a lively rocker with some typically witty imagery which made the Top 30 on both sides of the Atlantic, and then 'No Particular Place To Go', a grown-up version of Berry's 1957 composition, 'School Days': the tune is identical but Berry replaces innocent adolescent routine with hedonism and lust. As such, it struck a chord both in the US, where it was his biggest hit for seven years, and in the UK, where it reached number three and coincided with his first-ever tour there which began in May 1964.

But his finest effort of the year was 'You Never Can Tell', a tale of a teenage couple who achieve happiness despite the gloomy portents. Much of the quality is in the arrangement, which features riffing saxes and a clanking piano redolent of the low-budget wedding reception suggested in the song; but, as ever, it is Berry's witty lyrics and wry delivery that elevate the record to its classic status – in 1994 Quentin Tarantino used it for a key scene in his award-winning film *Pulp Fiction*.

In contrast, the fortunes of Chuck Berry's fellow rock and roller, Fats Domino, could not have been much lower in 1964. It was the first year for a decade that he had no record in the national charts. His record label, Imperial, had been sold the year before and he was now at ABC-Paramount, recording in Nashville under the supervision of Felton Jarvis. Jarvis was a gifted producer who went on to work with Elvis Presley for the last eleven years of his life, but his collaboration with Domino was nowhere near as productive as that with his co-writer, arranger and producer Dave Bartholomew in their native New Orleans. The picture was much the same for many Crescent City acts who had prospered in the late 1950s and early 1960s. Clarence Henry, Lloyd Price, Jessie Hill, Lee Dorsey, Ernie K-Doe, Chris Kenner and Larry Williams, all of whom had previously enjoyed national hits, were entirely absent from the American singles chart in 1964.

As far as New Orleans was concerned it was the female artists who continued to fly the flag. The most successful group were The Dixie Cups who, as noted in Chapter 2, reached number one in June with 'Chapel Of Love'. But although she had only one national hit, the outstanding New Orleans artist in 1964 was Irma Thomas. By the time she was nineteen Thomas had been married twice and had four children – little wonder that her first record, issued in 1960 and a number 22 hit on *Billboard*'s R&B chart, was entitled 'You Can Have My Husband (But Please Don't Mess With My Man)'. This was followed by other minor successes including, in 1963, 'It's Raining' and 'Ruler Of My Heart', both poignant ballads written by Allen Toussaint (under the pseudonym Naomi Neville) and delivered with the utmost sensitivity.

A year later, Thomas's contract was bought by Liberty Records, who took her to Los Angeles to record one of the greatest double-siders of the decade, 'Wish Someone Would Care'/ 'Break-A-Way'. The 'A' side was her own composition, an emotive ballad into which she packs her life experience to date into a controlled but soulful performance:

Sitting home alone, thinking about my past
Wondering how I made it, and how long it's gonna last
Success has come to lots of them, and failure's always there
Time, time waits for no one and I wish, how I wish, someone would care.

'Break-A-Way' is in many respects a contrast: a full-blooded rocker written by Jackie De Shannon and Eddie Cochran's former fiancée,

Sharon Sheeley. But again it is underscored by melancholy – the plight of someone irresistibly drawn back to her lover despite her efforts to escape – and Thomas handles the complexities inherent in the song with assurance.

'Wish Someone Would Care' entered the US singles chart on 25 April 1964, made number seventeen and became her first and only national hit. But it was the follow-up, 'Anyone Who Knows What Love Is' – or more correctly, its flipside – that was to have the greater impact. 'Time Is On My Side' was written by Jerry Ragovoy (as Norman Meade) and was first recorded by the jazz trombonist Kai Winding in October 1963. Thomas uses extra lyrics by Jimmy Norman that were completed only minutes before the studio work began, but there is no suggestion of a rush-job as she soars over Eddie Ray's epic production. Particularly striking is her spoken interlude with wild blues guitar accompaniment. The Rolling Stones picked up on the Thomas record and based their rendition on hers to achieve their first American Top Ten hit. The day after it entered the chart on 8 November 1964 they made another version which was later included on the album *The Rolling Stones No. 2* – but neither held a candle to Irma Thomas's magnificent recording.

Her next single, Van McCoy's 'Times Have Changed' was in the same vein and of similar quality, and to cap off an outstanding year came another fine double-header, 'He's My Guy'/ '(I Want A)True, True Love', both powerful ballads interpreted with feeling and authority.

If New Orleans – with the exception of Irma Thomas – was in the doldrums, there were signs of optimism elsewhere in the South. In Memphis, Tennessee, Jim Stewart and Estelle Axton had established their record label Stax, a conflation of their surnames, in an old cinema at 926 East McLemore Avenue and were starting to make an impression with their roster of local acts that included Carla Thomas, whose 'Gee Whiz' was a US number ten hit in 1961, and house band Booker T and The MGs, who got to number three a year later with the instrumental, 'Green Onions.' But their hottest property was a singer from Macon, Georgia, by the name of Otis Redding.

In his early career Redding was heavily influenced by fellow Maconite Little Richard, but by the time he joined Stax in 1962, he was well on the way to his unique singing style. Has range was narrow and his pitch sometimes uncertain but Redding more than made up for these minor shortcomings by the emotional intensity he brought to every song – not in the uninhibited, free-flowing manner of, say, Aretha Franklin, but packed tight into explosive outbursts of aching, straining balladry. His first records for Stax, 'These Arms Of Mine' and 'Pain In My Heart', an adaptation of Irma Thomas's 'Ruler Of My Heart', betray these qualities in abundance.

Both appear on his debut album, *Pain In My Heart*, which was released on 1 January 1964. Five of the twelve tracks were written by Redding himself, including 'These Arms Of Mine', 'Security' and 'That's What My Heart Needs' (the latter two both singles from the previous year). He also collaborated with Booker T and The MGs' guitarist, Steve Cropper, for the punchy single 'Mr Pitiful', a title which seemed to embody Redding's methodology; equally good was the ballad on the other side, 'That's How Strong My Love Is', written by Roosevelt Jamison for OV Wright's debut single and covered by The Rolling Stones on the 1965 album *Out Of Their Heads*.

In 1964 Redding, and Stax in general, presented an alternative to Motown. Less polished and professional but more grounded and gospel-flavoured, it would soon become known universally as soul music. As Peter Guralnick has written,

> Unlike Motown, which attempted to provide a totally controlled environment, Stax encouraged individual initiative within the context of corporate development, and Jim Stewart's first organizing principle of business seems to have been … to surround himself with people not simply of talent but of character, people on whom he could rely, individuals who were capable of growth. In Otis Redding he found the exemplar of these qualities. For Otis Redding was the heart and soul of Stax. (*Sweet Soul Music*, p. 131)

Other 'people of talent' who joined Stax during 1964 included Donald 'Duck' Dunn, whose bass playing was the cornerstone of so many classic soul records, and Isaac Hayes, who became one of the best known figures in the history of African-American music.

New York's Atlantic Records bought into Stax in every sense. Their vice-president, Jerry Wexler, a former journalist who had coined the term 'rhythm and blues' in 1948, was leasing their product as early as 1960. As Stax built both its roster and its reputation, Wexler was keen to attract Atlantic artists to the Memphis studios and/or have their records released on the label. One such was Don Covay, whose 'Mercy Mercy', recorded with The Goodtimers and allegedly featuring Jimi Hendrix on guitar (though Ronnie Miller is also credited), was a national hit in autumn 1964 and influenced Mick Jagger's singing style. Another was Joe Tex who recorded the expressive ballad 'Hold What You've Got' at the Muscle Shoals Sound Studio, Alabama, in late 1964 and took it into the national Top Five at the beginning of the following year; and a third was the incendiary vocalist Wilson Pickett who signed with Atlantic in 1964 after writing one of Solomon Burke's biggest hits, 'If You Need Me'.

Burke's 1964 record releases are discussed in Chapter 2. He was crowned King of Rock 'n' Soul the same year at a ceremony in Baltimore's Royal Theatre, a typical incident in the colourful career of this larger-than-life character. According to his obituary by Steve Jones in *USA Today* (10 October 2010), Burke sold popcorn between his sets at the Apollo, sang for the Pope in the Vatican and once turned up at a concert to find it was a Ku Klux Klan rally, but as his honorary coronation suggested, he was one of many former R&B stars who metamorphosed into soul artists in 1964, with mixed results.

One of the great R&B singers, Etta James, turned 26 in January, so was still young enough to be re-branded as soul, but none of three excellent singles she made for Chess during the year made the national chart. 'Lovin' You More Every Day', an attractive medium-tempo piece, begins conventionally enough but before long James rips it apart with a breathtaking display of sustained aggression. Her hard-nosed romanticism divests the ballad 'Bobby Is His Name' (which she co-wrote with Ed Townsend) of any sentimentality, and the pulsating 'Breaking Point' would have been a credit to any of the leading lights on Stax or Atlantic.

James Brown had been at the top of the R&B tree since 1957 but was embroiled in a legal battle which meant that after July 1964 he was unable to release any records for a year. Two months before the axe fell, however, he came up with a single that would give his fans more than enough sustenance to tide them over. 'Out Of Sight' was an entirely contemporary song that managed to anticipate the future while at the same time looking back to what had gone before. In many forms of music around the world, particularly African, melody is sublimated to rhythm, giving a continuous, almost hypnotic flow. In 'Out Of Sight' Brown taps into that tradition by bringing bass and drums, so often relegated to supporting roles, to the fore and converting his tightly riffing horn section into a quasi-rhythm instrument. He then overlays this taut backcloth with a suitably sparse, controlled vocal and intermittently raises the temperature with an impassioned phrase or monosyllabic cry. 'Out Of Sight' proved to be both eminently danceable and, in R&B terms at least, revolutionary, moving away from the traditional emphasis on the second and fourth beats of the bar to the first and third. In short, it marked the birth of funk, an idiom that Brown himself was to preside over from 1965 onwards as 'Soul Brother Number One' and 'The Godfather of Soul'.

Away from the studio Brown was a dominant force on the live music scene – justifying two more of his nicknames, 'Mr Dynamite' and 'The Hardest Working Man in Show Business'. This is amply illustrated by his appearance at the TAMI (Teen Age Music International) Show in October 1964, a two-day concert at the Santa Monica Civic Auditorium. Filmed by a team from *The Steve Allen Show*, including director Steve Binder, the TAMI Show has passed into legend thanks to its all-star cast – Jan and Dean, The Beach Boys, The Supremes, Marvin Gaye, The Miracles, Chuck Berry, Gerry and The Pacemakers, The Rolling Stones – and to Brown's remarkable performance, a bewitching combination of high energy and melodrama. The Stones had the misfortune to follow Brown on stage, as Bill Wyman related to Philip Norman:

> "We were all in the dressing room beforehand, really scared. And Marvin Gaye and Chuck Berry came in to see us. Marvin Gaye said, 'Are you guys nervous?' We said, 'Petrified.' He was really nice. He said, 'Hey, go out there and just do your best. Nobody wants to know if you're better than anybody. They only want to know that you're on.'"
>
> The Stones did not expect to surpass that. But they still gave a performance impressive enough for "Mr Dynamite" to grant them an audience in the dressing room where he sat, surrounded by black retainers and stage shoes and tubs of champagne on ice. (*ibid.*, p. 152)

Norman reports that Giorgio Gomelsky dates the TAMI show, and Brown's influence on him there, to Jagger's growth in confidence as a live performer: "'That was when the Mick Jagger we know began ... When Mick got off the plane in London, he was doing the James Brown slide.'"(*ibid.*, p. 153)

★ ★ ★ ★ ★

In spite of James Brown's impact on The Rolling Stones, the band's main inspiration, as we saw in Chapter 4, was the blues, especially the urban variety purveyed by the likes of Howlin' Wolf, Jimmy Reed and Muddy Waters. It was a cruel irony that as The Stones and their followers began to achieve chart success in the US, the authentic artists who influenced them were finding it hard to make a living. As Michael Haralambos has shown (*Right On: From Blues To Soul In Black America*, p. 16), there were only 80 blues records issued in 1964, as opposed to 230 ten years previously.

The decline in recording opportunities for blues artists was not a direct result of the 'British Invasion' of 1964, which was spearheaded by The Beatles and other groups in the Mersey Beat mode like The Dave

Clark Five and Freddie and The Dreamers, most of whom were too lightweight to be seen as competitors to the heavy hitters of Chicago, although by autumn blues-based bands were beginning to make their presence felt in much the same way as they were in the UK. On 5 September, The Animals hit number one with 'The House Of The Rising Sun', a feat repeated seven weeks later by Manfred Mann with 'Do Wah Diddy Diddy'. The latter, whose frenetic debut single '5-4-3-2-1' was the theme music for *Ready Steady Go!*, were thus the first group from the South of England to have an American number one, pre-dating The Rolling Stones by nine months. But – at least until the second British Invasion of the late 1960s – they continued to be outnumbered by the teenybop bands whose continuing success surprised many back home. Herman's Hermits, for example, had seventeen Top 40 hits there between 1964 and 1967, five more than in the UK during the same period.

It can be argued with greater certainty that the threat to blues in 1964 came from a renaissance in pop music in general; just as output of blues records had dipped by 20% in 1956 with the arrival of rock and roll, now the genre bore the brunt of another boom – this time in the demand, not just for white music based on black sources but for African-American music itself, in the shape of Motown and soul. In fact so popular was black pop music that *Billboard* ceased the publication of a separate R&B chart for the whole of 1964.

So where did this leave blues? The short answer is: in some confusion. Neither the blues artists themselves, nor their record companies, had any expectation of outselling pop artists; moreover, there was still a market for their records among the older members of the African-American community and, increasingly, young whites trying to escape the commercialism of mainstream pop. Indeed, elderly country blues singers were constantly being 'rediscovered' during this period, in the same way that, two decades previously, the reaction against swing and bebop had seen zealous purists bring New Orleans pioneers like Bunk Johnson out of the woodwork. 1964 was a particularly fertile year in this respect, with the return of the Delta Blues greats Nehemiah 'Skip' James and Eddie

'Son' House, neither of whom had made a record for decades. Therefore despite the natural evolution of blues towards what would shortly be known as rock music, there was an equally strong compulsion to pull it backwards to the acoustic era.

One of the greatest blues singers of all time, Muddy Waters, epitomised this dilemma. In the late 1950s, Muddy was at the cutting-edge of Chicago blues: he was, indeed, one of its creators, having arrived in the city in 1943 from Clarksdale, Mississippi. There was nothing new about adapting the African-American idioms of the South to the urban conditions of the North; as early as 1923 King Oliver's Creole Jazzband were delighting audiences and fellow musicians alike with the music they had brought to Chicago from their native New Orleans. In the late 1930s, and again principally in Chicago, artists like Big Bill Broonzy and Sonny Boy Williamson began to translate country blues – traditionally the province of the solo artist – into small group settings, a kind of halfway house to the blues bands that were to follow. But Muddy accomplished something which had consequences far beyond his immediate environment: the conversion of the Delta blues, into a new, electrified – and electrifying – form of music. Chicago blues, as we have seen, became the foundation on which rock was built.

Not everyone, however, appreciated such innovations. On his visit to the UK, in 1958, Muddy's amplified sound was greeted with disdain, an experience that shook his nerve and led to modifications for his tours here in 1963 and 1964. Prejudice against adulteration by electrification was common in the UK – Alexis Korner's threat to blackball Brownie McGhee was noted in Chapter 4, and the accusation of 'Judas' was famously levelled at Bob Dylan at Manchester's Free Trade Hall in 1966 – but it was not an exclusively British phenomenon. In 1963, the leading producer and talent scout Ralph Bass persuaded Muddy, against his better nature, to make, in the words of Bass's sleeve note, 'an LP depicting the blues without any stigma of commercialism attached to it.'

The title of the record, released in January 1964, was a statement of this intent – *Muddy Waters: Folk Singer.* Bass acknowledges that the term 'folk' is a loaded one, more to do with marketing than with music, but true to his intent, the album is entirely acoustic. Yet Muddy is not satisfied merely to turn the clock back 20 years but brings to bear all the intensity of his band performances – and then some. Of the nine tracks only one, the gently undulating 'Good Morning Little School Girl', gets anywhere near medium pace. The rest are slow, often painfully so, with the remarkable 'My Captain' pretty much abandoning regular meter altogether. Muddy's brooding, confessional vocals frequently descend to a barely audible whisper; at other times, he seems ready to roar, but never quite does so. On the normally rollicking 'Big Leg Woman', the lugubrious tempo and delivery are incompatible with the lyrics, but everywhere else they fit the material like a glove. 'My Home Is In The Delta', 'Long Distance', 'You Gonna Need My Help', 'Country Boy', 'Cold Weather Blues' and 'Feel Like Going Home' are yearning, aching epics, richly evocative and immaculately executed, and all but the last featuring the virtuosic yet sensitive guitar of Buddy Guy. In 2005, *Muddy Waters: Folk Singer* was voted number 277 in a poll conducted by *Rolling Stone* for the 500 Greatest Albums of All Time – a creditable result for a non-rock record/non-anthology. Presumably no-one spotted the irony of the artist to whom the magazine owed its name finishing in such a comparatively lowly position.

Only an artist of the stature of Muddy Waters could be handed such a dud brief as *Folk Singer* and come up with such a gem. In the absence of an invitation to do otherwise, most of his urban blues confreres carried on regardless, and produced some excellent records during 1964. One such was Jimmy Reed, who, while past his best, hit the jackpot with the wailing, walloping 'I'm Going Upside Your Head', the opening track on the *Jimmy Reed At Soul City* album. On 30 April Sonny Boy Williamson II cut the typically rambunctious 'One Way Out' at, appropriately, one of his last sessions for Chess; four months later in the same studio Howlin' Wolf recorded the strutting 'Killing Floor', successfully covered four years later by jazz-rock band The Electric Flag, who used a snippet of a speech by LBJ as an ironic preface.

Buddy Guy played on both of the last two records and in June made a classic of his own, 'My Time After A While'. Among its many outstanding features are the interplay between his elegant guitar-playing and anguished vocals and the understated but incisive horn arrangement. For sheer consistency he was matched only by BB King, ten years his senior and a recording artist of fifteen years standing by 1964. During the course of the year King released three superb singles: the buoyant 'Beautician Blues' and 'You're Gonna Miss Me', both with exquisite guitar solos, and the rumbling, insidious 'Rock Me Baby' which caught the imagination of the rock generation, spawning numerous covers including an incendiary version in 1967 by The Jeff Beck Group.

In addition, some exciting new blues artists appeared on the scene in 1964. Among them was Tommy Tucker who, backed by fellow Ohioans Weldon Dean 'Cousin Sugar' Young on guitar and Brenda Lee Jones on bass (alias the former early sixties duo Dean and Jean), released 'Hi-Heel Sneakers', an easygoing, relaxed number with a sting in the tail instrumentally, via Young's biting guitar, and lyrically. Not many songs have been covered by Elvis Presley, Paul McCartney, The Rolling Stones and Chuck Berry (plus some 200 other versions) but 'Hi-Heel Sneakers' is one of them; it entered the US singles chart on 29 February 1964, reaching number eleven, and made number 23 in the UK a few weeks later.

'Hi-Heel Sneakers' was, however, a drop in the commercial bucket as far as blues records were concerned in 1964. Although there seemed to be more blues artists around than ever, most of them were making ends meet not through their album or singles sales, but either – for the very lucky ones – from royalties for a composition recorded by a successful white band such as The Rolling Stones or from constant touring with Europe an especially favoured destination.

Since 1961, the German impresarios Horst Lippmann and Fritz Rau had organised the American Folk Blues Festival, a touring troupe of blues acts which traversed the continent from Sweden to Switzerland, Scotland to Spain. Each package consisted of around ten artists and the 1964 line-up was one of the best, a well-balanced blend of the famous and the obscure, the city and the country. The big names were Howlin' Wolf, Sonny Boy Williamson II and the mournful Texas singer-guitarist Lightnin' Hopkins, but perhaps the most intriguing participants were the legendary country bluesman, Sleepy John Estes and his long-term accompanist, harmonica-player, Hammie Nixon. In addition there was Sugar Pie DeSanto, whose sexy 'Soulful Dress', one of the blues hits of the year, was related stylistically and sartorially to 'Hi-Heel Sneakers'; and the veteran slide guitarist John Henry Barbee. The latter, plucked by Willie Dixon from a job serving ice cream, bought a car with the proceeds from the tour but, tragically, ran over and killed a man with it and died in prison of a heart attack on 3 November 1964. The company was completed by Dixon and drummer Clifton James, Muddy's accompanists on the *Folk Singer* album, and Wolf's regular guitarist, Hubert Sumlin.

In the UK, the 4th National Jazz and Blues Festival was held at the Richmond Athletic Club between 7 and 9 August 1964. True to the spirit of the times, the bill was a mixed bag comprising British R&B, modern jazz and trad. Despite the presence of Manfred Mann and The Rolling Stones, pride of place went to the American guests: pianist/singer Memphis Slim, then resident in Paris, and blues shouter Jimmy Witherspoon, backed by the Chris Barber Band, were the headliners on the Saturday night, and on Sunday the big name was Mose Allison, a unique artist combining a cool, blues-inflected vocal style, wry lyrics and a fearsome jazz piano technique. The Festival is often remembered, however, for a jam session at the end of The Yardbirds' set featuring Eric Clapton, Jack Bruce and Ginger Baker who two years later would form the seminal rock band, Cream.

British enthusiasm for blues was also reflected on TV at various points in the year. The BBC filmed sessions with John Lee Hooker and Champion Jack Dupree and on 2 October 1964 Hooker appeared on *Ready Steady Go!* But Granada TV scooped the pool with its documentary of the extraordinary Blues and Gospel Train package that pulled into Manchester on Thursday 7 May 1964. Under the auspices of Newport Jazz Festival director George Wein and stage-managed by Joe Boyd, who later produced Fairport Convention, The Incredible String Band and Nick Drake, the show took place on the disused Wilbraham Road railway station in the Chorlton-cum-Hardy district of the city (specially erected platform signs were painted 'Chorltonville' – an attempt to make the US visitors feel at home as well as a jokey reference to the nearby garden suburb of the same name). The mouth-watering line-up comprised Muddy Waters; his brother-in-law Otis Spann, possibly the finest of all post-war blues pianists; gospel stars Sister Rosetta Tharpe and the Reverend Gary Davis; the New Orleans pianist Cousin Joe Pleasants; and the perennially popular duo of Sonny Terry and Brownie McGhee. As the film illustrates, every one of the artists rose to the occasion, none more so than Sister Rosetta who, complete with fur coat and double-cutaway Gibson guitar, defied the inclement weather with a vigorous version of 'Didn't It Rain'.

But equally remarkable are the shots of the audience, arriving by train and rushing across the platform to get the best vantage point. On the other side of the tracks, in all senses, from the performers, they are a cross-section of middle-class British youth – CND members, trad fans, mods, students – in short, the generation who, despite the fresh-faced innocence they exhibited in 1964, would shortly join together with their American counterparts to challenge the prevailing structures and drive a permanent wedge between the orthodox and the alternative.

CHAPTER 6:

Meditations On Integration

The growing realisation that blues was the foundation of rock music helped at least some of its practitioners to survive during the early to mid-1960s. Moreover as musicians, and fans, delved beyond the big names like Muddy Waters, Jimmy Reed and Howlin' Wolf, they began to uncover a whole crop of blues singers of commensurate quality: Otis Rush, Elmore James, Robert Johnson, Charlie Patton and Skip James. John Mayall and Eric Clapton's *Blues Breakers* album of 1966 featured material by the likes of Johnson and Rush and, building on the interest in the music that The Rolling Stones and others had already created, it stimulated a second wave of enthusiasm – a phenomenon which became known as the 'Blues Boom.' This new trend was especially strong in the UK, where bands such as Fleetwood Mac, The Groundhogs, Chicken Shack and The Aynsley Dunbar Retaliation were at the forefront of developments. Such was their success that in 1968 they were satirised by both The Liverpool Scene ('I've Got The Fleetwood Mac-Chicken Shack-John Mayall-Can't Fail Blues') and The Bonzo Dog Band:

> And now it's getting near the time I gotta make the scene,
> I change out of my dark-grey mohair suit, pull on my dirty jeans,
> The band comes round to pick me up, I holler: "Hello, boys,
> I gotta mess my hair up and gotta make some noise – blues!"
> Can blue men sing the whites?
> Or are they hypocrites? …

The Bonzos' 'Can Blue Men Sing The Whites' contrasted the affluence of the young white bands with the humble origins of the artists whose music they were plundering, a well-made point in view of the fact that although constant touring, particularly in Europe, and composer royalties were alleviating the poverty for some, most authentic blues singers were much less prosperous than those who were imitating them. Yet on another level white blues was morally justified, for it quickly merged with psychedelic rock to form the music of the late 1960s counterculture, for a few brief years a force for change, and all of it for the good.

But blues was not an overtly political music; like gospel, it concealed its message in day-to-day imagery and most of its exponents were, in any case, of a generation that was unaccustomed to speaking out against things they didn't like. In 1964 there were signs of militancy among some of the younger musicians, a tendency that was to intensify with the assassination of Martin Luther King and the escalation of the Vietnam War. For the moment, however, the clearest voices of protest in the African-American community came from R&B/pop artists like Sam Cooke and Curtis Mayfield or, increasingly, from jazz musicians.

As we saw in Chapter 1, jazz had been a revolutionary music since its inception, constantly changing and challenging the precepts of the previous generation, but by 1964 it had also – through the work of Charles Mingus, Max Roach and Oscar Brown Jr in particular – become a vehicle for unrest. As with blues, the British Invasion of 1964 meant a decline in work opportunities and this forced some leading artists to take more commercial directions and/or to tour more relentlessly, with Europe again the destination of choice; others retreated into studio work or gave up playing altogether. But the prophets of doom were all too quick to pronounce the death of jazz at this point, especially those who were, in any case, out of sympathy with the newer paths the music was following. Much vaunted writers from other fields such as Philip Larkin and Kingsley Amis, both of whom had a pathological hatred for any jazz produced after World War II, were especially gloomy. Another non-specialist, the Marxist historian Eric

Hobsbawn, who wrote on jazz under the pseudonym Francis Newton, did eventually chronicle a revival, though he, too, had been at a low ebb:

> Three years after 1960, when the golden age was at its peak, in the year of the Beatles' triumph across the world, jazz had been virtually knocked out of the ring. "Bird Lives" could still be seen painted on lonely walls, but the celebrated New York jazz venue named after him, Birdland, had ceased to exist. To revisit New York in 1963 was a depressing experience for the jazz-lover who had experienced it in 1960. (Quoted in Miles Kington – *The Jazz Anthology*, p. 301)

What these writers were missing, from their far-off vantage point of English academia, was both the message and the music of a coterie of young musicians, most of them under 40, and many under 30, who were to make 1964 an outstanding year for jazz – in many respects, the most remarkable it had ever seen.

★ ★ ★ ★ ★

In 1964 the foremost musician in contemporary jazz was Miles Davis. He had ascended to that elevated position gradually, first finding fame in 1945 as the trumpeter with Charlie Parker's group and then leading the 'cool' jazz movement of the early 1950s. More recently he had been celebrated for the outstanding creativity of his late 1950s quintet, which featured tenor saxophonist John Coltrane; three highly praised collaborations with the arranger Gil Evans, culminating in 1960's *Sketches Of Spain*; and the immortal *Kind Of Blue* which popularised modal jazz – based on scales rather than chords – and became the biggest-selling jazz album of all time. At each of these junctures, he had reassessed his role before heading in a radical new direction, and 1964 found him in one of those periods of transition.

Davis was from a well-to-do African-American family but had both experienced racism first-hand and seen its effect on the careers of fellow jazz stars like Billie Holiday and Thelonious Monk. Up to 1964, he had said little publicly on the subject of Civil Rights but early in the year chose to make a high-profile statement by playing a benefit concert to support voter registration in Mississippi and Louisiana, with the proceeds going to the NAACP, CORE and SNCC. This was no casual gesture: ticket prices were as high as $50 when the top price for a Broadway show was then $10, and Davis waived his own, and his group's, fee (a matter that caused some discontent within the band). Whether by design or happy accident the concert, at Lincoln Center's Philharmonic Hall, took place on 12 February, Abraham Lincoln's birthday.

As well as its political importance, this concert enjoyed considerable aesthetic significance. The entire event was recorded by Columbia, but at first only half the performances were issued, on an album entitled *My Funny Valentine*. This proved a sound decision commercially, since it sold well enough to make the US pop charts, but one inadvertent consequence was to throw Davis's experimentation into relief. For the album consists, by and large, of the slow pieces from the show and these were the ones that most clearly illustrate the beginnings of his next musical metamorphosis.

Some of them, such as 'My Funny Valentine' and 'Stella By Starlight', were well-known items in the Davis canon but, as Ian Carr has written, they were transformed that night at the Lincoln Center: 'On the later versions, there is strong movement away from romanticism and towards abstraction, and the emotional range is very much greater' (*Miles Davis*, p. 174).

Both are astonishing performances. On 'Valentine', after a brief introduction, Davis soars without warning into the upper register and plunges back again – from then on, he gives us only fragments of the melody, interspersed with further trips to the stratosphere and terse, anguished phrases. The rest of the group – pianist Herbie Hancock, bass-player Ron Carter, drummer Tony Williams and tenor saxophonist George Coleman – are cast very much in a supporting role, though Hancock takes inspiration from Davis in his own solo and Carter does some effective probing. Towards the end, Davis once again hits the high notes but this time spreads them sparsely, conveying a sense of abandonment and isolation and bringing to the piece a layer of meaning scarcely dreamt of by Richard Rodgers and Larry Hart when they wrote it back in 1937. On 'Stella', Davis stumbles into the melody like the love-struck subject of the song, but once there confidently enfolds it with long, strong lines. A shout of approval comes from the audience, there is applause when bass and drums come in, and Davis stacks up the bravura flourishes before shattering his solo into splinters of sound. Coleman restores normal service, a duet between Hancock and Carter blends the warm and reassuring with the querying and questioning, and the leader closes the number out with a stately reprise of the theme over Hancock's rippling piano.

Eventually Columbia issued the balance of the recordings as *Four & More* (both records are now available together on a double CD, *The Complete Concert 1964*), allowing us to discern Davis's methodology across groups of pieces. One favourite technique, exemplified by the ballads ' I Thought About You' and 'There Is No Greater Love', is to play around with the melody, juxtaposing long notes with short, aggression with reflection, fast tempos with slow. Another, evident on 'All Of You', 'Walkin' and 'Joshua', is to dispense briefly and cursorily with the tune before leading the band into headlong improvisations.

Despite Davis's domination, he depends heavily on the excellence of his colleagues. Coleman is the most conventional musician in the group but, as Ian Carr points out, his straight-ahead approach sometimes comes as welcome relief from Davis's explorations; Hancock's imaginative playing reflects a myriad of influences, and his solos on, in particular, 'Seven Steps To Heaven' and 'There Is No Greater Love' are exhilarating *tours de force*; while Carter's sense of adventure often matches his leader's. The high proportion of ballads means that Tony Williams has limited chances to display his formidable skills, but when the opportunity does arise, on 'All Blues', 'Four' and 'So What', he seizes it with relish, his sizzling cymbals, rapid-fire snare and thundering bass drum pushing the front-line musicians to ever more exciting heights. Eighteen years and two months old on the night of the concert, Williams was to hit a creative peak during

1964: thirteen days later he was a major contributor to Eric Dolphy's ground-breaking *Out To Lunch!* and in August he recorded his own debut album as leader, the superb *Life Time.*

Davis was very satisfied with the Lincoln Center concert. Ostensibly dismissive of contemporary *avant garde* jazz – probably because many critics were entranced by it, at what he considered to be his expense – he had brought its influence into his own playing without compromising the lyricism for which he was renowned. His technique was secure, his conceptions were working and he had a group that shared his vision and included some of the best young musicians around. No-one could view him now as a man of the 1950s. Only two issues remained: one, his repertoire could do with updating – of eleven numbers performed at the Lincoln Center, five were standards he had played for some time and three of these were written in the 1930s – and two, Coleman did not really fit into the group; while an accomplished musician, he wasn't audacious enough. In summer 1964, Davis solved both problems at a stroke by hiring Wayne Shorter.

★ ★ ★ ★ ★

The Quintet led by Davis and featuring Hancock, Carter, Williams and Shorter went on to be one of the most famous groups in jazz history and the signs are there to see on *Miles In Berlin,* recorded live at the city's Philharmonie concert hall on 25 September. The repertoire is familiar, and it is one of the characteristics of this line-up that in spite of the wealth of excellent new material on their studio albums they tended to opt for established numbers when playing live, using them as a framework for experimentation with sound and rhythm. Such is the case here. 'Stella By Starlight', inexplicably omitted from the original LP release, is very different from the Lincoln Center rendition: Davis veers from confidence to fragility and back again, exploring not the just the structure but the meaning of the song. On 'Autumn Leaves', his solo verges on the psychotic, incorporating muted buzzing, disjointed blasts and the melancholic, lonely tones that were becoming his trademark. But Shorter is the revelation, matching Davis's enterprise without sounding anything like him. His restless searching drives the group's music to new levels of intensity on 'Milestones', 'So What' and 'Walkin'' and on the two ballads his manipulation of melody and metre liberates the rhythm section to set off on paths of their own.

Davis had wanted Shorter in his band since 1961 but had been unable to prise him from the clutches of Art Blakey, for whom he was both a star soloist and composer. After George Coleman left the Davis group there was a lot of speculation that he might hire Eric Dolphy, whose virtuosity on alto saxophone, flute and bass clarinet had made him much sought after by a variety of big-name bandleaders.

Few contemporary jazz musicians were more enigmatic than Dolphy – mild-mannered and dreamy, he was at the same time a ferocious and uncompromising improviser, a paradox explained by John Litweiler as follows:

> There's a great sense of wonder about all his playing , a purity of scope and intention on the surface that seems almost innocent next to the emotional complexities of [Ornette] Coleman, [Cecil] Taylor, and Coltrane. (*The Freedom Principle*, p. 63)

As such he was different, too, from other innovators of the time such as pianist Andrew Hill and vibraphone player Bobby Hutcherson, musical intellectuals who were linking what was past with what was to come. His approach was more akin to Tony Williams, whose utter disregard for convention and phenomenal technique made him attractive to a range of bandleaders (Litweiler states with unerring accuracy that, 'Davis used him specifically to assault the nerves' – *ibid.*, p. 116). But whereas Williams had a touch of arrogance about him – he was less than complimentary, for example, about George Coleman, an experienced musician ten years his senior – Dolphy was sweet-tempered and liked by everyone – even Davis, who all the same detested his playing, saying that he sounded 'like somebody was standing on his foot' (*Miles: The Autobiography*, p. 259). There was therefore never any question of his joining the trumpeter's group.

By 1964 Dolphy had been a professional musician for nearly 20 years, including a spell at the Naval School of Music, and had worked with some of the major figures in jazz, such as Chico Hamilton, Mingus and Coltrane. Yet, to reinforce Litweiler's comments above, he seemed to approach every project and indeed every solo as if it was his first. The album he made on 25 February 1964 – the same day that, in another universe, George Harrison was celebrating his 21st birthday and The Beatles were recording 'You Can't Do That', 'And I Love Her' and 'I Should Have Known Better' – was especially notable for its freshness and sense of wide open space; it even had a novel cover, with no picture of Dolphy or his band but a locked door, a clock with multiple hands giving no clear time of return and the title, *Out To Lunch!*.

The name of the album was also a clever play on words, for 'out to lunch' was a slang term for 'crazy', a reference to how this music was seen at the time and possibly, in a gesture of mild self-mockery, how the musicians saw themselves. Eventually, as is common in slang, it came to mean the exact opposite, namely 'cool' or 'awesome' – a much more fitting description for one of the finest jazz records of the year, the decade and possibly the century.

Its success rested to a large extent on its personnel: five musicians of like mind who, nevertheless, had distinctive individual voices. Alongside Dolphy, Williams and Hutcherson, were bassist Richard Davis and trumpeter Freddie Hubbard, both of whom were capable of playing any style of jazz (Davis had experience, too, in classical music) but sublimated their virtuosity to the demands of the music. And these were considerable: Dolphy's writing was unorthodox and oblique with odd time signatures and unpredictable rhythms, sometimes abandoning any sort of tempo at all.

The opening 'Hat And Beard', a tribute to bebop pioneer Thelonious Monk, sets the tone. Commencing with a single, abrupt chord, it is a brisk, staccato theme in 5/4, moving swiftly to 9/4 – propelled by walking bass and martial snare. A strangulated bass clarinet solo by Dolphy is punctuated by Hutcherson's icy vibes and slicing hi-hat accents from Williams; Hubbard brings serenity and polish, and the closing section is a collage of variegated textures including more angular trilling by Hutcherson, Williams burrowing away on brushes, and Davis on bowed bass. In contrast, 'Something Sweet, Something Tender' is a neatly constructed showcase for Dolphy's whirling bass clarinet, while his fluent flute on 'Gazzelloni' is worthy of the Italian maestro to whom it is dedicated. The title track is a *magnum opus* of considerable complexity; the convoluted theme sets the leader up for an astounding alto solo that alternates sculpted melodic phrases with bloodcurdling emotional outbursts; Hubbard enters with a fanfare and sustains the momentum, only to see it dissipate as the tempo crumbles. Hutcherson's crystalline vibraphone emerges to lead the piece towards a climax that features chopped up interjections from Dolphy and Hubbard, plaintive bass by Davis and the shifting, dynamic drumming of Williams. The album concludes with 'Straight Up And Down' which, despite its title, is intended to simulate the lurching movements of a drunk and succeeds admirably thanks to swaying alto from Dolphy and a remarkable Hutcherson solo in which he scrutinises the sonic potential of his instrument rather like someone sozzled will investigate an object with disproportionate interest.

Out To Lunch! confronts the traditional framework of jazz whereby the theme or riff provide the stability and the soloist the spontaneity; here, composition is inseparable from improvisation and the music veers from discipline to near-anarchy and back in the space of a few bars, to gripping effect. Nothing quite like it had been heard before and, arguably, since. When, eighteen years later, Freddie Hubbard autographed the album sleeve for the author, he inscribed it 'New Music'. He could not have described it any better.

★ ★ ★ ★ ★

As noted in Chapter 1, Charles Mingus had nailed his political colours to the mast well before 1964 with 'Fables Of Faubus', 'Cry For Freedom (Prayer For Passive Resistance)', 'Non-sectarian Blues' and 'Suite Freedom'. But despite the strength of his convictions, he was no Black Muslim. In an interview with Stanley Dance for the November/December 1963 issue of *Jazz*, he stated,

> When these fellows start talking about their "black brothers and the weaker tribes", I think it's a lot of crap, especially when Muhammad X is lighter than Max Roach and as light as I am. (Quoted in Brian Priestley – *Mingus*, p. 156)

In truth, Mingus was not inclined to join any society, movement or pressure group; he was as independent in his opinions as he was in his music. His tendency to veer from unbridled aggression to conciliation and tranquillity was mirrored in many of his best compositions, especially those with a political dimension, such as 'Meditations On Integration'. This began life as 'Meditations', premiered at the New York Town Hall at an NAACP benefit on 4 April 1964 and was introduced by Mingus as follows:

> Eric Dolphy explained to me that there was something similar to the concentration camps once in Germany now down South … and the only difference between the barbed wire is that they don't have gas chambers and hot stoves to cook us in yet. So I wrote a piece called Meditations, as to how to get some wire cutters – before someone else gets some guns to us. (*ibid.*, p. 162)

Mingus's appearance at the Town Hall was recorded, as were no fewer than eight other concerts during the course of the year (he did not enter the studio at all during 1964), many of which were on his April tour of Europe, which was also filmed extensively by local television stations. The wealth of this material allows us to chart the evolution of 'Meditations' into 'Meditations On Integration'.

Dolphy had re-joined the band the previous August and his presence on the tour was critical to its success. He had, however, informed Mingus that he would be leaving as soon as it was over. According to Rob Bowman's notes to the Jazz Icons DVD, *Live In '64*, Mingus considered this group – Dolphy, trumpeter Johnny Coles, tenor saxophonist Clifford Jordan, drummer Dannie Richmond and pianist Jaki Byard – the best he ever worked with, and the material on the DVD provides some persuasive evidence for that view. The performances shown are from Norway, Sweden and Belgium, the latter two containing versions of 'Meditations On Integration' which, though separated by only two days, are quite different from each other. The first is lighter in mood and showcases the contrasting individual skills of the musicians while the latter, minus Coles who had collapsed on stage with a perforated gastric ulcer, is wilder, more intense and, possibly as a reaction to the trumpeter's absence, derives its energy from the collective effort. There is one remarkable passage, close to the end, in which Byard, Dolphy and Mingus weave an intricate improvised pattern, each taking turns to lead. Dolphy's playing is outstanding on both occasions, not least for its variety of execution and effect. In Sweden, his bass clarinet is commanding, in Belgium, it is angular and fragmented; his flute solo brings peace and calm to the latter performance, melancholy to the former.

When the tour was over, Dolphy stayed in Europe and on 11 June made an album in Paris with a group that comprised trumpeter Donald Byrd, tenor saxophonist Nathan Davis and a local rhythm section. On two of the four tracks he is on alto saxophone – '245' sees him using his vocalised tone to conduct a conversation with himself, commencing with a furious diatribe and developing into an exchange of animated phrases, and on 'GW' he whirls and swirls in dramatic fashion. But his work on bass clarinet is still more impressive. The epic 'Springtime' is a bewildering catalogue of sonic effects, underpinned by an unwavering rhythmic drive, and his solo on 'Serene' is bluesy and light-hearted. Eighteen days later, Eric Dolphy was in Berlin when he went into a diabetic shock and died, aged 36.

Dolphy had been central to Mingus's vision as he epitomised the interface between violence and peace that the bassist was looking to achieve in his compositions. Although it was not billed as such, Mingus's appearance at the Monterey Jazz Festival on 20 September 1964 seemed tantamount to a tribute to his former colleague. But the concert presented other contrasts, too, the most glaring of which was that between the music of the acknowledged master, Duke Ellington, and Mingus, the young pretender. Fortunately, it was recorded and released on the latter's mail-order Jazz Workshop label.

Of the three pieces played, the first is the Ellington medley, which Mingus begins in daring fashion with a bass solo, initially sticking to the tune of 'I Got It Bad But That Ain't Good' before creating melodies of his own. From then on, he and his group – Byard, Richmond, trumpeter Lonnie Hillyer and saxophonists Charles McPherson and John Handy III – interpret another five Ducal themes with some surprising and delightful results, including Hillyer's mournful interpretation of 'Mood Indigo' and Byard's uproarious unaccompanied solo in the stride idiom employed by Ellington when he began his career 50 years before. Some good-humoured announcements by Mingus lead into 'Orange Was The Color Of Her Dress, Then Blue Silk', one of the staples of the European tour and a richly-textured work blending balladry with blues.

Finally comes the 26-minute 'Mediations On Integration' in which the band is augmented by six musicians who add individual and collective strength and underline its viability as a composition, rather than a vehicle for jamming. The funereal, raga-like opening, played by bowed bass and tuba, seems to commemorate Dolphy as does the by-now familiar theme, described by Mingus in the sleeve note as 'deep and dolorous'. As the pace accelerates, the written and the spontaneous intertwine, cooling down to the flute interlude with bass and piano decoration; declamatory trumpet cuts through the ensuing out-of-tempo section that builds to an almighty tumult, followed by eerie tinkling piano and the concluding, crushing chord.

Mingus's performance at Monterey was greeted by a standing ovation, with organiser Jimmy Lyons proclaiming it – not unreasonably – 'a dream come true.' 'Meditations On Integration', in particular, had it all – Eastern and classical influences, swing, blues, *avant garde* jazz, written and improvised sections, large and small ensembles, individual excellence, fast and slow tempos – all of which so fully reflected the global nature of what he wanted to achieve – in his words, 'A prayer for peace, a prayer of love, a prayer for all people.'

★ ★ ★ ★ ★

In 'Meditations On Integration', Mingus worked through the conflict being played out politically between Martin Luther King and Malcolm X – that is, how to make the appropriate response to injustice and oppression. A necessary part of that was belligerence and anger: both were certainly present by the barrelful in Mingus's music, yet so was the desire for reconciliation and peace, and it was this that ultimately held sway. Having meditated on integration, he still preferred it to separation.

Seen purely in terms of jazz development, he had achieved a deftly calibrated balance between the old and the new and occupied a position at the halfway point to free jazz. Others, meanwhile, were 75% of the way there. One was the pianist Andrew Hill who recorded no fewer than five albums for Blue Note, the premier contemporary jazz label, between 8 November 1963 and 25 June 1964. All featured some of the best musicians of the period and attracted rave reviews. *Judgment!* and *Point Of Departure* were the only two both recorded (on 8 January and 21 March respectively) and released in 1964.

Hill's partners on *Judgment!* are Hutcherson, Richard Davis and Elvin Jones. The latter was Coltrane's drummer and a musician of formidable ferocity, yet the power of Hill's conception – cool, cerebral, classical – is so inexorable that even he conforms to it without complaint. The model is established on the opener, 'Siete Ocho', in which the apparently free association between instruments brings a sense of communal purpose that all but conceals the delicate melody underneath. Its equilibrium is replicated on 'Flea Flop' in which Hutcherson's shimmering vibes meet Hill's sinuous piano, 'Yokada Yokada' where the spiky, cyclical theme is offset by the fluency of the solos, and on the title track which balances Hutcherson's elegance with a volley from Jones. Rank is broken briefly on the closing 'Reconciliation' which is dominated by a tense, precise Hill solo betraying the twin influences of Bach and Monk.

Similar structures pervade *Point Of Departure*, though this time Hill is more concerned with the search for self-expression – hence the title – and, in the process, getting away from established chord patterns and predictable rhythms. In Eric Dolphy and Tony Williams, he found absolutely the right men to assist him; Dolphy was already liberated from traditional harmonic precepts, while Williams was given *carte blanche* to dispense with metronomic time-keeping. To retain some semblance of orthodoxy Hill chose trumpeter Kenny Dorham and tenorist Joe Henderson, both of whom had one foot in hard bop, the tough, no-nonsense offshoot from bebop that was doing good commercial business for Blue Note in the early 1960s. As a result, the record is fresh and uncluttered yet firmly grounded in reality: as Hill comments in the sleeve note, 'Anything "new" has to evolve out of the old.'

'Refuge' exemplifies this methodology; the theme is robust but at the same time edgy and anxious, and the individual contributions are carefully arranged to highlight the differences that exist between them. Hill leads off with a nuanced, intricate solo that quietly pushes the boundaries; in comparison, Dolphy's dazzling alto is like an electric shock. Dorham brings some stability then Richard Davis's bounding bass threatens to disturb it again, and Henderson draws the number to a close with a surge of emotion. The evocative 'Flight' features sprightly exchanges between trumpet and piano, buoyed by fluttering cymbals and buzzing bass clarinet; 'New Monastery' celebrates Thelonious Monk in its loping angularity; and the solemn 'Dedication' allows Hill the luxury of a long, cascading solo. But the multi-layered 'Spectrum' provides ultimate proof of Hill's intention to take jazz forward. As if the complexities of the writing were not enough, the piece contains a remarkable sequence of solos in which Dolphy's abandon tows Henderson and Dorham in his direction and Williams rounds things off with a ringing, reverberating drum feature.

Exactly five months later, Williams was in the studio recording *Life Time,* his first album as a leader. Still only eighteen, his playing and writing had already reached maturity. As a drummer he had few, if any, equals, for he was able to pull off the seemingly impossible trick of using bass drum, tom-tom, snare, cymbal and hi-hat as if they were separate instruments yet at the same time playing the whole kit as one integrated, flowing entity. Though few in number his compositions were varied and challenging, not least for their use of space and silence, and to interpret them he chose his personnel with exactitude.

Using two bass players in an ensemble was nothing new; Ellington had done so in the 1940s as had Hill on *Smokestack* the previous year. But no-one yet had opened an album, let alone their debut, with two soloing bassists, one *arco* and the other *pizzicato.* However, this is how '2 Pieces Of One (Red)' begins, before the two musicians in question, Richard Davis and Gary Peacock, give way to the twisting tenor saxophone of Sam Rivers. Williams confines himself to the occasional snare drum rap, but he is all over '2 Pieces Of One (Green)', driving Rivers to extremes and turning in two very different solos – the first, light, subtle and cleanly executed, the second a thunderous climax to the whole piece. 'Tomorrow Afternoon' is a three-way partnership between Rivers, Peacock and Williams, giving each man a turn to dictate the course of events, while 'Barb's Song To The Wizard' features only Herbie Hancock and Ron Carter who develop its simple melody with dexterity and grace. But the most compelling track of all is 'Memory', an evocation of childhood in which a range of percussive effects from Williams, Hancock's gentle piano and the clinking marimba of Bobby Hutcherson cohere to create a feeling of suspension in time and place.

Life Time shows that, despite his sense of adventure and quest for new sounds, Williams, like Hill, still valued organisation and discipline: he had gone to the brink of free-form but declined to jump in. Before long, in any case, he was to be involved in other musical revolutions.

★ ★ ★ ★ ★

In 1964 most African-American jazz artists who wanted to express their views on Civil Rights did so solely through their music. Tenor saxophonist Archie Shepp was not one of them. Well before turning professional, he had written an allegorical play entitled *The Communists* on the situation of black Americans. Shepp left his native Philadelphia for New York with the intention of becoming an actor but, finding work scarce, he threw in his lot with the pianist Cecil Taylor, who was viewed as one of the pioneers of 'free jazz', also known as 'free-form' or *avant garde* jazz.

Dispensing with the rules of melody, harmony and rhythm was not a new development. On 16 May 1949 Lennie Tristano had recorded 'Intuition' and 'Digression,' both of which were collective improvisations with no theme, fixed chord progression or tempo, as was Shelley Manne's 'Abstract No. 1' from 1954. Two years later, Taylor himself took a similar direction with the heavily percussive *Jazz Advance* while from 1958 onwards the alto saxophonist Ornette Coleman had released a series of innovatory records, culminating with *Free Jazz* in 1961 on which he used a double quartet structure featuring Dolphy and Hubbard. But when Coleman arrived in New York in November 1959 for a residency at the Five Spot Café, it sparked massive interest – and not a little controversy – in these radical approaches.

Although Shepp is not featured to best advantage on the records he made with Taylor, they did lead him to form the New York Contemporary Five with altoist John Tchicai, a quintet that at various times included trumpeter Bill Dixon, trombonist Roswell Rudd and the cornet player Don Cherry, who had played in Coleman's quintet. Finally, in 1964, Shepp got to make his first studio recording as a leader. For his producer, he started at the top – Bob Thiele had worked with many of the biggest names in jazz including the two giants of the tenor saxophone, Coleman Hawkins and Lester Young. In order to secure Thiele's services he first approached John Coltrane for a recommendation. Thiele suggested Shepp make an album of Coltrane compositions, but Trane proposed the inclusion of one of Shepp's own pieces, 'Rufus (Swung His Face At Last To The Wind Then His Neck Snapped)'. The result was *Four For Trane*, recorded (as were *Out To Lunch!*, *Judgment!*, *Point Of Departure* and *Life Time*) at the Van Gelder Studio, Englewood Cliffs, New Jersey, on 10 August 1964.

Even the cover photograph announces that this will be no ordinary tribute album; both men are pictured but it playfully implies that the seated, pipe-smoking Shepp is the senior partner – and as soon as the record hits the turntable it is clear that he intends to put his own stamp on what was, by then, familiar material. Three of the pieces, for instance, come from Coltrane's *Giant Steps* album of four years earlier. Shepp's own account of the up-tempo numbers, 'Syeeda's Song Flute' and 'Cousin Mary', entirely lack the bounce and exuberance of the originals and, instead, the theme statements are sparse and quickly set aside. The formerly dignified 'Naima' is raw, almost grief-stricken. But Shepp's real impact is as an improvising tenor saxophonist – despite sporadic references to past icons like Hawkins and Ben Webster, he bypasses both the historical and contemporary development of the instrument by revealing a style that consists of random runs, truncated phrases and strangled single notes and which is predicated on emotion rather than musical logic. To hear how he explicitly rejects the facility of Charlie Parker, the architectural sweep of Sonny Rollins and the relentlessness of Coltrane himself is little short of intoxicating.

Based not on clever but esoteric experiments with musical theory, but on sheer visceral instinct and guts, *Four For Trane* set a new benchmark for free jazz. Yet precisely one month earlier, a record had been made which, if anything, went further out. *Spiritual Unity* was the first album by another tenor saxophonist, Albert Ayler, who had moved to New York in 1963 and worked with Don Cherry the same year. Consisting of only four tracks, two of which share a tune, it has a playing time of less than half an hour but its content is sensational – virtually all free improvisation and completely stripped of gratuitous frills and niceties. The nearest it gets to normality is the 'Ghosts' theme, an unsteady march with a distinctly Caribbean gait. On 'Ghosts: First Variation', it heralds a frenzied, throbbing Ayler solo; Gary Peacock's bass is commensurately violent and only the hissing cymbals of Sunny Murray pull the piece together. 'Ghosts: Second Variation' follows a similar pattern but is marginally milder. Ayler invests 'The Wizzard' with a furious, charging motion, extracting from his instrument an amazing variety of sound from throttled shrieks to a rounded, brassy timbre; at other times his tone is so thin it sounds like a violin. The incantatory 'Spirits' sees him progress from agonised barks to a tender, quivering coda.

Neither Ornette Coleman nor Cecil Taylor released any records during 1964 so it was left to Shepp and Ayler to spearhead free jazz. Shepp went on to combine his music with his politics, beginning with 'Malcolm, Malcolm, Semper Malcolm' in early 1965, and became a role model for young jazz artists wanting to do the same. Ayler continued to shock both fans and critics yet he never acquired the sort of following acquired by Shepp, Taylor, Coleman and Coltrane; on 5 November 1970 he went missing in New York and three weeks later his body was found in the East River.

★ ★ ★ ★ ★

Most of the records discussed so far in this chapter were released on the Blue Note label, founded in 1939 by Alfred Lion, Max Margulis and Francis Wolff. As well as maintaining an excellent roster of traditional jazz artists, Blue Note had been interested in contemporary jazz from the start and recorded many of the great names of bebop such as Thelonious Monk, Bud Powell and Miles Davis. But today they are probably best known for their vast catalogue of releases in the style that succeeded it, hard bop. Following the digressions of cool jazz and Third Stream music (a fusion of classical music with jazz), hard bop represented a return to the basics. Usually played by a quintet or sextet – trumpet, saxophone, perhaps trombone, piano, bass and drums – it was direct, punchy and heavily influenced by blues and gospel, so much so that certain strands became known as 'soul-jazz'. As a result, it became popular with the general public and helped subsidise Blue Note's investment in artists with less commercial potential. It was also, almost exclusively, an African-American idiom, one of the few not to be appropriated and exploited by whites.

The origins of hard bop are to be found in the 1955 album *Horace Silver And The Jazz Messengers*, the line-up comprised of Kenny Dorham on trumpet, tenor saxophonist Hank Mobley, bass player Doug Watkins, drummer Art Blakey and pianist Silver, a former member of Stan Getz's group. Even the titles reflected the vernacular – 'Creepin' In', 'Hankerin'', 'Doodlin'' – and one track, 'The Preacher', was considered so corny by Alfred Lion that he almost didn't record it. But it was this piece, with its catchy tune and good-time feel, that caught the imagination of both jazz fans and record-buyers in general. The group, under Silver's nominal leadership, was more of a joint project between himself and Blakey, who continued to use the band name after Silver had left.

In 1964, both men were still going strong and getting excellent results from a formula that united tight ensemble control with individual freedom. Silver, despite having to deal with personnel changes during its creation, came up with one of the most enduring jazz records of the decade, *Song For My Father*. Two of the six tracks were made in October 1963, the rest a year later, by – other than Silver – an entirely different group, and it is two of these latter cuts that give the album its classic status. The title track is especially well-known, partly because Steely Dan used its intro for their 1974 hit, 'Rikki Don't Lose That Number'. Its melody, like most of those on the album, is robust and instantly memorable, hinting both at the blues and the then fashionable bossa nova; Silver's soulful solo is succeeded by a beautifully constructed effort from Joe Henderson which takes the temperature up to boiling point. The leader then cools things down again and brings the piece to a sudden, dramatic conclusion. 'Que Pasa' has a brooding, undulating tune built around an insistent, repeated piano chord while pounding bass and rumbling drums add to the foreboding atmosphere. Again, Silver and Henderson share the spotlight, the leader lithe and funky, the tenorist characteristically vigorous. Just over a month later, on 30 November 1964, Henderson was in the same studio making his first album as leader in his own right. Featuring 50% of The John

Coltrane Quartet – Elvin Jones and pianist McCoy Tyner – *The Inner Urge* is a varied, well-balanced record overflowing with top-quality musicianship; Henderson's mastery of all the contemporary jazz idioms is astounding.

Art Blakey had also fared well since splitting with Silver, indeed his Jazz Messengers had become the definitive hard bop outfit. The band was also a breeding-ground for new talent and in that respect the spring 1964 incarnation was one of its finest, with Lee Morgan replacing Freddie Hubbard on trumpet, Curtis Fuller on trombone, pianist Cedar Walton, bass player Reggie Workman and – just a few weeks away from joining Miles Davis – tenor saxophonist Wayne Shorter. All bar Workman and Blakey himself were also writers and *Indestructible,* made in April and May and the only album to be recorded by this line-up, includes pieces by each of them.

The first two tracks, 'The Egyptian' and 'Sortie', are riffy modal jazz compositions by Fuller, illuminated by Morgan's sparkling solos; the trumpeter's 'Calling Miss Khadija' is pleasingly old-fashioned with more than a hint of swing in conception and execution. Yet although it is yet to come to the maturity it acquired under Davis, Shorter's playing is the most absorbing aspect of the record – on his 'Mr Jin', explosions of energy generate new melodies, and on Walton's bittersweet ballad, 'When Love Is New', he eschews the lush vibrato of Hawkins and Webster to create an intensity all of his own.

Shorter was to go on to stardom with Davis and later Weather Report, but it was Morgan who was the bigger name in 1964, thanks to the enormous success of his album *The Sidewinder,* recorded at the end of the previous year. The infectious title track, with its insistent staccato riff and socking backbeat, caught on to such an extent that it made the US Top 100 singles chart and, for a time, Blue Note commenced all their albums with a comparably funky composition. Morgan's fluid, relaxed playing permeates every track, but he is run close by the seemingly ubiquitous Joe Henderson whose exuberant solo on 'Hocus-Pocus' shows the more affable side of his musical personality.

Morgan had strong political views and, far from letting the popularity of *The Sidewinder* drive him towards the mores of show business, became a vocal and active campaigner for equal rights. He joined forces with the multi-instrumentalist Rahsaan Roland Kirk to form the Jazz and People's Movement, the objective of which was to bring about fairer representation for African-Americans in the US entertainment industry. Among the main targets were the high-profile TV programmes hosted by the likes of Ed Sullivan, Johnny Carson and Dick Cavett. In 1971, for his last-ever show, Sullivan finally invited Kirk to appear. With a group comprising Mingus, Shepp and drummer Roy Haynes, he performed not, as scheduled, Stevie Wonder's 'My Cherie Amour', but a chaotic free-form version of the Mingus composition, 'Haitian Fight Song'. Some commentators, like Dan Morgenstern, editor of the jazz magazine *down beat* since 1964, deplored this action as counterproductive to the interests of the Movement since it could only alienate programme-makers still further. But in retrospect, it was an essential part of a struggle against discrimination that was to continue for some time. Morgan did not live to see it come to fruition, for the following year he was shot dead by his wife in a New York night club.

In many ways, Kirk was the most idiosyncratic of all the contemporary jazz artists operating in 1964. Blind from an early age, he was completely fearless as a man and as a musician, with an astonishing ability to play several saxophones at once. Such feats added to his reputation as an entertainer and, following a spell with Mingus in the early 1960s, he became an international attraction, not averse to taking a pop song like 'My Cherie Amour' or Aretha Franklin's 'I Say A Little Prayer' and adapting it for his own purposes – often with an element of parody lurking in the background. But alongside the showmanship, he was a hugely gifted musician.

Kirk recorded two albums in 1964: *I Talk With The Spirits*, on which he plays flute on all the numbers (which include 'Serenade To A Cuckoo', covered four years later by Jethro Tull) and *Gifts And Messages*, recorded in Los Angeles on 22 July and a representative cross-section of his music at this period. This comprised adaptations of works by such diverse composers as Pyotyr Ilyich Tchaikovsky ('March On, Swan Lake') and Sidney Bechet ('Petite Fleur') and six of his own pieces which included the darting 'Blues For C &T' and 'Hip Chops' on which, in between spoken interjections, he plays flute and tenor saxophone simultaneously; he need hardly ask at the end of the track, 'Who has the hippest chops in the world?' His dexterity also raises a smile on 'The Things I Love' where he switches with ease between multi-horn playing to successive solos on manzello – a reed instrument he had discovered during a visit to a music shop in his native Columbus, Ohio – and tenor saxophone. The more serious side of his personality is evident on the ballad 'Tears Sent By You', on which he avoids conventional romanticism in favour of hard, rounded sounds and long-held notes, and 'Where Does The Blame Lie?' with its remarkable tenor solo based on a cyclical, repeated phrase, that conveys how, in looking for scapegoats, one is apt to go round in circles.

What Kirk and the hard boppers demonstrated was that in 1964, amid the rampant radicalism of Dolphy, Shepp and Ayler, more traditional forms of African-American music – New Orleans, swing, gospel and, especially, blues – still had something to offer, albeit within a modern context. This new-yet-old approach was found most consistently in the work of the guitarist, Grant Green.

Green made no fewer than 29 albums for Blue Note under his own name, clear evidence that he caught the mood of a jazz public who wanted to keep up-to-date but were wary of the iconoclasts. Like Charlie Christian, his major influence, Green's phrasing resembled that of a horn player yet at the same time his feeling for the blues was on a par with the greats of the idiom such as BB King, Otis Rush or Buddy Guy. *Idle Moments* was his first release of 1964 and became one of his most acclaimed, thanks in part to the fifteen-minute title track which, due to a misunderstanding in the studio, turned out be twice as long as originally envisaged. It was subsequently re-recorded but the first take was considered so superior that other tracks were made again in shorter versions so as to fit the overall playing time. A luxuriantly slow blues, it is an oasis of calm. Green's solo unfolds quietly while its composer, the underrated Duke Pearson, adds some elegant touches; Joe Henderson's sound is warm and velvety and Bobby Hutcherson weighs each note with precision and care. 'Jean De Fleur' is pacy, 'Django' reverential, but it is 'Nomad', another Pearson piece, which compares best with 'Idle Moments'. With echoes of Davis's 'Milestones', it allows the musicians maximum room to manoeuvre: Henderson is loose-limbed and cliché-free, Hutcherson smooth and agile, and Green, without compromising his style in the slightest, displays an impressive range of ideas and effects, moving Henderson to make the comment quoted in the sleeve note that he had 'never heard a guitar sound like that before.'

But Green's enormous popularity was exceeded by that of the organist, Jimmy Smith. Indeed Smith had already reached number 21 on the US singles chart in 1962 with 'Walk On The Wild Side'. Like Green, Smith had come to prominence with Blue Note, for whom he made eleven albums in the first two years of his contract, but a move to Verve brought him into contact with the commercially-minded producer, Creed Taylor. The result was a flood of albums, commencing with *Bashin': The Unpredictable Jimmy Smith*, from which 'Walk On The Wild Side' was taken.

In 1964 he got to number twelve on the album chart with *The Cat*. This LP certainly made concessions to commercialism – none of the tracks run for over five minutes and arranger Lalo Schifrin creates some irresistible riffs – but Smith is more animated than on *Bashin'* and his by-then familiar nimble runs and machine gun-like repetitions power 'Blues In The Night', 'St Louis Blues' and the title track; on Elmer Bernstein's 'Main Title From *The Carpetbaggers*' he reverses the normal process by acting as accompanist to the clamorous, brass dominated orchestra.

Smith's massive success, the continued appeal of Blue Note with its roster of hard bop artists and the renaissance of Miles Davis is proof that – assuming one were to disregard the innovations of Mingus, Dolphy, Hill, Shepp and Ayler as decadent diversions – jazz was by no means dead in 1964. What *was* under threat was its mainstream, and with it some of the figures who had dominated the music over the previous decades; but even they evolved strategies for survival that, in many cases, supported them well into old age. And there was also the overarching vision of the jazz musician who more than anyone else embodied the spirit of '64, John Coltrane.

★ ★ ★ ★ ★

The presidential election of 1964 provided the first chance for African-Americans to give their verdict on Johnson and his response to Civil Rights. In the jazz community, some felt progress had been too slow while others brought a lighter note to the campaigning:

> In a lampoon candidacy, jazz trumpeter Dizzy Gillespie was also running for president in 1964. His platform included changing the name "White House" to "Blues House," disbanding the FBI and Senate Internal Security committee, legalizing the numbers racket that paid the mob so well in black neighborhoods, and forcing job applicants to wear sheets so potential employers could not tell their race. Gillespie named fellow jazzmen Miles Davis his future CIA head, Max Roach his Minister of Defense, and Charlie Mingus his Minister of Peace. (Guido van Rijn, *President Johnson's Blues*, p. 17)

On the whole, however, Johnson was the favoured candidate, especially among the more established stars of the music. The vibraphonist Lionel Hampton, for example, stated in his autobiography:

> I may be a Republican, but I'm first of all an American, and I thought that what President Johnson was doing was good for the country. So in 1964, when he ran for election as president, I jumped party lines to support him. I had nothing personally against Barry Goldwater – in fact, we were good friends – but Johnson had signed the 1964 Civil Rights Act and said, "We shall overcome," and he was the man I wanted to support. (*Hamp*, p. 143-4)

For his part, Johnson asked Count Basie and Duke Ellington to play at his inaugural ball, one of seven times he invited Ellington to the White House during his presidency.

But there were occasional dissenting voices, too. Oscar Brown Jr – who, as recounted in Chapter 1, had partnered Max Roach for 1960's *We Insist! Freedom Now Suite* and released his incendiary debut album *Sin And Soul* the following year – was to a large extent the musical counterpart of his friends Lorraine Hansberry and James Baldwin, who were both successful African-American playwrights. 1964 saw the premiere of Baldwin's *Blues For Mister Charlie*, his reflection on the murder of Medgar Evers, and the publication by the SNCC of a book of photographs on the theme of Civil Rights entitled *The Movement*, to which Hansberry provided the commentary. Brown had no albums out that year but put together a one-man show, *The Many Characters Of Oscar Brown Jr*, and made a much-praised appearance at the Newport Jazz Festival on 5 July 1964. Roach had played the whole of the *Freedom Now* suite the previous day and Brown joked with the audience, 'Many of you were lured here with the promise of a jazz festival, but a few insiders know that in reality this is a political rally.' He referred to Gillespie's spoof candidacy in his introduction to 'When My Baby Is The First Lady In The Land' and poked fun at the promise given to freed slaves in his poem 'Forty Acres And A Mule'; but there was a serious intent behind it all, underlined by the sombre anti-war protest song, 'Muffled Drums'.

Brown was such a talented writer and performer that he may well have made the transition to superstardom, were it not for his reputation as an outspoken social commentator and Civil Rights activist. It was much safer to keep your views to yourself and go with the flow, even if that led to compromises along the way. For many of the biggest names in jazz, this meant coming to terms with pop music: Duke Ellington, Ella Fitzgerald and Count Basie all made pop albums in 1964 and Louis Armstrong had a massive world-wide hit with the show tune, 'Hello, Dolly!'.

Predictably, Ellington's take was the most interesting. In April 1964 he recorded the tracks for what would be the *Ellington '65* album, including the aforementioned 'Hello, Dolly!' which he had the sense to convert to a tenor saxophone feature for Jimmy Hamilton, set to a shuffle beat, thus avoiding comparison with the Armstrong version. But closer listening to these sessions and to those that took place in autumn for his *Mary Poppins* album reveals that whenever the shuffle rhythm is employed, parody is not far away. The most extreme case is the April version of 'Blowin' In The Wind' where Dylan's melody is mocked by the plaintive wah-wah sound of three trumpets in unison. This satire on protest music was a follow-on from the previous year when he had given his attempt at merging classical music with jazz the ironic title of 'Non-Violent Integration'. Frustratingly, the tunes most deserving of such treatment do not get it: 'Stranger On The Shore', for example, with its sonorous baritone saxophone solo by Harry Carney, is treated with reverence, as is 'I Left My Heart In San Francisco', though the latter comes inadvertently close to *self*-parody by piling a sugary Lawrence Brown trombone solo on top of the already sentimental tune.

Duke Ellington Plays With The Original Score From Walt Disney's Mary Poppins is the cumbersome title of a record commissioned by Disney himself with the words, 'I just want to hear what you're going to do with it!' *. He was in for a surprise. The clue is in the name of the album: Ellington 'plays with' the score rather than simply 'plays' it. There were many versions of this hit soundtrack during 1964 but none with the ambiguity of Ellington's, where the dividing line between caricature and creativity is often wafer-thin. We may be fairly sure that 'A Spoonful Of Sugar' occupies the former territory since the first notes we hear come from Willie Dixon's heavyweight blues number, 'Spoonful' – a more contrasting composition is impossible to imagine. The shuffle beat is in evidence and it features, too, on 'I Like To Laugh', while the use in this piece of a range of comic effects, including the dreaded wah-wah trumpets, may well relate to its title.

Sometimes the humour comes not from Ellington or his arranger

---

* Sleeve note by Mark Tucker to *Duke Ellington: The Reprise Studio Recordings*.

colleague, Billy Strayhorn but from the soloists. In 'Supercalifragilisticexpialidocious', tenorist Paul Gonsalves quotes from 'We're In The Money', which Mark Tucker suggests was 'a dig directed toward Ellington (or Reprise) for producing such a baldly commercial recording project.' Certainly there was no question about the motivation behind an album that – with seven of its eleven tracks under three minutes and all well under five – was made in September and in the shops the following month.

This is not to say the record lacks quality. The creamy alto saxophone of Johnny Hodges elevates 'The Life I Lead' and 'Let's Go Fly A Kite'; trumpeter Cootie Williams growls to great effect on 'Chim Chim Cheree'; and Ellington's imaginative, swinging arrangement of 'Sister Suffragette' hints at what might have been done with 'Blowin' In The Wind', a not dissimilar tune. Although *Mary Poppins* may not rank with his finest work, it is a tribute to Ellington's undiminished powers that, exactly 40 years after his first record, he was able to fashion something of lasting value out of such unpromising material.

As we saw in Chapter 5, Louis Armstrong had long been taken to task for 'going commercial' and by the late 1950s corresponded to many people's definition of the acquiescent African-American, the 'Uncle Tom'. But beneath the genial veneer, Armstrong was a firm believer in Civil Rights who occasionally confounded his audience, and his management, by speaking out. In 1957, for example, he denounced Governor Orval Faubus and stated that, 'President Eisenhower should go there [Little Rock] and take those little children by the hand and lead them into that school.' Statements like this led to his being monitored by the FBI for the rest of his life. Yet to all intents and purposes he remained the ambassador of jazz, taking the music far and wide both internationally and within the frontiers of the US. It was during one such trip that he heard that a song he had recorded some months before but considered 'lame' had hit the top of the charts. His bassist, Arvell Shaw, recalls,

We were out somewhere in the wilds of Iowa, Nebraska, doing some one-nighters ... Every night the audience would be calling, "Hello, Dolly!", "Hello, Dolly!" ... Louis said, "What's 'Hello, Dolly!'"? ... We were so far out in the woods he didn't realise he had a hit record. (DVD *Masters Of Jazz: Jazz Pioneers*)

'Hello, Dolly!' made number one on the US chart on 9 May 1964 and number four in the UK a couple of months later. It is not difficult to see why it was such a huge success: Armstrong's personality is all over the record, his ebullient, gravelly vocals offsetting his inimitable trumpet bravura, and though the same can be said of countless other recordings throughout his career, this one had the advantage of a catchy chorus and instantly memorable punch-line. But perhaps, too, it represented a reaction against a music scene being swamped by youth and, in particular, The Beatles.

It was not the only jazz record to make the national singles chart in 1964. 'The Girl From Ipanema', by Stan Getz and Astrud Gilberto, was a hit on both sides of the Atlantic during the summer when its gentle samba rhythm transported the listener direct to the Brazilian beach on which it was set. Two years previously tenor saxophonist Getz had released the popular *Jazz Samba* album and the follow-up, *Jazz Samba Encore!*, sold over a million copies in 1964.

In general, however, jazz musicians were not relying on record sales to earn them a living. Some were fortunate enough to get studio work or jobs in the resident bands for TV shows; the big name artists, in contrast, derived most of their income from constant touring, a life many of them had known since they turned professional. The concert halls of Europe were frequented by the jazz aristocracy, while others found an appreciative audience in the jazz clubs that had proliferated across the continent since the War. An insight into the quantity and quality of music on offer in one city, Manchester, is provided in Bill Birch's book, *Keeper Of The Flame: Modern Jazz In Manchester 1946-1972* (p. 214-217). The schedule for 1964 reads:

29 February: Duke Ellington and his Orchestra (Free Trade Hall)
8 April: Ella Fitzgerald, Oscar Peterson (Free Trade Hall)

25 April: The Modern Jazz Quartet (Free Trade Hall)

17 May: The Cannonball Adderley Sextet (Palace Theatre – presented by Vic Lewis and Brian Epstein)

6 June: The Dave Brubeck Quartet (Free Trade Hall)

8 June: Jimmy Witherspoon (Club 43)

6 July (for a week): Mel Tormé (Palace Theatre)

11 July: Ray Charles (Free Trade Hall)

12 and 19 September: Jimmy Witherspoon (Club 43)

17 October: Erroll Garner (Free Trade Hall)

21 November: Mark Murphy (Club 43)

Some of these American visitors were also able to get spots on British TV. The Adderley group, for example, recorded a memorable session for the BBC's *Jazz 625* programme. 'Work Song' features the leader's full-blooded alto saxophone and a writhing tenor solo by Charles Lloyd and 'The Song My Lady Sings' spotlights the bittersweet muted cornet of Nat Adderley. Joe Zawinul, later to join Wayne Shorter in Weather Report, contributes some soulful piano to Nat's 'Jive Samba'.

Europe was seen as such a hospitable destination that many African-American jazz musicians decided to settle there: the pay was often better and they felt they were treated as creative artists and not a target for racial slurs. One of the first to emigrate was the drummer Kenny Clarke, who came to live in Paris in 1956. He was followed by fellow bebop stars Bud Powell, in 1959, and Dexter Gordon, who moved to Copenhagen in 1962. As the DVD *Jazz Icons: Dexter Gordon* demonstrates, Gordon – who epitomised the freewheeling, improvising tenor saxophonist – was at the peak of his powers in 1964. On 8 January, he recorded a session in Brussels comprising 'Lady Bird' and 'Body And Soul'. On the former he stays very much in the middle register, yet without a hint of repetition or cliché, while on the latter his solo displays s sense of near-architectural construction. Even better is the performance filmed on 29 July for Dutch TV. This time Gordon is in front of a club audience which seems to inspire him to greater heights; on 'A Night In Tunisia' he positively

214

gallops through the chord changes and tacks on some high-register overblowing as a nod to the *avant garde*. The ballad 'What's New' is rendered with sentiment but without sentimentality and his big sound and unremitting creativity illuminate 'Blues Walk', which also includes a fine solo by the Swiss pianist, George Gruntz.

Trumpeter Chet Baker had a more prosaic reason for coming to Europe: his convictions for drug offences meant he could not get work at home. He was immediately in demand for record dates and live appearances, but his addiction to heroin persisted and by April 1961 he was incarcerated in the Italian town of Lucca. Released early, he spent time in Germany, Switzerland, Britain and France, his nomadic existence dictated by a series of deportation orders. Just before returning to the States in the spring of 1964, he recorded a session for the Belgian TV programme *Jazz Pour Tous,* which is now available as a *Jazz Icons* DVD and demonstrates that Baker, despite the upheavals in his personal life, was still capable of making music of exceptional quality. At a time when jazz was hurtling towards uninhibited free expression, Baker's creativity results from restraint. The tunes are familiar, the tempos predictable and, as ever, his playing is anchored in the middle register. But his solos are endlessly inventive, whether in the relaxed, easy paced-setting of 'Bye Bye Blackbird' and 'Isn't It Romantic' or on the ballad 'Time After Time' which is also graced by his quietly intense, sensitive vocals.

Two giants of jazz went beyond merely escaping to Europe: Sonny Rollins and Ornette Coleman dropped out of music altogether. Rollins was considered one of the greatest tenor saxophonists in jazz history when he took his first 'sabbatical' between 1959 and 1962. His seemingly inexhaustible flow of ideas and phenomenal facility attracted the attention of numerous bandleaders including Miles Davis, with whom he worked in the early 1950s. He was at his best, nevertheless, when leading his own groups, as evidenced by such excellent albums as *Saxophone Colossus* (1956) and *Way Out West* (1957). Rollins maintains that he quit jazz in order to take stock of, and refine, his music, but it is hard to resist the idea that he was taking a broader view of his environment, for when he returned his music was edgier and more challenging than before. 1964's *Now's The Time* suggested a return to former glories with his leathery tone and cascading runs complemented by the contemporary sensibilities of pianist Herbie Hancock.

Alto player Ornette Coleman, as we have already seen, had created a sensation in the late 1950s with his radical approach to individual and collective improvisation – in Frank Tirro's words, 'a distillation or abstraction of bebop stylistic elements which are reorganized and combined with some of the newer musical thoughts that no longer derive from jazz' (*Jazz: A History*, p. 346). But, like Rollins, Coleman wanted to enhance his music – in his case, by learning trumpet and violin – so he made no recordings at all during 1964, leaving John Coltrane as the unquestioned figurehead of the new developments in jazz.

★ ★ ★ ★ ★

As the year 1964 progressed there was a sense that what had seemed like domestic and localised issues were actually part of a global pattern; that some of the major changes taking place were not isolated incidents but representative of a wider movement across the world. This was much accelerated by the rapid evolution in communications technology – for example, the satellite Syncom 3, which was launched in August 1964 and allowed the Tokyo Olympics to be transmitted live to the USA.

The struggle for Civil Rights in America was echoed in protests against racial segregation in Sydney, Australia and at the Notting Hill Carnival, organised by the London Afro-Caribbean community in response to the parlous state of race relations in the UK. Fears of new intercontinental conflagration were heightened by the escalation of the Vietnam War and – within a two-day period – the removal in the Soviet Union of Nikita Khruschev, seen by the hardliners as too soft, and the testing by China of their first atom bomb. In the same month, October, the UK and the USA seemed to be moving to the left, with election victories for Harold Wilson and Lyndon Johnson, who achieved 61% of the vote and the biggest majority in American history.

This global vision was a distinct feature of African-American culture in 1964. Chapter 5 charted the development of Malcolm X's philosophy that began with pan-Africanism and came to see Islam as a force for universal unification; this ideology spread to others in the Black Muslim community including the many musicians who had converted in the 1950s and early 1960s. One of these was the saxophonist, Yusef Lateef, who began to incorporate Eastern influences into his work in 1961. On *Jazz 'Round The World*, recorded in late December 1963 and released in 1964, his musical journey extended to Nigeria ('Abana'), France ('Yusef's French Brother'), Russia ('The Volga Rhythm Song'), the UK ('The Good Old Roast Beef Of England'), Israel ('Raisins And Almonds') and Japan ('Ringo Oiwake'). As may be guessed from these titles, there was an element of humour in Lateef's method, but it was balanced with serious intent – 'India', for example, is a moving composition featuring the leader's mournful oboe and the stately trumpet of Richard Williams.

John Coltrane was not a Muslim, but had experienced a spiritual awakening in 1957 when he kicked his drug and alcohol habit and moved from Philadelphia to New York. His wife, Naima, was, however, and she gave him unstinting support during this period of re-birth, as did his mother, a devout Christian. The first fruits were evident in *Blue Train*, an album of crystal-clear conception and execution. But it was not until 1961 that compositions with religious overtones began to appear regularly in his repertoire: 'Dahomey Dance' (*Olé*), 'Africa' (*Africa/Brass*) and 'Spiritual' (*Live At The Village Vanguard*). Two years earlier he had begun to play the soprano saxophone, with which he could impart an Eastern flavour to his work, as in his famous recording of 'My Favourite Things' (1960). By 1963 his music was intensifying at a rapid rate: at the Newport Jazz Festival in July, for instance, his versions of 'I Want To Talk About You' and 'My Favourite Things' were positively electrifying, the first featuring an epic cadenza of unflagging invention, the second a thrilling, vertiginous soprano solo that ranks among his very best performances. Four months later, in response to the Birmingham bombings, he recorded 'Alabama', a sombre, imposing piece laden with barely-suppressed emotion.

In 1964, Coltrane combined all of this – spirituality, innovation, technique – in two major album releases. The first, *Crescent*, was recorded on 27 April and 1 June with his long-standing group of pianist McCoy Tyner, Jimmy Garrison on bass and drummer Elvin Jones. At this time he was one of the best-paid, and most controversial, musicians in jazz so it is surprising to find that, amid all the brouhaha, this is a record of considerable restraint and dignity. The title track begins with Trane's contemplative tenor floating over flowing piano and crashing drums; even when the pace picks up, there is an unhurried quality to his playing despite its characteristic volubility. 'Wise One' is in similar vein: his first solo is lyrical, his second, though persistently chasing the same three-note phrase until there are no options left, still lacks the sense of grandiloquence with which he was most associated. On 'Bessie's Blues' he is much less uninhibited, bounding along in a manner redolent of the great swing tenorists before Tyner drops out to leave him free to roam. As its title suggests 'The Drum Thing' is a feature for Jones, who maintains metronomic regularity despite flailing all around the kit to impressive effect, and 'Lonnie's Lament', one of Coltrane's most poignant compositions, includes some scintillating piano from Tyner and a bass solo by Garrison which betrays Eastern influences.

All in all, this was a strong performance by the whole group, particularly Coltrane who seemed to be reaching a new level of expression. In the sleeve note, he is quoted as saying, 'I don't know what I'm looking for … something that hasn't been played before. I don't know what it is. I know I'll have that feeling when I get it.' It is fairly safe to assume that he found what he was seeking in his next album, *A Love Supreme*.

So much has been written about this album – indeed, Ashley Khan has devoted an entire book to it – that it can be difficult to evaluate it dispassionately. Interpretations seem to fall broadly into one of three categories. First, and most in line with Coltrane's own comments, it is a statement of devotion to God. This much is clear from his declaration on the sleeve, the title of the suite and of each of its parts – 'Acknowledgement', 'Resolution', 'Pursuance' and 'Psalm'. Others, with some justification, have seen it as a reflection of African-American consciousness – for example, Khan quotes Max Roach's statement that,

"I heard many things in what Trane was doing. I heard the cry and wail of the pain that this society imposes on people and especially black folks." (*A Love Supreme: The Creation Of John Coltrane's Classic Album*, p. 76)

Another school of thought advocates a purely musical analysis. Setting aside any notions of the record's social or religious significance, these observers concentrate on the technical factors and the place *A Love Supreme* holds in Coltrane's linear development as a composer and saxophonist.

All of these views are seductive, though for this writer none fully embraces his intention, conscious or otherwise. It is my opinion that Coltrane – rather like Mingus, who reconciled the apparently incompatible standpoints of Martin Luther King and Malcolm X in 'Meditations On Integration' – was offering a response to the instability and conflict in the world as a whole in 1964, looking back at a year of turbulence and, in the wide scope of the music presented, providing a commensurately universal answer.

'Acknowledgement' starts with a clarion-call by Coltrane, gripping the attention and sustaining it with the insistent four-note melody, ('a-love supreme') played by Garrison. Then the leader takes over with a scorching solo that uses simple phrases and embroiders them *ad infinitum*. Fervent shrieks and convoluted runs follow, before he settles on the theme again, first on tenor and then chanting the mantra himself: here is a musical account of the trials and tribulations experienced by Coltrane and, by extension, the world.

The piece ends with unaccompanied bass which segues into 'Resolution', another painful process evoked by the driving, restless theme, Tyner's cascading solo and Coltrane's torrent of notes that display logic and precision within the maelstrom. 'Pursuance' continues the mood: opening with a walloping solo by Jones, it features quicksilver piano from Tyner and a tempestuous tenor work-out over more volcanic drumming.

This is Coltrane at his most harrowing and it is easy here to understand the inferences drawn by Roach.

'Psalm' is introduced by a long Garrison solo with still clearer echoes of the Indian raga. Jones sets up a cycle of booming tom-toms and crashing cymbals behind the slow, inexorable theme. Trane moves from serenity to a pleading, impassioned climax before murmuring bass and gentle cymbal strokes close both the movement and the suite – a cathartic conclusion to a piece of music of heroic proportions.

The impact of *A Love Supreme* has proved lasting and indelible: in 2005, it was voted number 47 in the *Rolling Stone* 500 Greatest Albums of All Time, ahead of such eminent releases as Presley's first LP, *Electric Ladyland* by Jimi Hendrix, The Rolling Stones' *Sticky Fingers* and *Bridge Over Troubled Water* by Simon and Garfunkel. Strong evidence suggests it had a profound effect on early hippie philosophy – but that was in 1965 and beyond and so belongs to another story.

CHAPTER 7:

Break-A-Way

The period immediately following the Second World War was dominated, inevitably, by its after-effects – a legacy that differed enormously from country to country and from continent to continent. The USA and Russia had profited most from the War; the latter in terms of territorial control, the former, as we saw in Chapter 1, in a booming economy and rapid technological progress. Britain had fared less well. With no material gains to speak of and a weakened infrastructure, it continued for some time on a quasi-wartime footing; rationing, for example, continued up until 1954. The rejection of Churchill – despite his superhuman wartime leadership – at the General Election of 1945 was symbolic of both a desire to make a fresh start and a mistrust of the established order. For the next two decades, British authority and tradition were regularly challenged and often irreparably damaged – not just within the institutions and culture of the country but on a worldwide basis, as more and more nations sought independence from the British Empire. 1964 was a particularly significant year on both counts, marking the culmination of some of these processes and the beginning of others.

The transformation in attitudes to, and of, the working class was central to the post-war political, social and cultural upheavals. British servicemen had returned home with high hopes that their efforts would lead to a bright future for themselves and their families and initially their optimism seemed justified. The in-coming Labour Government created the Welfare State, with the National Health Service as its centrepiece, and new housing estates sprang up to replace inner-city slums. But there was hardship, too, as unemployment increased and shortages of essential goods continued. No-one minded privations during the War itself, but it was hard to bear when these continued deep into peacetime, especially as we had been on the winning side.

As early as 1947 there was a cinematic attempt to portray post-war misery: Robert Hamer's *It Always Rains On Sunday*, based on the novel by Arthur La Bern, was one of the early 'kitchen sink' dramas. Thwarted ambition and resentment of the middle classes was at the root of John Osborne's 1956 play, *Look Back In Anger*, which gave rise to the expression 'angry young man', a sobriquet for a school of playwrights and novelists – not always men – whose unflinching accounts of working-class life were often adapted by British New Wave film directors like Tony Richardson and Karel Reisz. Richardson directed both the theatre and cinema versions of *Look Back In Anger*, *A Taste Of Honey*, based on the 1958 novel by the nineteen year-old Shelagh Delaney and *The Loneliness Of The Long Distance Runner*, originally a short story by Alan Sillitoe. Reisz, whose *We Are The Lambeth Boys* depicted working-class London youth, made his feature film debut with an adaptation of Sillitoe's *Saturday Night And Sunday Morning*. However, the terse documentary style of the British New Wave eventually gave way to a more spectacular and colourful type of film-making, epitomised by the James Bond films. 1964 was, in fact, the beginning of the new era, the last vestiges of grim reality having disappeared the previous year with Reisz's production, *This Sporting Life*.

Yet working-class culture continued to be a subject of fascination, both as a means of entertainment – for example, TV soap operas such as *Coronation Street* and a proliferation of Northern presenters, comedians and musicians – and as an area of academic study. Other than reporting on their living conditions, education and health, nobody had paid much attention to what working-class people actually did – their experiences, customs, lifestyle and attitudes – until the 1950s. The Cambridge don Raymond Williams, himself from humble origins in rural Wales, was among the first to suggest that the culture of ordinary people was just as rich, varied and potentially worthy of study as that of the upper classes.

His 1960 novel , *Border Country*, illustrates the strengths of Welsh working people and their traditional way of life and draws a contrast with both the inhumanity of economic 'progress' and the remote world of academia. He returned to this latter subject ten years later in a BBC documentary of the same name which made an even starker comparison between the university's staff and students and the Cambridge residents who worked in menial jobs within it. Williams's vision of culture was all-encompassing, with no material, intellectual or spiritual boundaries, but shaped according to the conditions and systems that prevail at any one time. He also provided the vocabulary for what came to be known as 'cultural studies', a term coined by another academic to emerge from the working classes, Richard Hoggart.

In *The Uses Of Literacy*, published in 1957, Hoggart provided both a graphic description of working-class culture and of the forces that threatened it, in particular, the large-circulation magazines and the tabloid newspapers. Furthermore he deplored the practice of democratisation – that is, allowing everyone to have the freedom to say what they want – seeing it as illusory and false, since in actual fact the media continued to manipulate opinion. One can see the truth of this over 50 years later: reality TV, social networking, and the endless requests from presenters to email or text them may flatten the hierarchy of communication but seldom result in anything other than inanity. Some of Hoggart's *bêtes noires*, in particular, the influence of American culture, now seem quaint; even his prophetic powers could not have helped him foresee that, through The Beatles and others, it would be converted into something that was unmistakeably British. But on the whole *The Uses Of Literacy* proved remarkably durable and, indeed, laid the foundations for an area of academic study we now take for granted.

Hoggart's concern was to understand and interpret the way people go about their daily lives and this inevitably led him into conflict with the bastions of 'high culture'. Called as a witness for the defence in the 1960 trial of Penguin Books for publishing the unexpurgated version of DH Lawrence's *Lady Chatterley's Lover*, his testimony – together with that of

Raymond Williams and other prominent intellectuals – proved critical to their acquittal. He later stated that the trial had revealed 'a gulf in British society between those who thought of themselves as the guardians of established morals and most people'.

That those 'guardians' continued to function despite their abject defeat at the *Lady Chatterley* trial was nowhere better illustrated than in the higher education sector where, in spite of Hoggart's increasing profile, cultural studies was slow in gaining recognition as an academic discipline. But a new era was ushered in when, in 1964, the University of Birmingham established its Centre for Contemporary Cultural Studies, with Hoggart as its first Director.

From the outset it was clear that the Centre would adopt a wide-ranging and multi-disciplinary methodology: Hoggart himself defined the 'foundational disciplines' as history, philosophy, sociology and literary criticism. To the contemporary reader, accustomed to a sociological approach to culture, this last emphasis may seem strange, but of all the influences on the way the Centre operated, at least in this first year, it was the most important. For Hoggart and his colleagues were following a line of development that reached back to the likes of Matthew Arnold, whose collection of essays, *Culture And Anarchy*, published in book form in 1869, argued that culture – that is, high culture – was the uppermost state that could be aspired to and the solution to all of society's ills. In so doing Arnold constructed a literary premier league, headed by Shakespeare and Milton, by whose standard everything else should be measured. By the mid-20th century the eminent critic FR Leavis had added Jane Austen, George Eliot and Joseph Conrad to this illustrious list. In fact, it was Leavis's unreserved cultural elitism that percolated through to Hoggart, who himself was so scathing about mass culture in *The Uses Of Literacy*. Unlike Leavis, though, he was fascinated by it and under his stewardship the Centre for Contemporary Cultural Studies diversified to encompass such topic areas as music, film and sport and indeed, the way in which the whole of the popular mass media operated.

But the importance of the Centre lay in the fact that it not only vindicated the study of areas of activity that had previously been viewed as trivial and tangential, but it also inspired action to correct the misconceptions and prejudice that marginalisation had brought about. It is possible to attribute some of the progress made in women's rights and race relations, for example, to the work of the Centre, since one of its major, and most controversial, purposes was to empower people to understand the relationship between culture and the sources of power and thus develop strategies for survival.

The Centre was therefore considered a hotbed of radical thinking – and with some justification. It is no exaggeration to state that much of the intellectual force behind the left-wing student politics of the 1960s and of the New Left in particular was generated there; this was partly because cultural studies is, by its very nature, related to Marxism, the notion of class division within a capitalist society being fundamental to both. The distinction made by leading figures of the Centre between the Marxist's inclination to view economic factors as determining history and the at least equal importance of culture is probably too fine for many observers to grasp, but the fact remains that it was wider in its political scope than is often suggested.

Just as profound an influence as Marxism was the impact on the Centre of what are sometimes described as the 'colonial intellectuals'. In its infancy, as we have seen, cultural studies in Britain drew from the native tradition of literary criticism; it was also dominated by figures from the New Left which had formed in reaction to, amongst other things, the revival of the Conservative Party in the 1950s. But increasingly the New Left became a refuge for Commonwealth citizens who found the traditional left-wing institutions such as the Labour Party and the TUC less welcoming. One such was Stuart Hall, who had won a scholarship to Oxford University in 1951 and was invited by Hoggart to join the staff of the Centre at inception; five years later he became its Director.

Hall's forensic analysis of the way in which media communications are transmitted and received was echoed across the Atlantic by the publication in 1964 of *Understanding Media: The Extensions Of Man* by the

Canadian writer Marshall McLuhan. This proved to be a seminal work, advancing as it did the notion that it is the medium, not the content, which is most important in people's lives: effectively – as McLuhan was widely quoted as proposing – the medium *is* the message. He went on to differentiate aspects of the media in terms of their effect on individuals, drawing a distinction between the 'hot' – assailing multiple senses simultaneously and requiring little effort on the part of the receiver – and the 'cool', which allows the opportunity for reflection and analysis and hence greater participation. It is not difficult to see how the former tendency has come to dominate film and television in the 21st century, many would say to their detriment.

Understanding Media had an enormous impact, especially among the American student population, who accorded McLuhan the status of a prophet. In spite, or, more likely, because of, this acclaim, he has acquired numerous detractors in the intervening years; he also recorded a disastrous interview for the BBC where he was so incoherent and incomprehensible that it was never broadcast. Yet his ability to coin new and apposite phrases ('the global village' was another one of his best known expressions), to foresee the future – he predicted the development of the internet over 30 years before it was invented – and, most significantly, to query accepted thinking makes him a major contributor to the history of ideas. He also symbolised the mood of challenge that permeated 1964, not just in Western academic circles but in communities and countries across the world.

★ ★ ★ ★ ★

1964 was a pivotal year in the history of Africa. Some countries, notably Nigeria and Ghana, were experiencing their first crisis since independence; others – Malawi and Zambia – became independent during the course of the year; and elsewhere, notably Rhodesia, the struggle to break free of colonial control was reaching a peak. There were revolutions in Zanzibar and the Congo, armed conflict between Ethiopia and Somalia, guerrilla warfare in Mozambique and, in South Africa, one of most momentous events of the 20th century: the imprisonment on Robben Island of Nelson Mandela.

The West African nations of Ghana and Nigeria, separated, at the narrowest point, by the 110 miles of coastline which now belong to the countries of Togo and Benin, achieved independence from Britain in 1957 and 1960 respectively. Though demographically and politically different, both countries followed a similar path, which was to become sadly familiar across the continent. Beginning with proclamations of freedom and democracy, both deteriorated into repression and corruption and their inevitable consequence, a military coup.

By 1964 Ghanaian politics had been dominated for over a decade by Kwame Nkrumah, whose energy, vision and ambition had propelled his country towards self-determination. On becoming its first president, however, he soon let his success go to his head and began to view himself as not just the figurehead of one country but as the potential leader of Africa as a whole. As early as 1958 he organised an All-African People's Conference, attended by several representatives who would later head their own governments, including Patrice Lumumba from the Belgian Congo, Hastings Banda from Nyasaland and Kenneth Kaunda from Northern Rhodesia. While at that time he was a source of inspiration to them Nkrumah ultimately alienated his fellow African leaders by talking down to them and intervening in their internal affairs.

Within five years of independence, Nkrumah had squandered Ghana's plentiful natural resources through lavish government expenditure on rewards for his cronies and a range of projects aimed at self-aggrandisement rather than public benefit. His megalomania gradually increased to the exclusion of all opposition, and on 31 January 1964 he held a referendum that proposed amendments to Ghana's constitution. Supported by an unlikely 99.91% of voters, it had the effect of turning the country into a one-party state on 21 February, with Nkrumah as president for life.

Meanwhile parallel developments were taking place in Nigeria, a populous and complex nation with distinct ethnic groupings to the north, west and east. Each had its own political party, the Northern People's Congress (NPC), the Action Group, and the National Council of Nigerian Citizens (NCNC) respectively. The tale of the first years of independence was one of serial attrition, alliance and counter-alliance, all with the purpose of gaining overall control of the country, and once a party gained the ascendancy it instantly forgot the drive to improve the well-being of Nigeria in the rush to appropriate public funds for personal gain. By 1964, the eastern and western factions were in cahoots with each other, but the subsequent election, held in December in the hope of resolving matters, degenerated into farce when the NPC obstructed the registration of opposition candidates and the NCNC withdrew in retaliation. Thus democracy in Nigeria collapsed and would not be revived for fifteen years.

Both Nigeria and Ghana began their slide towards military rule in 1964. The Congo too was heading in that direction, following a year of unprecedented turmoil, confusion and bloodshed. As recounted in Chapter 1, there had been internal strife since Independence Day itself which culminated in the assassination of Prime Minister Patrice Lumumba five months later, on 17 January 1961. Over the next two years the main cause of tension was the proposed secession of the south-eastern territories of Katanga and South Kasai, both of which possessed considerable natural resources. Neither issue was resolved until the successful military intervention by the United Nations in December 1961 (South Kasai) and December 1962 (Katanga).

A year later, the geographical emphasis shifted. As a result of the perpetual wrangling and squabbling among its deputies, the Congolese parliament was dissolved in September 1963. Feeling that their democratic rights had been flouted, a group of disaffected opposition politicians, many of them former supporters of Patrice Lumumba, reacted by forming the CNL (Conseil National de Libération). The CNL was openly encouraged both by neighbouring Congo-Brazzaville and by the government of Burundi, from which it orchestrated a rebellion in the eastern provinces of the Congo, former stronghold of Patrice Lumumba.

In the summer of 1964, town after town fell to the insurgents, culminating in early August when the principal city of Stanleyville came under their control. It was there, on 5 September, that they proclaimed a 'People's Republic of the Congo' and executed thousands of people considered counter-revolutionaries in front of Lumumba's memorial. It will be remembered that Lumumba had a close relationship with the Soviet Union (he even appeared on a stamp there) and the CNL was backed by Cuba, Algeria, Egypt and – in particular – China; Pierre Muléle, a former minister in the Lumumba administration and one of the founders of the CNL, had received his guerrilla training there.

The involvement of socialist/Communist countries inevitably aroused the interest of the United States, but decisions on how and when to act were complicated by the need to work in concert with the UN and the Congolese government, of which Moïse Tshombe, formerly leader of the Katangan secessionists, was now Prime Minister. In the end, no immediate action was required, since internal disagreement and indifferent leadership were already corroding the rebel ranks. Tshombe had recruited white mercenaries and former Katangan gendarmes to fortify the Congolese army, and this combined force began to regain the lost territory.

The rebels responded by holding 1500 white Europeans hostage in Stanleyville: the self-styled rebel President, Christophe Gbenye, threatened to 'grill them alive'. Unsurprisingly this provoked worldwide condemnation and in November a joint Belgian-American task force was assembled to rescue them: on the 24th, 350 Belgian paratroopers were dropped on Stanleyville and all but around 30 hostages evacuated to Léopoldville Airport in US transport planes.

Despite the success of the operation, Tshombe was criticised for allowing the US and, especially, the hated Belgians such a prominent role. President Kasavubu and the Army Chief of Staff, Joseph-Désiré Mobutu were both displeased, as were other African leaders; Moscow called the rescue a 'criminal act' and the Cuban revolutionary Che Guevara denounced it at the UN General Assembly on 11 December 1964. Four days later, the rebels slaughtered a group of white missionaries.

CHANGING TIMES

★ ★ ★ ★ ★

During the entire revolution, Congolese musicians played on, though they were not unaffected by the conflict. Bombing by urban guerrillas interrupted a concert by OK Jazz in Léopoldville's Parc de Bock and the same band lost three of their number – Edo Ganga, Daniel Lubelo (known as 'De La Lune') and Michel Boyibanda – to Congo-Brazzaville when Tshombe began to order the expulsion of aliens. Yet there was a constant demand for their music, both at home and abroad, and in spite of some rough patches (at one point, according to his biographer, Graeme Ewens, Franco had to hide their instruments from the bailiffs), OK Jazz retained their status as the country's leading band. Ewens writes that

> OK Jazz made a spectacular return to popularity with a song which Zaïrean commentators still regard as a milestone, considered to be the first successful synthesis of popular music with folklore not to be based on the rumba or one of its "Latin" relatives. Ngai Marie Nzoto Ebeba ("I, Marie, Whose Body Is Crumbling") was a satire on modern morality, sung on the part of a woman (Marie) who lives by her charms and is being besieged by some of the married women whose husbands support her. (*Congo Colossus*, p. 101)

Yet in Franco's music, songs about men and women are often allegories referring to the relationship of the individual to the state, so it is quite feasible that this song is one such, describing a now-obscure aspect of contemporary politics.

Edo, De La Lune and Boyibanda returned to the group in 1964, as did 'Vicky' Longomba, and with the addition of new faces like saxophonist Dele Pedro OK Jazz swelled to 20 musicians. It was a period of triumph, with their first foreign tour, to Nigeria, and a number of outstanding recordings that include the single 'Nakobanga Mangungo Te'/ 'Tolobi' and a series of EPs entitled *OK Jazz 1964*. Both sides of the former were written by Jean Munsi – 'Kwamy' – who also contributed 'Bilongo Na

230

Bougie' to the fourth EP in the sequence: its staccato guitar and vocals and cheery, chugging rhythm typify the band's contemporary sound. But Franco was still very much the main man and his compositions on the same record show two sides of his musical personality – the fleet-footed 'Polo' has spirited guitar and tenor saxophone (possibly by Pedro) whereas 'Nionga Na Yo Nakofuta Te' is morose vocally and instrumentally.

OK Jazz 1964 No. 5 includes three up-tempo numbers – 'Le Temps Passe', with an insouciant solo from the leader, 'Ngaï Nde Rideau Ya Nakado', featuring more pungent saxophone, and Pedro's light-hearted 'Si Tu Bois Beaucoup', which hints at the band's freewheeling live sound. This was characterised by the 'sebene', described by Ewens (*ibid.*, p. 96) as 'a kind of open-ended reverie', whereby repeated, improvised phrases mesmerised the audience, especially the dancers. It has to be said, however, that the EP's other track, 'Alphonso' – while at only medium pace – is equally hypnotic.

OK Jazz were not the only band at the top of the Congolese musical tree in 1964 – African Fiesta, formed in 1963 when African Jazz split up – were giving them a run for their money through hits like the Tabu Ley song 'Permission', a pacy, purposeful piece with meaty percussion and horn section. Bantous De La Capitale were another formidable outfit; their 'Kumbele Kumbele' echoes (presumably inadvertently) the Latin melodies of 'La Bamba' and 'Twist And Shout' but with a much greater feeling of space and 'Bantous Pachanga' is an exciting mix of propulsive drumming, breezy flute and energetic vocals. But despite the quality of the opposition, it was Franco who occupied a special place in the affections of both the people in general and the politicians in particular. This was to come into focus a year later when, following a *coup d'état,* Joseph-Désiré Mobutu seized power in the Congo.

Elsewhere in Africa, Malawi (formerly Nyasaland) and Zambia (formerly Northern Rhodesia) achieved their independence on 6 July and 24 October respectively. But whereas the repressive regime of Malawian President Hastings Banda discouraged music, and the arts in general, it was a very different story in Zambia. Music was seen as vital to the emerging identity of the new country and the Zambia National Broadcasting Corporation gave a high priority to the work of native artists performing in their own languages.

Across the border in Southern Rhodesia, the tide was running the other way. The Rhodesian Front, a white right-wing party committed to suppressing African nationalism, had come to power in the December 1962 election. But as well as pursuing rigorous anti-black policies the Rhodesian government was also at odds with Britain whom it felt was not doing enough to protect the interests of the white citizens of what was still, at that stage, one of its colonies; indeed, Britain was unwilling to grant independence without majority (that is, black) rule.

The relationship with Britain took a turn for the worse on 13 April 1964 when Ian Smith became the new Prime Minister of Southern Rhodesia. Smith immediately scotched any suggestion of majority rule and imprisoned all of the black nationalist leaders. This sparked off riots in the capital, Salisbury, but Smith was undeterred: in August he banned black nationalist organisations altogether. Comprising only 3% of the population, white Southern Rhodesians (or, simply, Rhodesians, as they now began to call themselves) felt that, despite – or perhaps because of – such actions, somehow Britain would impose majority rule. But Smith persisted, no doubt fortified by developments across the border in South Africa.

★ ★ ★ ★ ★

Dr Hendrik Verwoerd, the Prime Minister of South Africa, had managed to stave off majority rule, in spite of immense pressure from both within and outside the country. This he had achieved, not simply by subjugating the 'non-white' population – though there was plenty of that – but by arguing that no one ethnic group actually constituted a majority. In that sense he was correct – the Xhosa, Zulu and white populations all numbered around three million each, the 'coloured' (including those of European ancestry) about 1.5 million and the rest of the groups put together just over four million. But of course Verwoerd had no intention of creating a government which represented all of these interests – his mission was to set up each group as a separate nation. The starting-point was that whites had evolved as far as it was possible to go, hence would retain overall control while the others caught up to the extent that they could govern themselves. Exactly when this would kick in seemed to vary according to whom Verwoerd and his government were talking at the time: when addressing National Party members, it was a remote prospect; when dealing with members of the international community, impatient for progress, it became more imminent.

The whole system rested, in fact, not just on the notion of separate development but on racial segregation, that is, apartheid. It was therefore unpalatable to African nationalists, and black South Africans in general, who quite reasonably argued that as the non-white population as a whole numbered over twelve million and the white just over three, then Verwoerd and his colleagues should scarcely have any sort of foothold in government at all.

So resistance continued. As both the ideology and the practices of the white regime became more brutal so the nationalists became more aggressive in their methods. An armed section entitled Poqo ('pure') was formed within the PAC and Umkhonto we Sizwe ('the spear of the nation'), later known simply as 'MK', grew out of the ANC, a break with their tradition of non-violent protest. Nelson Mandela, its first commander-in-chief, called it a response to 'savage attacks on unarmed and defenceless people'. Both organisations advocated a general uprising by black South Africans: Poqo stated openly that the slaughter of whites would be part of the process, thus redoubling the efforts of the government to suppress it. By mid-1964, the Minister of Justice, John Vorster, was able to announce that Poqo had indeed been destroyed, following the arrest of over 3,000 members.

MK was also in disarray – in May 1963, the police picked up a member of its Eastern High Command , Vuyisile Mini, together with two prominent members of the ANC, Wilson Khayinga and Zinakile Mkaba;

two months later almost all of MK's national leadership were captured in a raid on their hideout in Rivonia, a suburb of Johannesburg; Mandela had already been in jail for nine months.

Mini had a long history of campaigning against the South African government. Involved in trade union activities since his teens, he joined the ANC in 1951 and MK ten years later. Although he had fallen foul of the law before, this time the charges were more serious – sabotage and complicity in the murder of an alleged police informer, Sipho Mange. The outcome of his trial, which took place in Port Alfred in the Eastern Cape, was something of a foregone conclusion since his defence lawyer was not permitted to leave Durban, some 400 miles away. However, when Mini and his two colleagues were given the death sentence in March 1964, it caused outrage both within Africa and across the world. There were protests by President Nasser on behalf of the Non-Aligned Movement and by the UN Secretary-General, U Thant. But they were to no avail. Mini, who loved music and was a former member of the Port Elizabeth Male Voice Choir, went to the gallows on 7 November 1964, singing his own composition, 'Nants' Indod' Emnyama' ('Beware, Verwoerd'), which became one of the most important freedom songs of the 1960s. (Miriam Makeba's rendition appears in the 2002 film *Amandla! A Revolution In Four Part Harmony,* directed by Lee Hirsch and part-financed by rock musician Dave Matthews, which traces the role of music in the struggle against apartheid.)

On 7 October 1963 charges were brought against seven of those arrested in Rivonia. Documents found during the raid also incriminated Mandela, and so all eight were indicted for offences under the Suppression of Communism and Sabotage Acts. Controversy still rages as to whether Mandela was a Communist. The South African Communist Party was certainly instrumental in the creation of MK and the African Studies Centre at the University of Leiden has discovered evidence not only of his membership but also of his role as an official, possibly as part of its Central Committee. However Joe Slovo, MK's Chief of Staff, who *was* a member of that Committee has stated that Mandela respected the Communist

Party but was not a member, while the Director of the Royal African Society, Richard Dowden, claims he was more of an Africanist than a Communist. But the accusation of sabotage was more credible. Details, including maps, of over a hundred potential targets were discovered in Rivonia, with some of the material in Mandela's own handwriting.

The trial got under way in Pretoria on 3 December 1963. Mandela and his fellow defendants pleaded not guilty; their view was that it was the South African government who should be brought to account for its misdeeds, and – despite being warned by the judge, Quartus de Wet, not to use the trial to make political speeches – all except one said so in court when entering their plea. Over the succeeding months, state prosecutor Dr Percy Yutar presented a mass of documentation demonstrating their involvement in plans for insurrectionary activity. Some of this related to Operation Mayibuye, which was to be, in effect, a revolution by black South Africans, sparked off by guerrilla warfare. Mandela had nothing to do with planning Operation Mayibuye – he was in prison at the time – but there were sufficient papers implicating him in other plots for it not to make any difference. Yutar also produced over 170 witnesses, including two former MK commanders, Bruno Mtolo and Patrick Mthembu, able to testify against the accused.

The case for the defence opened on 20 April 1964. Despite the judge's admonition Mandela decided, since he was sure he would be found guilty, to make a statement explaining his beliefs and the actions they had led to. This lasted for almost five hours and is considered the greatest speech of his career (it was also to be his last for 26 years). He was especially anxious to convey his fundamental opposition to violence – this had only been contemplated, he emphasised, as a last resort. He also averred his patriotism and desire for South Africa to be seen not as a racist pariah state but as a country worthy of international investment. Mandela concluded:

During my lifetime I have dedicated myself to this struggle of the African people. I have fought against white domination, and I have fought against black domination. I have cherished the ideal of a democratic and free society in which all persons live together in harmony and with equal opportunities. It is an ideal which I hope to live for and to achieve. But if it needs be, it is an ideal for which I am prepared to die.

This speech caught the imagination of the world's press and there were pro-Mandela demonstrations in Europe and the USA; the United Nations Security Council also called for all the defendants to be released. But there was no way that was going to happen; with only one exception, they were found guilty as charged. In fact, Mandela and his colleagues were fully expecting to hang; so when, on 12 June 1964, Judge de Wet sentenced them to life imprisonment, his decision was greeted with some relief, both within the court room and outside, where the crowd began to sing the Xhosa pan-African liberation anthem 'Nkosi Sikelel' iAfrika' – 'Lord Bless Africa'.

But temporary celebrations soon gave way to horror at the enormity of the South African regime, and the exodus of dissenters continued. Prominent musicians such as Hugh Masekela and Miriam Makeba had already left – now they were joined by the country's leading jazz group, The Blue Notes. As a valedictory statement, they recorded a live album in Durban during the early summer, around the time of the Rivonia Trial. *Live In South Africa 1964* includes no political material as such (though titles like 'Coming Home' and 'Now' are pregnant with implication) but the very existence of The Blue Notes was a political act with its combination of one white and five black South African musicians. The former, pianist Chris McGregor, contributes two compositions, alto saxophonist Dudu Pukwana four, and there is one standard, 'I Cover The Waterfront', which features tenor player Nick Moyake. Shortly afterwards the band set off for the Antibes Jazz Festival, never to return, but Moyake soon became homesick and came back to South Africa where he died five years later.

Meanwhile Masekela and Makeba were achieving fame across Europe and America. Makeba's 1964 album *The Voice Of Africa*, made in New York and arranged and conducted by Masekela, seemed to give her a representative role, not just for her country but for her continent. The overall message is resolutely upbeat, with 'Nomthini', 'Langa More', 'Shihibolet', 'Uyadela' and 'Mamoriri' being driven along by galloping percussion and Makeba's exultant vocals; 'Mayibuye' ('Let It Return') is in the same vein, and it is perhaps stretching it to see any connection with the ill-fated plan of the Rivonia plotters. Some of the best moments come at gentler tempos – 'Qhude', written by the two principals, matches Makeba's strong, clear voice with a chanting chorus and 'Lovely Lies' is a vehicle for her rich vibrato. 'Le Fleuve' (sung in French), the Latin-flavoured 'Tuson', 'Willow Song' from *Othello*, and the dramatic spiritual 'Come To Glory' all serve to underline her versatility and confirm that she was in transition to international stardom.

Back in South Africa, her countrymen were striving to develop the domestic music scene in the face of all the year's pressures and disruptions. Former Blue Notes drummer Early Mabuza formed a quartet which included saxophonist Barney Rachabane (later a member of Paul Simon's band); this transmuted into the influential Early Mabuza Big Five featuring the bassist Ernest Mothle who emigrated to the UK in 1973 and appeared at the Nelson Mandela 70th Birthday Concert at Wembley Stadium. Among the many other notable jazz musicians were pianist Pat Matshikiza and Mackay Davashe, composer of the aforementioned 'Lovely Lies'. Producer Rupert Bopape, who had written the 1958 international smash, 'Tom Hark', for Elias and his Zigzag Jive Flutes, created opportunities for local musicians when he moved from EMI to Gallo, South Africa's first independent record company with a long tradition of employing black artists. Bopape took with him some of the top session players and formed a production company, Mavuthela, which brought numerous new and talented acts under his management.

But perhaps the most significant event in South African music took place late in 1964 when the British singer Dusty Springfield, having stipulated in her contract to tour the country that she would sing only to integrated audiences, was arrested for doing so, confined to her hotel and then deported. Although the comic singer George Formby had refused to play to segregated audiences in 1946, nothing like this had been seen in the era of apartheid. Springfield came in for considerable criticism from fellow artists, many of whom continued to visit South Africa; however it was they, not she, who became the object of derision. The evils of apartheid were already well known to Western governments and those who followed world affairs, but by and large this did not include pop fans. Springfield's action suddenly brought the issue to their attention and so played its part in the politicisation of young people which, inspired by the protest singers, intensified during 1964.

★ ★ ★ ★ ★

In many ways, there could have been no greater contrast with South Africa than Jamaica. Newly independent, it was apparently free from white influence – a milestone marked on 10 November 1964 by the return from London of the remains of Marcus Garvey Jr, who had opposed colonial rule so implacably. Garvey was declared Jamaica's first National Hero and his body reburied in an area designated as National Heroes Park, an event commemorated during a remarkable series of recording sessions that took place the same month.

Ska was fast becoming the dominant style in Jamaican music. It seems to have started as an adaptation of the New Orleans shuffle rhythm whereby the second and fourth beats of the bar (the 'off' beats) were given additional emphasis. As to who was responsible for this innovation, debate has raged for many years. Often attributed to Prince Buster and his guitarist Jerome 'Jah Jerry' Hinds, a counterclaim was lodged by Ernest Ranglin, another guitarist, who stated that producer Clement 'Coxsone' Dodd had developed it with a group including himself and bassist Cluett Johnson (also known as Clue J). But in his series of radio programmes for the BBC, *From Mento To Lovers Rock*, Linton Kwesi Johnson argued that ska was a natural progression from earlier types of Jamaican music.

Whatever the case, ska – an onomatopoeic name allegedly derived from the terse upstroke made by the guitarist on the off beat – began to take root in the late 1950s and early 1960s. But 1964 was, as reggae historian Lloyd Bradley has written (*Bass Culture*, p. 150), the year 'ska broke through. Big time.' First there was the huge international hit 'My Boy Lollipop' by Millie Small – a cover of the 1956 R&B original by Barbie Gaye, a record that seemingly so impressed songwriter Ellie Greenwich that she chose Ellie Gaye as a pseudonym. The Millie version retains the brisk tempo and substitutes a lively harmonica break for the saxophone solo; but the record's success was predicated on the ska beat and the singer's refreshingly naïve vocals: it reached number two in both the UK and US singles chart in spring and summer respectively.

Then there was the formation of The Skatalites, an instrumental super-group of session musicians including Johnny 'Dizzy' Moore on trumpet, saxophonists Tommy McCook, Roland Alphonso and Lester Sterling, guitarists Ranglin, Hinds and Harold McKenzie, Jackie Mittoo on piano, bassist Lloyd Brevett, drummer Lloyd Knibbs and Don Drummond, described by jazz pianist George Shearing as one of the world's finest trombonists. The band's first gig was at the Hi-Hat Club in Rae Town on 27 June; a couple of months later they made the catchy 'Man In The Street' which superimposes assured solos by Moore and Drummond, its composer, on a sparse but jubilant riff. Released under Drummond's name, 'Man In The Street' became one of the best known of all ska numbers, especially in the UK where the audience for the music was to remain strong for the rest of the century.

In November The Skatalites, under the supervision of producer Justin Yap, came to Coxsone Dodd's studio in Brentford Road, Kingston, for the aforementioned series of recording sessions. The five best pieces were all written by Drummond (though Yap is also sometimes credited). 'Confucius' starts with a rousing drum lick, launching a socking backbeat with cymbal accents; the band develop the riffy theme only to truncate it for Drummond's soulful solo. Knibbs is again to the fore on 'Smiling' which employs an attractive call-and-response pattern, while 'Chinatown' contrasts the animation of the rhythm section with the mournful horns; Drummond's fluent playing integrates relaxation and drive and demonstrates why the trombone is the archetypical ska instrument. His other two compositions are those which refer to the arrival and re-interring of Garvey's body. 'Marcus Junior' is set at an appropriately stately medium pace, thus prefiguring reggae, and 'The Reburial' combines crashing drums and pithy piano with a tugging rhythm and cool horns. The remaining tracks – the slower, more strident 'Ringo' and the jolly but incongruously titled 'Ghost Town', a cover of Phil Upchurch's 'You Can't Sit Down' – are not quite in the same league but very acceptable. Taken as a whole, these tracks crystallise ska and represent the final stage in the breakaway from traditional Jamaican music and the beginning of a vibrant musical culture which was to influence pop and rock music to an extent that is impossible to quantify. Unfortunately Don Drummond was not around to profit from that: on 1 January 1965, he murdered his girlfriend, Marguerita Mahfood, and was subsequently committed to Belle Vue Mental Hospital where he died four years later.

Even a musician of Don Drummond's stature would, however, have found it impossible to eclipse the eventual popularity of the year's emerging star, Bob Marley. Released in 1962 under the name of Bobby Martell, his first single, 'One Cup Of Coffee'/ 'Judge Not', had not made much of an impression, but things began to look up the following year when he was reunited with three friends he had sung with back in 1961 as The Teenagers. Marley, Peter Tosh, Bunny Livingston and Junior Braithwaite called their new group The Wailing Wailers, though this was inevitably shortened to simply – The Wailers.

In their way, The Wailers were the Jamaican equivalent of The Beatles: four talented personalities who each contributed to the group's overall sound, and success. Lead vocal duties, for example, were shared, and their eclectic mix of material allowed for a wide range of individual expression, further augmented by the addition of backing singers Beverly Kelso and Cherry Smith. In mid-1963, The Wailers made two recordings produced by Coxsone Dodd, 'I'm Still Waiting' and 'It Hurts To Be Alone', the first sung by Marley and the second by Braithwaite; these were so well received that Dodd arranged a follow-up session, this time with The Skatalites in tow. The resulting single, Marley's 'Simmer Down', rates with almost anything he ever produced in terms of political impact.

By 1964, fissures were opening up in Jamaican society that few had foreseen in the run-up to independence. The governing Jamaican Labour Party (JLP) was ostensibly, in spite of its name, more right wing than the opposition People's National Party (PNP). Yet as Lloyd Bradley has pointed out, there was little difference between them in reality:

> Both sides glossed over the issue of massive social inequality, opting instead to pander to any remaining post-independence spirit of optimism with largely empty slogans and promises tailored to take full advantage of the masses' hopes and dreams. Public money was spent outside the ghettoes, among the influential upper classes and where it would impress/benefit visitors to the island from "a foreign".
> (*ibid.*, p. 177)

Rising unemployment, particularly among the young male population of Kingston, was one such issue, leading to disaffection, delinquency and the formation of the 'rude boy' subculture with its distinctive sharp suits and predilection for gang violence.

'Simmer Down' was a direct appeal by Marley to the rude boys, but adroitly avoids condemning them outright. He was not unsympathetic to their situation – indeed The Wailers had been known as The Wailing Rude Boys for a spell – and the song comes over accordingly as a piece of advice from an elder brother who can see the futility of what they are doing. In any case, his message was well received by a sizable section of the population and 'Simmer Down' went to the top of the Jamaican charts in February 1964.

Commenting on politics through music was nothing new – as Steve Barrow and Peter Dalton have noted (*Reggae: The Rough Guide*, p. 7), 'Well before the advent of recording in Jamaica, street singers would make up lyrics about the latest goings-on and sell them in tract form for a penny a copy.' Social comment was also fundamental to mento, the island's equivalent of the Trinidadian calypso form, which thrived in the early 1950s. Later in the decade, however, the giant sound systems began to dominate the urban landscapes, and their owner/operators became powerful figures in their own right. The leading names were Coxsone Dodd, Duke Reid and Vincent 'King' Edwards who, like the other two, went into record production, though he left music in 1964 to become a member of parliament for the PNP. But the relationship between Jamaican music and politics was embodied most completely by Edward Seaga.

In 1959, Seaga founded West Indies Recording Limited (WIRL) and achieved immediate success with 'Manny, Oh' by the vocal duo Higgs and Wilson (Joe Higgs, subsequently mentor to Bob Marley, and Roy Wilson) – often cited as early ska but in reality a lively R&B number. 'Manny, Oh' proved so popular that Seaga could not get copies pressed fast enough to meet demand. Later in the year, he was appointed by Alexander Bustamente to the Upper House of the Jamaica Legislature, where he helped design the island's constitution; following independence he became JLP MP for Western Kingston and immediately entered the Cabinet as Minister of Development and Welfare.

An opportunity soon arose for Seaga to market Jamaica, and its music, to an international audience. The organisers of the 1964 World's Fair, scheduled to take place in New York between April and October, were especially keen to recruit exhibitors – partly because their decision to charge for space had alienated the Bureau of International Expositions (BIE) and hence led to a boycott of the Fair by 40 BIE member countries including several European nations, Canada, Australia and the Soviet Union. But Jamaica was not a member country, and Seaga eagerly arranged a team of artists to perform both at the event and other venues in the city.

Seaga's priority was to promote Jamaican tourism, and though music was a vital part of that, it had to be of the more accessible variety, the sort of music, in effect, that Seaga had favoured at WIRL. So while there was criticism in some quarters – especially from Jimmy Cliff, one of the artists on the trip – at his choice of the middle-of-the road Byron Lee and The

Dragonaires as the house band, it made commercial sense. No doubt some of the concerns stemmed from the fact that Seaga had just sold WIRL to Lee as part of his exit strategy from the music business.

Nevertheless, the World's Fair line-up was still a strong one, featuring as it did Cliff, Prince Buster, Millie, Eric 'Monty' Morris and The Blues Busters. Certainly the ska purist – if there was such a thing in 1964 – may have cringed when Seaga had Carol Crawford, who the previous year had won the Miss World title for Jamaica, join a group of dancers to demonstrate its potential as a dance craze, but there was no denying that his efforts to draw the music to the attention of the US media were at least partially successful. *The Clay Cole Show*, then second only in popularity to *American Bandstand*, ran a feature on ska, and Millie replicated her British success with 'My Boy Lollipop' and its follow-up, the similar but equally joyous 'Sweet William'.

But Seaga's real achievement lay in his efforts to market the island as a holiday destination: 1965 was Jamaica's best-ever year for tourism with over 316,000 visitors bringing in £23 million in revenue. The World's Fair initiative had been an important part of that and enhanced his reputation as a resourceful man of action; three years later he became Minister of Finance in Hugh Shearer's administration and in 1974 the leader of the JLP itself. In 1980, he was sworn in as Jamaica's fifth Prime Minister.

As to Jamaican music, it did not quite establish the hoped-for foothold following the World's Fair. There *was* a market for ska in America but it consisted largely of ex-pats and, in any case, it was up against the insuperable competition of Motown and soul. So for the moment musicians like Cliff and Buster – let alone The Skatalites and The Wailers who had been left at home – had to be content to ride the crest of the new wave in their native country.

And there it was sweeping all before it; some idea of the infectious, irrepressible energy of the music can be gleaned from the short film *This Is Ska!* (Iva/Maverick Productions) made in 1964 and featuring all of the World's Fair artists, and others, playing for dancers at two locations. Lee and his band provide the steady, idiomatic accompaniment and there are fine performances from, in particular, the sweet-voiced duo Roy and Yvonne ('Two Roads Before Me') and from Toots and The Maytals, who draw heavily an Southern soul and gospel for 'Treat Me Bad' and 'She Will Never Let You Down'.

In the space of a decade, ska would lead to rocksteady, rocksteady to reggae, and the US – and the rest of the world – would finally take notice.

★ ★ ★ ★ ★

The American response to ska was symptomatic of the way in which what we would today describe as 'world music' was perceived in both the US and the UK – that is, as interesting but peripheral. Individual artists like Miriam Makeba had gained a measure of acceptance and some jazz musicians, such as John Coltrane and Yusef Lateef, were successfully integrating Eastern elements into their work, but as a general rule if American or British musicians employed sounds from Africa, South America, the Caribbean or Asia it was little more than gimmickry.

By far the most innovatory approach came from France, in the person of Serge Gainsbourg. Poet, songwriter, singer, actor, director, Gainsbourg saw 'the bigger picture' and was comfortable synthesising disciplines in the cause of creativity. He had no problem, therefore, in absorbing diverse musical sources, although to begin with he stuck fairly close to the traditional French song format, the *chanson*. Between 1959 and 1963 he wrote a number of songs for the bohemian sex symbol, Juliette Gréco, who released her own beautiful collection of *chansons* – *Les Grandes Chansons De Juliette Gréco* – in 1964, just as Gainsbourg was heading into a more ambitious direction with his album *Percussions*.

Three tracks were derived from the 1959 album *Drums Of Passion* by the Nigerian musician, teacher and political activist Babatunde Olatunji (whose composition 'Abana' had appeared on Lateef's *Jazz Around The World*). All of them feature percussion and vocals only. On 'Joanna' ('Kiyakiya'), Gainsbourg sets up a call-and-response pattern with a shrill chorus of female backing singers; 'Marabout' is an urgent, staccato piece based on 'Jingo-Lo-Ba' (covered by Santana on their 1968 debut album and by Cuban percussionist Candido Camero in 1981). On 'New York USA' ('Akiwowo') he intones a list of buildings – 'First National City Bank', 'CBS Building', etc. – in mock wonderment.

Other tracks – 'Couleur Café', 'Ces Petits Riens' – use Latin rhythms to set up a softer, more romantic feel while, in contrast, the organ/saxophone combination all but immobilises the already lugubrious melody of 'Machins Choses'. Gainsbourg is at his best, however, when he uses all the resources at his disposal, including studio technology and effects as well as music. 'Coco And Co.', for example, simulates the ambience of a jazz club, complete with audience chatter, applause and Gainsbourg's half-spoken vocal bisecting the instrumental solos. 'Les Sambassadeurs' is tantamount to cinematic in its vision: whistles, chanting voices and fireworks overlay a relentless samba beat to conjure up a carnival atmosphere.

Gainsbourg's experimentalism in the pop field had its counterpart in contemporary classical music – indeed, the space between the two was becoming narrower, with the middle ground occupied by *musique concrète*, that is, the use of recorded sounds, emanating from both musical and non-musical sources, electronically reprocessed for compositional use. Pierre Schaeffer had coined the term in 1949 to describe his own work in fulfilling the musical potential of 'concrete' (that is, natural, unadorned) sound, and during the course of the 1950s the practice became widespread – even the BBC, seen at the time as the very epitome of stuffy conservatism, established its own Radiophonics Workshop in 1958, initially to provide special effects for radio programmes such as *The Goon Show*.

Also in the late 1950s, the Columbia-Princeton Electronic Music Centre was established with the support of the Rockefeller Foundation, and the composer Milton Babbitt was commissioned by RCA to work there to investigate the potential of its Mark II Synthesiser. The results included *Composition For Synthesiser* (1961) and, in 1964, Babbitt's most famous work, *Philomel*, in which he creates a dialogue between the conventionally recorded soprano, Bethany Beardslee, and an array of electronic noises including the synthesised and distorted voice of Beardslee herself. The effect is heightened when Babbitt introduces a series of mechanical, almost industrial, sounds to offset Beardslee's crystalline purity.

Some seven months later, on 2 September 1964, John Cage wrote the score for *Electronic Music For Piano* in a Stockholm hotel room, and premiered it in the same city eight days afterwards. The piece is of indeterminate length (performances have been known to last for up to twelve hours) and allows the player to tape and play back, using an electronic oscillator, the sounds he/she is creating acoustically, whether on the keyboard or inside the instrument. As in *Philomel*, it is the juxtaposition of natural and artificial sounds that creates the tension, but here it is stretched almost to breaking-point by the many long periods of silence which permeate the piece.

Karlheinz Stockhausen also used live electronics to produce two important works during the year. *Mixtur* brings together an orchestra, four ring modulators and four sine wave generators (a form of oscillator, much loved by contemporary composers) and creates, in particular, some astonishing textures in the string section. But of possibly greater significance is *Mikrophonie I*, written for the tam-tam, an enormous gong-like instrument that Stockhausen purchased at a music fair in Frankfurt and installed in his garden since it was too large to fit in the house. In this piece, one player strikes or scratches the tam-tam, while another records these sounds with a microphone as instructed in Stockhausen's score – 'playing' it like a musical instrument. The third member of the group uses an electrical filter to produce the final result which is relayed to the audience via four loudspeakers.

Mikrophonie I ebbs and flows in the manner of a more traditional work, and Stockhausen compared the extraction of these inner sounds of the tam-tam with a doctor examining his patient with a stethoscope. As such, he considered it a breakthrough and saw no reason why the same methodology could not be applied to non-musical objects such as a Volkswagen car. Premiered in Brussels on 9 December 1964, *Mikrophonie*

I was succeeded the following year by the third in his trilogy of live-electronics pieces, *Mikrophonie II* – but using a Hammond organ rather than a car.

Luciano Berio had been one of the first composers to use electronics and was recognised as an authority on the subject, but 1964 saw him taking his music in other directions. *Sincronie* for string quartet is an arresting work which combines some fearsomely percussive ensemble passages with a bewildering variety of individual instrumental sounds. Similarly, in *Chemins I*, he extends and transforms the timbres of the harp, this time with a full orchestra for company. The outcome is dramatic, especially when the dialogue builds to a mighty crescendo. As a complete contrast, Berio began his series of *Folk Songs For Mezzo Soprano*, a project that was to last for nine years. In all, eleven songs are included, from the USA, Italy, France and Eastern Europe, and the orchestrations are suitably varied, subtle and imaginative. Sadly Berio and Cathy Berberian, one of the most distinguished interpreters of the *Folk Songs*, were divorced in 1964, not long after they were first performed.

Berio and Stockhausen were well into their thirties when 1964 began, Cage was in his fifties. Although all three continued to dominate contemporary classical music, a younger generation was beginning to make its presence felt. Berio had taught some of them, including Steve Reich, destined to become one of the great minimalist composers, and Louis Andriessen, whose politics were as radical as his music; Cage had been particularly influential on La Monte Young, who moved from California to New York in 1960. But Young also drew inspiration from other sources, including jazz and Indian music – as did his almost exact contemporary, San-Francisco-based Terry Riley.

La Monte Young is sometimes described as the first minimalist composer and by 1964 he was experimenting with drone music – that is, a penetrating, siren-like monotone which, devoid of tempo, seldom wavers but has the effect of mesmerising the listener. *Pre-Tortoise Dream Music* is played by The Theatre Of Eternal Music, a group comprising sopranino and soprano saxophones, violin, viola, a sine wave generator and voice –

while the individual instruments are scarcely distinguishable within the drone, the core crying sound comes from the strings. 1964 also heralded the first phase in Young's continuous composition, *The Tortoise, His Dreams And Journeys.* Here the violin and viola, played by Tony Conrad and John Cale, are more prominent and seem to give a firmer, more resolute feel to the piece, yet the sustained nature of the drone makes it difficult to judge whether it is the listener's perception, or the music itself, that grows more intense as it progresses. But the most famous minimalist work to be composed in 1964 was undoubtedly *In C,* by sometime Theatre Of Eternal Music member Terry Riley.

Riley had returned to his native California early in the year and made ends meet by playing piano in bars. He wrote *In C* shortly afterwards, but as Keith Potter relates:

> The initial San Franciscan performances evolved "by consensus, almost", without any written instructions, and the composer has himself done much over the ensuing years to encourage performances of In C to be conceived more as contributions to an ongoing exploration of its potential than as merely a faithful reproduction of the score. (*Four Musical Minimalists*, p. 109)

When it was first performed, in November 1964, the ensemble comprised two trumpets, accordion, recorder, clarinet, soprano and tenor saxophones, five electric pianos (two played by Steve Reich and Riley himself) and organ, although Riley scored it for any number or type of instruments, and indeed the make-up of the group varied from rehearsal to rehearsal . He also expected the piece to change with every performance and therefore did not indicate a specific duration.

In C is essentially a rolling, repetitive, hypnotic work which generates an inexorable rhythm. 53 modules appear on the single-page score but each shift is subtle, almost imperceptible, and does nothing to disturb the cool, flowing motion of the piece. But within what at first seems a tight and compact framework, there is room for individual and collective improvisation – not as an anarchic free-for-all, but within the discipline of Riley's modular structure: in Potter's words,

> The self-expression of each performer characteristic of all improvisation is here channelled through a collective vehicle that yields expressive results which go beyond individual tastes and intentions, "transport[ing] us suddenly out of one reality into another", as Riley has described the experience. (*ibid.*, p. 148)

1964 was an auspicious year for classical music; it marked the 100th anniversary of the birth of Richard Strauss and Alexander Gretchaninov, there were new works by Shostakovich, Britten and Stravinsky (including *Elegy For JFK*), and The Guarneri Quartet, the leading string quartet in America for the next 40 years, was formed at Marlboro College, Vermont. But the appearance of *In C* was, perhaps, the most significant event of all. As we have seen, Riley was not the first to introduce unplanned, random elements into contemporary classical music, nor was he the first minimalist composer; but as with any evolving genre, a time comes when a definitive work is produced and to all intents and purposes, in terms of minimalism, *In C* was it. Its influence was ubiquitous, and not just within contemporary classical music: there were repercussions both in rock (The Who's 'Baba O'Riley', 1971) and jazz *(Kaleidoscope Of Rainbows* by Neil Ardley, 1976).

Yet in terms of impact upon rock music, it was those compositions consisting entirely of electronics that in retrospect seem to be the most important. A good example is Joji Yuasa's *Projection Esemplastic For White Noise*, also from 1964. One way of interpreting this piece is as a kind of tone poem, its array of expressive sounds suggesting at various points an Arctic snowstorm, the take-off of a jet aeroplane or a hissing locomotive. But a more productive approach is to view it as pure music, albeit the white noise of its title, moulded into phases of increased or diminished intensity, before fading away into silence. Whatever the case, it is not difficult to hear echoes of *Projection Esemplastic* in the work of Pink Floyd, Tangerine Dream, Jean Michel Jarre, Vangelis and Kraftwerk.

A common characteristic of the leading contemporary classical composers of 1964 was to collaborate with artists from other fields. Yuasa, for example, helped form the multi-media group Jikken Kobo (or Experimental Workshop), in the early 1950s, while Riley, Young and Cale were associated with Fluxus, an international network of artists founded by George Maciunas, himself inspired by John Cage's compositional ideas and methods.

There were numerous areas of overlap between the Fluxus artists and the groups that preceded them, such as the Situationists and the Dadaists. The former were more political and aimed to shock people out of their apathy (as such, they were the modern counterparts of the Japanese Zen artists who used similar tactics to foster Buddhist enlightenment). Dada, formed in 1916, had an anti-war focus but was primarily a cultural movement.

Fluxus, however, was sufficiently loose and diverse to encompass the principles of both Situationism and Dadaism, as well as their sub-groups and associated organisations. Among the concepts it espoused were:

- Alienation from bourgeois society and the art it produced
- A corresponding desire to create more positive, communal social models
- The rejection of conventional artistic structures, methods and tools
- An emphasis on improvisation and the spontaneous creation of art/performance in any location, often known as a 'happening'
- The absorption into art of everyday occurrences and materials
- An espousal of the abstract, the radical and the anarchic

Apart from Young and Riley, several other Fluxus members helped determine the path taken by the arts in 1964. We saw in Chapter 4, for example, the effect of Gustav Metzger and Yoko Ono's auto-destructive art on the young Pete Townshend. Ono herself first performed her *Cut Piece* in 1964, a piece of performance art (and undoubtedly a happening) whereby volunteers from the audience cut away her clothing until she was naked, symbolic of, among other things, the suppression and abuse of women. 1964 also saw the publication of Ono's book *Grapefruit*, a list of instructions or 'event scores' for the reader to enact, an idea that originated from John Cage's Experimental Music Composition classes and was followed up by, in particular, George Brecht in works such as *Solo For Violin* in which the musician is directed simply to polish his instrument.

Carolee Schneemann advanced the cause of performance art with her happening *Meat Joy*, in which eight naked people drenched themselves in paint and picked over pieces of raw fish, sausage and chicken. She also began work on *Fuses*, a film of her and her boyfriend, the composer James Tenney, having sex, which she then subjects to a variety of artistic effects – the intention being to compare and contrast her own version of pornography with that routinely produced by men.

Of the older generation of Fluxus artists, Robert Watts was among the most radical. In 1962 he had produced the event score *Casual Event*, a six-line instruction to burst a car tyre; during the same year he organised the Yam Festival, a series of happenings not dissimilar to the activities being co-ordinated by Fluxus. Watts helped pioneer the production of Flux boxes, which contained event cards and other objects produced by artists such as Brecht and Ono. *Flux Box 1* appeared in 1964, the first in a series of Flux products. For example, the first Flux Kit – an attaché case full of various Fluxus paraphernalia and retailing at $100 – was launched in June, to be followed by such initiatives as the *Flux Atlas*, designed by Watts and comprising stones from countries around the world, and even a *Flux Mass*.

Watts was one of the artists featured at a watershed exhibition held in 1964 at Paul Bianchini's Gallery in the Upper East Side and entitled *The American Supermarket*. Visitors entered through a turnstile made by Richard Artschwager to find a replica of their everyday shopping experience, complete with muzak and neon lights. Alongside genuine food items there were works of art such as chrome fruit, wax eggs and plaster pumpernickels made by Watts, a giant plastic turkey produced by Tom Wesselmann and shopping bags by Roy Lichtenstein. But perhaps the most notable works in the exhibition were those of Andy Warhol – a painting of a can of Campbell's Soup, valued at $1500, and a stack of original cans which Warhol sold for $6 each.

The exhibition was not without repercussions: later in the year, Christo, who would become famous for wrapping gigantic natural features and man-made edifices, established himself as an international artist with a series of installations entitled *Store Fronts*, using materials found on demolition sites. But these works are darker in nature, more akin to Claes Oldenburg's *The Store* (1961), the re-conversion of his studio into its former incarnation as a shop. Rather, the significance of *The American Supermarket* lies in the fact that it represented the zenith of US Pop Art, at once celebrating and satirising the design, packaging, marketing and consumption of mass-produced goods and, by implication, making a sardonic comment on art itself. It confirmed, in particular, the status of Andy Warhol who also exhibited his *Brillo Boxes* and *Campbell's Tomato Juice Box* at the Leo Castelli Gallery during the year.

Some of the artists who contributed to the exhibition continued to betray the influence of British Pop Art, which had flowered rather earlier. For example, as Michael Archer points out (*Art Since 1960*, p. 21), Wesselmann recalls Richard Hamilton's renowned collage *Just What Is It That Makes Today's Homes So Different, So Appealing?* in his 1964 tableau *Great American Nude No. 54* – though with the addition of contemporary devices such as taped sounds. But the transatlantic influence ran both ways. America was more advanced than the UK when it came to abstract expressionism, and the leading British abstract painter, John Hoyland, went to New York in 1964 to experience the scene first-hand.

Hoyland's work was characterised by bold splashes of colour, often revolving around a central nucleus in a manner which seemed to have as much to do with science as with art. As such he perfectly caught the mood of the period, in which technological progress ran alongside the explosion of energy in the arts. He was called 'Europe's answer to Mark Rothko' but in truth Hoyland's work has a good deal more optimism. His first solo show was held at Marlborough New London Gallery in 1964 and he was also one of the artists included in the groundbreaking *New Generation* exhibition held between March and May at the Whitechapel Gallery. Here were some of the newest stars of British art – Hoyland, David Hockney, Bridget Riley, Patrick Caulfield, Paul Huxley, Peter Blake, Allen Jones, all in their twenties or early thirties – being introduced to a wider public for the first time. Between them they were to dictate the course of British art for many years to come and, especially in Blake's case, create a new dynamic between art and pop music.

In the meantime, as one British artistic movement gathered speed, another fell into decline. In August 1964, the Cornish landscape painter Peter Lanyon died, effectively marking the end of the St Ives School which had flourished for a quarter of a century. Its origins lay in a visit made by Christopher Wood and Ben Nicholson to the town in the late 1920s, where they discovered the untutored, naive work of local fisherman Alfred Wallis. Nicholson and his wife, Barbara Hepworth, moved to St Ives in 1939, signalling an influx of abstract artists including Naum Gabo, Patrick Heron, Terry Frost, Wilhelmina Barns-Graham and Sven Berlin. But by 1964, most of them had moved away or were no longer active.

Nicholson and Hepworth were divorced in 1951 and although Nicholson left for Switzerland seven years later, Hepworth stayed in St Ives to produce some of her finest work and consolidate her reputation as one of the foremost sculptors of the 20th century. Her largest and most important work, *Single Form*, was unveiled on 11 June 1964; located in United Nations Plaza, New York, it was a memorial to the UN Secretary – General, Dag Hammarskjöld, who had been killed in a plane crash three years before. In a year when so much activity in academia, international politics and the arts was concerned with breaking away from traditional structures, the eloquent simplicity of *Single Form* seems to signify a reconciliation of the adventurous and radical with the established and the conventional.

Yet there were still many who resisted the changes that were going on around them and in some cases actively campaigned against them. In 1964, this led to some extraordinary developments on the Right of the political divide; it was also, coincidentally or otherwise, a vintage year for mainstream culture. And it is in these directions that we are heading next.

CHAPTER 8:

Hold What You've Got

Speaking from his home in Phoenix, Arizona, Senator Barry Morris Goldwater announced on Friday 3 January 1964 that he would be seeking nomination as the Republican candidate for the Presidential Election to be held in November. The timing and location were a surprise to many, including his own campaign team: such declarations were usually made from New York or Washington, and on a day of the week more likely to attract media attention. But it was not the first occasion, nor would it be the last, that Goldwater had done the unexpected.

Even in 1964, politics was a slick business, with opinions and behaviour carefully manicured to avoid giving offence; projecting a wholesome image, especially at election time, was of the highest priority. Goldwater, however, was not in that mould. Candid, outspoken and undiplomatic, he was the very antithesis of North Eastern politicians such as John F Kennedy and Goldwater's principal opponent in the contest for the Republican Presidential nomination, the Governor of New York, Nelson Rockefeller. Yet it was those qualities that made him stand out from the crowd and gained him considerable popular support. Add to the mix his ultra-conservative standpoint, and you had a combustible combination which had the potential to set the electorate on fire.

Goldwater was vehemently opposed to the direction in which he saw the US going – too much government, too much welfare spending, too little encouragement for business, taxes too high – all perfectly orthodox conservative attitudes. What endeared him to the more extreme elements of the Party were his opposition to Civil Rights (he was one of 27 in the

Senate to vote against the Civil Rights Act in June), his hard line on Vietnam, and his belief that the US should withdraw from the United Nations if Communist China were to be admitted. But he seemed to be entering the outer limits of even that universe with his casual attitude to nuclear weapons and his apparent willingness to devolve responsibility for their use to NATO commanders. This gave him a reputation as a trigger-happy individual, unsuited to high office, which was to prove a handicap during the run-in to the Election; parodying Goldwater's campaign slogan 'In your heart you know he's right', the Democrats came up with 'In your guts you know he's nuts'.

By the time of the Republican National Convention in July it was certain that Goldwater would get the nomination. He had effectively neutralised some heavyweight opponents including Rockefeller (who had done himself no favours by divorcing his wife of 31 years and, in May 1963, marrying a 36 year-old, herself a divorcee); Governor William Scranton of Pennsylvania; Governor George Romney of Michigan; and Henry Cabot Lodge, US Ambassador to Vietnam, who had been Richard Nixon's running-mate in 1960. Nixon himself had not sought the nomination, although he was still held in high esteem by many Republicans despite his defeat by Kennedy; he cropped up frequently as a write-in candidate during the primaries and could have mounted a charge had the circumstances warranted it.

But they didn't; Goldwater was the clear choice to run against Johnson. In his no-nonsense, unsophisticated way he had tapped into something that his more moderate rivals had not – the feeling that the 'permissive' society, albeit then in its infancy, was already going too far. Times were changing at too great a rate: previously disenfranchised groups such as African-Americans, women and young people were beginning to have their say; in addition the US was in danger of forfeiting its supremacy – militarily, diplomatically, materially, and in the spheres of science, sport and entertainment. All of this had to be stopped, and quickly: Goldwater seemed the only candidate capable of doing it.

Yet at the November Presidential Election he failed abjectly, gaining only 36% of the vote and carrying only six states. In his book *A Glorious Disaster*, J.William Middendorf II, Goldwater's campaign treasurer, attributes his defeat largely to negative press coverage and Democratic efforts to deride him as a dangerous maniac. Middendorf also acknowledges weaknesses in the administration of the campaign and in the candidate himself, who was frequently rude to potential allies and refused to indulge in the traditional candidate pursuits of glad-handing and baby-kissing. But it is hard to attribute the massive scale of Goldwater's defeat to these factors alone.

An alternative explanation is that, although the rumblings of discontent were getting louder, the US was not yet ready for a conservative President. By and large, Johnson was presenting a positive picture with his ambitions for a Great Society; he also had a good record on the economy and was apparently in control of events in Vietnam. Furthermore just before the Election the Warren Commission concluded that Lee Harvey Oswald had acted alone in assassinating Kennedy, thus drawing a line under the death of the former President and bringing to a conclusion a protracted period of national mourning. Above all, there was hope in the air, especially among the young – largely inspired, as we have seen, by The Beatles.

But Goldwater had planted seeds which would reach spectacular fruition in future years. He had, for example, shifted the Republican power base from the North and East to the South and West, a strategy that, in time, affected the Democrats, too. Of the eight Presidents who followed Johnson, only two (George HW Bush and George W Bush) were born in the East – and they made their political careers in Texas; furthermore, at least two of them shared Goldwater's predisposition for straight talking, despite the risk of ridicule. Equally, he and his supporters brought about the renaissance of the American New Right, a dominant force in national, and international, politics nearly 50 years on.

★ ★ ★ ★ ★

In pop music, too, there was resistance to the way the wind was blowing.

The biggest-selling act in the UK in 1964 was not The Beatles, nor The Rolling Stones, nor even Cliff Richard, but the Texan country singer, Jim Reeves. With his rich baritone voice and relaxed, almost soporific, delivery, Reeves was a bigger star in Britain than in the US, where his run of hits had dried up in 1960. In March 1964 he reached number five with Leon Payne's sentimental ballad, 'I Love You Because', and followed it up with two Top Ten albums, *Good 'N' Country* and *Gentleman Jim*. Another single, the slow waltz 'I Won't Forget You', entered the chart on 18 June, eventually making number three; its B-side, 'A Stranger's Just A Friend', written by Gilbert Gibson, was taken from the film *Kimberley Jim*, directed by Emil Nofal and starring Reeves alongside former Miss South Africa second runner-up Madeleine Usher.

Kimberley Jim was both set and shot in South Africa, where Reeves was hugely popular – more so, in fact, than Elvis Presley whose African-American vocal inflections probably did him no favours. Reeves, on the other hand, epitomised Aryan respectability and old-fashioned values and was consequently a welcome visitor. *Kimberley Jim*, the story of a Southern songster/gambler trying his luck in the diamond mines of the late nineteenth century, was made when he was on tour in 1963; rush-released in South Africa in 1965, it never saw the light of day in the US.

On 31 July 1964 Jim Reeves was killed when a plane he himself was piloting crashed near Brentwood, Tennessee. In the UK, reaction to the tragedy was swift and unequivocal: within three months there were no fewer than eight Reeves albums in the chart. A single, coupling Ray Baker's conventional country number 'There's A Heartache Following Me' with another song from *Kimberley Jim*, 'Diamonds In The Sand' – again written by Gibson, this time with Taffy Kikillus – made number six later in the year.

America, however, was largely indifferent to Reeves's death, although in August he did achieve a posthumous number one on the country chart with 'I Guess I'm Crazy'. Elsewhere on the country music scene there were three number ones for Buck Owens and the huge crossover hit for Roger Miller, 'Dang Me'. But one of the greatest achievements of the year

was Connie Smith's 'Once A Day' which created two new milestones –
the first instance of a debut single by a female artist reaching number one
on the country chart and the longest-running country number one ever
by a female artist. Set to a cantering rhythm with pedal steel guitar to the
fore, it tells the familiar story of a woman heartbroken at losing her man,
but Smith delivers it with both strength and sincerity; it was therefore no
surprise that she went on to have nineteen more hits.

Back in the UK, interest in country music was beginning to grow:
after Reeves, the most popular singer was former rock and roller Brenda
Lee, who got to number five early in the year with the plaintive ballad 'As
Usual' and had four subsequent hits. But at that time there were no
home-grown country acts to speak of. The nearest equivalent was the
Dublin vocal trio The Bachelors whose predilection for smart suits and
unashamed nostalgia got them into the Top Five on five occasions in 1964,
most notably with 'Diane' and 'Ramona' – which originated in 1927 and
1928 respectively – and 'I Believe', an enormous UK hit in 1953 for
Frankie Laine.

The other major bulwark against The Beatles and the new wave of
pop groups was Roy Orbison, who had been a big name for the last four
years on both sides of the Atlantic. In truth, his pedigree stretched back
earlier than that, for he had been a key artist on the Sun Records roster
along with Presley, Carl Perkins, Jerry Lee Lewis and Johnny Cash. In
spite of the fact that he made a big impression with hard-driving rock and
roll numbers like 'Ooby Dooby', 'Rockhouse' and 'Domino', his career
was just beginning to tail off when he joined Monument Records. Here,
he rose again like a phoenix and from 1960 onwards unleashed a series of
dramatic ballads, many of them co-written with Bill Dees and produced
by label owner Fred Foster.

Orbison's quivering voice was deceptively strong and he specialised
in building up a song from a subdued opening to a thundering crescendo.
1964 was a vintage year for him, particularly in the UK, where each of his
four hits was something special:

'Borne On The Wind' – in which the floating melody and percussive Spanish guitars conspire to evoke indelible images of the Wild West. Entered the chart on 20 February, made number fifteen.

'It's Over' – a martial drum beat gives immediate urgency; Orbison's vocal gradually intensifies until the emotional temperature reaches boiling-point. Entered the chart on 30 April, made number one.

'Oh, Pretty Woman' – cleverly constructed song whereby the optimism created by the whacking snare and five-note guitar riff offsets the minor-key moments of doubt. Entered the chart on 10 September, made number one.

'Pretty Paper' – written by Willie Nelson and kept just on the right side of sentimentality by a deft vocal performance. Entered the chart on 10 November, made number six.

Orbison's UK fans tended to be older than those of The Beatles – not much older, but given the rapidity with which trends change in pop music, even two or three years make a crucial difference. His appeal was more akin to that of another American singer, Gene Pitney, who was likewise more popular in the UK than in his home country. But unlike Orbison, Pitney's anguished intonation often took him into melodrama, even on good quality material like Burt Bacharach and Hal David's 'Twenty Four Hours From Tulsa', 'That Girl Belongs To Yesterday' by Mick Jagger and Keith Richard, or 'I'm Gonna Be Strong' by Barry Mann and Cynthia Weil, all UK hit singles during 1964.

The generation of British male singers who had ruled the roost in the very early sixties was beginning to fade away, their brand of maudlin balladry laid waste by The Beatles, The Stones and Motown. Billy Fury, for example, had made the Top Ten on nine occasions between 1960 and 1963, but only did so once in 1964, with his cover version of Conway Twitty's overwrought 'It's Only Make Believe'. Mark Wynter, who had had seven Top 40 hits, was riding high at the start of the year with the sentimental medium-pacer 'It's Almost Tomorrow', but his chugging revival of The Platters' 'Only You', which entered the chart on 9 April, proved to be his last.

Their American counterparts were faring little better: neither Bobby Vee nor Bobby Rydell, frequent hit-makers for the previous four years, made the US charts in 1964; it was left to the third Bobby – Vinton – to fly the flag for the boys-next-door: on 4 January, he hit number one with 'There I've Said It Again', repeating the feat on 7 November with 'Mr Lonely'. Both were slushy ballads – the very antithesis of what The Beatles were doing – but Vinton did not go away; indeed he proved to be a long-term antidote to rock music, with seventeen further hits, culminating in 1975 with the 'Beer Barrel Polka'.

Some former teen idols, however, were heading in new directions. Lesley Gore, for example, who had three Top Five hits in 1963 including the number one, 'It's My Party', entered the US chart on 11 January with 'You Don't Own Me'; written by John Madara and David White, it can lay claim to being the first feminist pop record of the 1960s:

> Don't tell me what to do
> And don't tell me what to say
> And please, when I go out with you
> Don't put me on display
> 'Cause you don't own me

Although going right against the grain of traditional teen ethics, 'You Don't Own Me' clearly struck a chord with many young record-buyers: it stayed at number two for three weeks, only kept out of the number one spot by 'I Want To Hold Your Hand'.

After five years of making hit records, Bobby Darin had all but retired from singing, concentrating instead on his TM publishing and production company, housed in the Brill Building. It was there that he employed and mentored Roger McGuinn. The success of The Beatles had impressed McGuinn, but he was equally drawn to the Greenwich Village folk scene; both influences would merge in the summer of 1964 when, with Chris Hillman and Gene Clark, he formed The Jet Set, soon renamed The Byrds.

Marketed as America's answer to The Beatles, The Byrds were also credited as the inventors of folk-rock. Both descriptions stretch the truth, in particular the second; as we have seen, Dylan and Simon and Garfunkel had already set off down this path by late 1964. But even they were not alone: there was a more general espousal of American roots music during the course of the year. Some, like Ian and Sylvia (who were in fact Canadian) came at it from the folk side with the lively 'You Were On My Mind' while others like the Nashville-based Newbeats, whose raucous 'Bread And Butter' made number two in the summer, had a more pronounced pop sensibility. A third category mixed folk and pop in equal parts; it included The Byrds and one of the most underrated acts of the 1960s, Sonny and Cher.

Sonny Bono, assistant to Phil Spector and co-composer, with Jack Nitzsche, of 'Needles And Pins', married his girlfriend Cherilyn Sarkasian LaPier on 27 October 1964. The previous month the duo had released their debut single, 'Baby Don't Go', written by Bono and built around Cher's underprivileged upbringing:

I never had no money
I bought at the second hand store
The way this old town laughs at me I just can't take it no more
I can't stay
I'm gonna be a lady someday

Underpinning the well-crafted, touching lyrics is a gently rolling beat, not too distantly removed from ska, and pithy punctuation from a harmonica, words and music combining elegantly to make a wonderful single which, nevertheless, did not become a hit until the duo broke through the following year with 'I Got You Babe'. Nevertheless, it added to the growing evidence that America would fare better by drawing on its own traditions rather than trying to ape Mersey Beat or British rock; it was a lesson well understood by the big names of subsequent decades such as Bruce Springsteen and REM.

Some of that tradition was still present in the African-American musical mainstream of 1964. Whereas some giants of the pre-Beatles era were becalmed (Ray Charles, for example, was reduced to making concept albums about crying and laughing – *Sweet And Sour Tears* and *Have A Smile With Me*), a new group of singers were, outside the influence of soul and Motown, reaffirming the values of articulation, phrasing and timing within a conventional musical context. Chief of these was Dionne Warwick.

Her album *Make Way For Dionne Warwick* was released on 31 August 1964 and was her first to enter the US chart. It was produced by Burt Bacharach and Hal David, who also wrote all but three of the twelve tracks, which include 'Walk On By' and 'You'll Never Get To Heaven'. Here, and throughout the record, the interest lies in the interface between Bacharach's imaginative arrangements and Warwick's vocals – ostensibly controlled but betraying an emotional profundity that occasionally rises to the surface. On 'A House Is Not A Home', for instance, she handles the tender-to-tough transition with assurance, keeping her feelings in check until the song reaches its dramatic conclusion, while 'Reach Out For Me' pitches her gentle entreaties against choir, strings and booming tympani. Other tracks, however, give her the chance to show her versatility: she is assertive on 'They Long To Be Close To You', appropriately dreamy on 'Land Of Make Believe', and on 'Get Rid Of Him' she even indulges in a bit of rap. Only Bob Merrill and Jule Styne's 'People' puts her in a sentimental strait-jacket.

Make Way For Dionne Warwick was not just the foundation of a glittering career; it also proved that in spite of the universal impact of The Beatles and the other British groups, there was still room in 1964 for pop music that was quintessentially American – but only just.

★ ★ ★ ★ ★

British influence was not confined to pop music; in cinema, too, the time-honoured supremacy of the USA was under threat from a second transatlantic invasion. The 37th Academy Awards, for films made in 1964, were dominated by *My Fair Lady*, set in Britain and with a predominantly British cast. In all it received eight Oscars, including Best Picture, Best Actor (Rex Harrison) and Best Costume Design – Black and White (Cecil Beaton); in addition Gladys Cooper was nominated for Best Supporting Actress and Stanley Holloway for Best Supporting Actor (an Award which went to another Briton, Peter Ustinov, for his role in *Topkapi*). A second musical set in Edwardian London, *Mary Poppins,* received a record thirteen nominations and netted the Best Actress Oscar for Julie Andrews. *Becket*, the story of Henry II's conflict with his Archbishop of Canterbury, was not far behind with twelve nominations, including Richard Burton (Best Actor), John Gielgud (Best Supporting Actor) and Peter Glenville (Best Director). In addition, Alun Owen received a Best Original Screenplay nomination for *A Hard Day's Night*.

Peter Sellers was a Best Supporting Actor nominee for *Dr Strangelove Or: How I Learned How To Stop Worrying And Love The Bomb*, a trenchant satire on the nuclear arms race preoccupying both the media and the general public (*Fail-Safe*, directed by Sidney Lumet, was another 1964 film on the same theme). His nomination marked a memorable year in which he had also starred in the second 'Pink Panther' film, *A Shot In The Dark* and another satire, the TV movie *Carol For Another Christmas*, in which he played opposite the Swedish actress Britt Ekland whom he had married in February.

There was a strong British presence, too, in the action films of 1964. *Zulu* was a critically acclaimed, full-blooded account of the 1879 Battle of Rorke's Drift between the British Army and local tribesmen and starred Stanley Baker, Jack Hawkins and Michael Caine (in his first major role); the narration was provided by Richard Burton, the music by John Barry. But it was *Goldfinger*, directed by Guy Hamilton and starring Sean Connery and Honor Blackman, that had the greater long-term impact. Released on 17 September, five weeks after the death of Ian Fleming, on whose novel it was based, it was the third of the James Bond films, and undoubtedly the best so far. The previous two, *Dr No* and *From Russia With Love*, were disjointed efforts with uneventful interludes and sporadic action. In contrast, *Goldfinger* was pacy, exuberant and stylish. The screenplay – which brought together the two writers, Paul Dehn and Richard Maibaum, who had worked individually on its predecessors – established the tradition for witty one-liners and gentle self-mockery that would sustain Bond films right through into the Roger Moore era and beyond, and the Aston Martin DB7, with its ejector seat, bullet proof screen and other gadgetry, symbolised the technological spirit of the age. After a period in which British film was synonymous with grim and gritty realism, *Goldfinger* was a glamorous new departure and set a course for action films that is still being followed.

Yet for all its accomplishments Britain was just one part of a 1964 film industry that had a distinctly cosmopolitan flavour. *Zorba The Greek,* for example, directed by Michael Cacoyannis and with an unforgettable soundtrack by Mikis Theodorakis, was one of the films of the year, earning Academy Awards for Best Supporting Actress (Lila Kedrova), Art Direction – Black and White (Vassilis Fotopoulos) and Cinematography – Black and White (Walter Lassally). Other highlights included the aforementioned *Topkapi,* set in Istanbul with a cast including actors from Switzerland and Greece, the heart-rending Danish film *Gertrud,* and *Kwaidan,* a quartet of chilling Japanese ghost stories directed by Masaki Kobayashi. But most significant of all was the Italian-made *A Fistful Of Dollars.* An early spaghetti Western, it was the first in the series of 'Dollars' films, all of which were shot in Spain and directed by Sergio Leone, with music by Ennio Morricone. Tough, tense and highly atmospheric, it was as influential in its way as *Goldfinger,* creating a blueprint for contemporary Westerns that its star, Clint Eastwood, has especially profited from.

While it was certainly true that the US still provided the finance, and much of the artistic direction, for most major feature films, few wholly American pictures could compare with such quality. The entertaining romantic comedy *Father Goose* – a typical Hollywood tale of a whisky-loving seadog trapped on a Pacific Island with a group of girls and their teacher during World War II – was one of the better ones, and did well at the Oscars but even this had the French actress Leslie Caron co-starring with Cary Grant (and he was born in England!).

Grant's successor as America's leading comic actor, Tony Curtis, starred in a more up-to-date comedy, *Sex And The Single Girl*. Based on Helen Gurley Brown's advice manual of the same name, it cleverly both lampoons and defends the idea of women's sexual independence proposed by Brown (played by Natalie Wood), but the wit and sophistication are dissipated by the protracted and unnecessary car chase that constitutes its climax. Although no actual sex is shown, the film symbolises Hollywood's newly found confidence in dealing with overtly sexual themes, also exemplified in 1964 by *The Carpetbaggers*, adapted from the lurid novel by Harold Robbins, and *A House Is Not A Home*, the biopic of New York's notorious madam, Polly Adler. But such films were some way from what was happening in European cinema: none of them could match the heady mix of eroticism and satire served up by Luis Buñel's *Le Journal D'Une Femme De Chambre*.

In the wider scheme of things, however, America was less concerned about international incursions into the film, and music, industries – indeed, at times, it seemed to encourage them – than it was about competing in matters of science and technology with its principal rival, the Soviet Union. There was the ever-present worry, in particular, that the Russians were winning the space race, a fear further fuelled on 12 October 1964 when *Voskhod 1,* the first spacecraft to carry more than one crewman, went into orbit. Next to this, American Jerrie Mock's achievement in becoming, in April, the first woman to fly solo around the world seemed like something from a bygone age. Even Europe was catching up: in July, *Blue Streak*, formerly a medium-range ballistic missile, went into orbit from Woomera, Australia, as a European space probe. And at sea, the Japanese launched the first-ever super-tanker – the 205,000-ton *Idemitsu Maru.*

Americans did, nevertheless, have a share in the major advances in both physics and computer science made during the year. Gerald Guralnik and CR Hagen, working with the Briton Tom Kibble, co-discovered, together with Peter Higgs, also from Britain, and the Belgians François Englert and Robert Brout, the Higgs boson particle – or at least, proposed its existence. The particle, still proving elusive 50 years later, was and is considered crucial to our understanding of matter and what took place in the first second that the universe was created – the latter question leading to the Higgs being termed the 'God particle'. Meanwhile Thomas Eugene Kurtz and the Hungarian-born John George Kemeny were inventing the BASIC computer language.

Some American scientists were responsible for key innovations on their own: Robert Moog demonstrated his synthesiser for the first time in 1964 and, after getting his preliminary draft approved by none other than Isaac Asimov, Robert Ettinger published *The Prospect Of Immortality* in which he provided the scientific basis for cryonics – the preservation of humans for whom current medical practice cannot avert death, or who have actually died, until science evolves to the stage where they can be revived. Immediately after the book came out Ettinger became a celebrity and while his ideas still attract controversy, he himself has been cryopreserved following his death, in the conventional sense, in July 2011.

But of perhaps more immediate significance than any of these developments was the increased progress made in 1964 by US environmentalists. The realisation that man was in the process of destroying the environment had been growing for some years and was accelerated by the publication in 1962 of the American marine biologist Rachel Carson's *Silent Spring*, in which she outlined the damaging effect of pesticides. Such a stance took considerable courage in the face of powerful industrial interests and at a time when concern about the environment was not as widespread as it is today. In 1964 it was followed up by the Citizens For Clean Air movement, founded in New York by British-born Hazel Henderson and by the pioneering work of the botanist Mildred Mathias, one of the first academics to draw attention to the destruction of the rainforests and its effect on the world's ecosystems; Mathias was named Woman of the Year by the *LA Times*. At the same time the veteran scientist Farrington Daniels was publishing his prophetic *Direct Use Of The Sun's Energy*, one of the earliest books on solar power. Finally, there was evidence that the US government was starting to take environmental concerns seriously: on 3 September 1964, Congress created the National Wilderness Preservation System, thus conserving for the nation nine million acres of open and untamed land.

★ ★ ★ ★ ★

There was further encouragement for the US in the world of sport. The year did not begin especially well, for at the Winter Olympics, held in Innsbruck between late January and early February 1964, they gained just one gold medal, in the men's 500 metre speed skating. Such a disappointing return was at least partly attributable to the fact that three years earlier the entire US figure skating team had been killed in a plane crash en route to the World Championships in Prague. However this did not make the Russian dominance of the event any easier to bear. In all the Soviet team picked up one-third of the golds on offer and their overall total of 25 was ten higher than any other nation.

As the Summer Games approached, there seemed every chance that the Soviets would confirm their supremacy there, too. After all the gap between the superpowers seemed to be widening: in the Melbourne Olympics of 1956, the Russians had won 37 golds to America's 32, and 98 medals of all kinds to 74 by the US. Four years later, in Rome, the respective ratios were 43 to 34 gold and 103 to 71 overall. Yet at the 1964 event, held in Tokyo between 10 and 24 October, it was a different story. This time the US topped the medals table, achieving 36 golds as opposed to Russia's 30 (although the total Soviet medal count was higher – 96 to America's 90).

The Tokyo Olympics were notable for other reasons. It was, for instance, the first time the Games had been held in Asia: Japan had been scheduled to stage the Games in 1940, but the offer was withdrawn owing to its invasion of China in 1937 (in the end, the outbreak of World War II meant the Olympics were cancelled altogether). As a symbol of peace, the Olympic flame was lit by Yoshinori Sakai, who was born in Hiroshima on the day it was devastated by the atomic bomb (6 August 1945). On a less positive note, South Africa was excluded because of its apartheid policies, a reminder of the link between sport and politics – indeed, four of the next five Olympics were marked by political turmoil of one sort or another.

While not the official theme song, 'Tokyo Melody', by Helmut Zacharias was used by the BBC for its coverage and proved to be one of the best compositions to be associated with that, or any other, Olympics; its rolling cadences and idiomatic melody made for a stirring combination and placed Zacharias, originally a violinist, in the big league of German bandleaders along with Bert Kaempfert and James Last, who formed his first orchestra in 1964.

As in all Olympics, there were many excellent individual performances. Don Schollander won four swimming gold medals for the USA and Australian Dawn Fraser won gold in the 100 metres freestyle for the third time in a row. New Zealand's Peter Snell took gold in the 800 and 1500 metres, Abibi Bakela of Ethiopia became the first athlete to win the marathon twice, and British hearts were in their mouths when Ann Packer burst through from sixth place to win the 800 metres in world record time.

Elsewhere in sport, the big news of 1964 was the victory of Cassius Clay over Sonny Liston in the world heavyweight boxing championship. Since the Rome Olympics, where he had won the light-heavyweight gold medal, Clay's rise to the top had been meteoric with no defeats and nineteen wins – including fifteen knockouts. But it was not just his success in the ring that made Clay such a charismatic figure: his brash displays of self-confidence included predicting the outcome of his fights, deriding his opponents and frequent and vehement declarations that he was 'the greatest'. Seen from today's perspective, there was a fair amount of flippancy in these actions for Clay was essentially a serious young man with deep political convictions. He was an associate of Malcolm X and planned to become a Muslim.

He was dissuaded, however, from announcing his intention to convert before the Liston fight. Ironic though it may seem in view of his subsequent canonisation by boxing writers, fans, as well as the general public, his braggadocio had already made him deeply unpopular, and it was feared that a stated relationship with a man like Malcolm, already loathed by large sections of the white community, might bring extra adverse publicity and hence damage commercial interest in a contest for which Liston was already the odds-on favourite.

Clay made the necessary compromise and the fight went ahead on 25 February. When asked beforehand how he would approach it, he coined the immortal couplet

> Float like a butterfly, sting like a bee:
> Your hands can't hit what your eye can't see

In the event, Liston refused to come out for the seventh round, claiming a shoulder injury, but by then it was clear that Clay was the superior fighter (a fact underlined by the 1965 rematch in which he knocked Liston out in the first round). On 6 March Elijah Muhammad stated that Clay would henceforth be known as Muhammad Ali, a signal that he had joined the Nation of Islam. Clay himself said that he had been interested in Islam for six years and that his religious convictions had helped him defeat Liston when '99 out of 100 seemed to see no possibility of me winning'.

It was a mixed year for UK sport. Great Britain could finish only tenth in the Olympic medal table, yet this was improvement on the twelfth place reached four years earlier. Britons took the first three positions in the 1964 Formula One Drivers Championship with John Surtees, Graham Hill and Jim Clark but in cricket the Ashes series went to Australia, who also occupied three of the Wimbledon singles semi-finals places and provided the winner of the men's tournament, Roy Emerson.

On the domestic scene, Liverpool won the First Division

Championship, much assisted by their fans, who appropriated numerous pop songs for their chants – among them were The Beatles' 'She Loves You' and Gerry and the Pacemakers' 'You'll Never Walk Alone', the latter becoming the club's anthem. The title was clinched with a 5-0 win over Arsenal. Worcestershire became county cricket champions for the first time, a massive 41 points ahead of nearest rivals, Warwickshire. Here the writer must declare an interest: a supporter of Liverpool *and* Worcestershire, he witnessed both triumphs first-hand.

★ ★ ★ ★ ★

What was it like to live in Britain in 1964?

In contrast to today, when the media is desperate to appeal to the young and no-one wants to be thought of as old, there was a distinct generation gap, with younger and older people seemingly quite content to play their separate roles. Being young for most – to me, it seemed like all – teenage boys largely amounted to football, pop music and the opposite sex (a combination of interests that, for many of us, has remained in place over the intervening 50 years). The idea of getting a job was often something to be postponed, for it was here that the real world kicked in – big-time.

Industry and commerce were indisputably controlled by adults and riddled with rules and regulations, many of which seem senseless now – indeed, they did so then – but there was always the fear of summary justice for those who transgressed. Yet at the same time workers could get away with practices which today would be considered unwise, unsafe or downright illegal. As 1964 began, John Greenway was working at a local newspaper in Manchester, having left school the previous summer. He recalls that,

> Newspaper production methods were frozen in time by union strangulation. Drastic change was not very far away but this was thought to be highly unlikely. As a young boy I saw a machine

gathering dust in the corner of the Publishing Room. Its purpose was for tying up papers for transfer to vans for dispatch. I asked why it was not being used and received a response not unlike the one Oliver Twist got when he requested seconds at the supper table. So the main task was tying up bundles of newspapers by hand, using a special knot and completing the job by cutting the twine with a blade inset in a tube called a piggy. It was impossible to hurt anybody with this, unlike an incident some years earlier when knives were used. A drunken argument about football, it was said, led to a fatal stabbing.

Offices were generally poorly furnished and shabby. Pre-computers, there were hand-cranked adding machines and comptometers, a dinosaur calculating device. Photocopiers were desktop models which took an age to produce one copy. This involved the use of chemicals which inevitably ended up on the user's hands. There was plenty of time to contemplate the harm you had caused yourself whilst waiting for the wet copy to dry out. Smoking was permitted in offices. Office managers were generally addressed as Mr and many of them showed little or no management skills. I actually saw someone with a forbidden cup of tea on his desk after lunch made to pour it away by his boss.

Little wonder that young employees took refuge in the local hostelries:

I can recall going into Yates's Wine Lodge with workmates and witnessing a stampede of customers towards a counter where a tray of steaming beef was being placed on sandwiches. A large copper contraption dispensed boiling water into a glass of Australian white wine and sugar known as a blob. Probably unique features in these licensed premises were posters displayed around the walls advising patrons not to drink too much! I sometimes used to take lunch in Seftons, the pub which many years later was at the seat of the IRA bomb. Another drinking establishment close to work was the Thatched House where some wag had displayed a notice, "Ice cold beer, Ice cold customers". Nearby was the Stock Exchange from which emerged many men wearing bowler hats, not unlike a surreal Laurel and Hardy film.

As to the musical diet,

> Music package shows were still popular and it was possible to see a few top acts in venues such as the Odeon. With two shows a night, the top of the bill – the likes of Roy Orbison – might get to perform for a maximum of twenty minutes. I saw Bo Diddley for half a crown [12 ½ pence] in a long-demolished club off Market Street. Record shops were the place to idle away Saturday afternoons. Here obliging assistants would play you records you were pretending to express a wish to purchase. Little listening posts were located around the room for this purpose. The two main record companies, EMI and Decca, both brought out monthly publications promoting their product. Decca's was in magazine format and featured articles on their latest LPs which were in fact rewrites of the album's sleeve notes. EMI's offering was a newspaper containing many reviews of their latest single releases. Strangely none were ever critical. What a waste of sixpence!

Big cities like Manchester, Liverpool and London may have led the way in 1964, but there was some sort of music scene in most towns. Even a comparative backwater like Worcester had its own band – in this case The Hellions, who in August 1964 secured an engagement at Hamburg's fabled Star Club and went on to sign a recording contract with the Piccadilly label. The pride of Burnley, Lancashire, were Kris Ryan and The Questions, whose repertoire included jazz and R&B as well as pop. Following a successful audition at a music shop in nearby Blackburn in spring 1964, the band met Philips record producer Johnny Franz and made a number of recordings, including a creditable version of Ben E King's 'Don't Play That Song'; they also worked as a warm-up act for the TV show *Top Of The Pops*.

Sadly, neither The Hellions nor Kris Ryan and The Questions hit the big time, although some of their members did go on to better things. The Hellions' Jim Capaldi and Dave Mason, for instance, subsequently joined Traffic, while The Questions' Jimmy Jewell became a noted session musician famous for his searing saxophone break on Joan Armatrading's 'Love And Affection'; their drummer, Geoff Wills, became a clinical psychologist and writer, combining both disciplines in his groundbreaking work on the stress experienced by jazz musicians.

It is a measure of the strength of British pop music in 1964 that such groups found it difficult to break through. Mersey Beat might be on the wane, but some Liverpool groups were having their best year yet. As discussed earlier, The Searchers made the charts on five occasions, including two number ones, and The Fourmost had their biggest hit to date with 'A Little Loving' – their first not to be written by Lennon and McCartney. Instead the wholesome duo Peter and Gordon were the beneficiaries of their compositional skills – the catchy 'World Without Love' reached number one on both sides of the Atlantic, with the follow-up, 'Nobody I Know', not far behind. Released in September, their third single, 'I Don't Want To See You Again', sounded like a cast-off from *A Hard Day's Night* and while that still made it superior to most of the competition, it failed to chart in the UK, an extremely rare occurrence for a Lennon-McCartney song.

The Dave Clark Five, from Tottenham, projected a different image from The Beatles, opting for dark blue blazers with shiny buttons, white polo neck sweaters and matching trousers. Their music was different too, more elemental and with a fuller sound, incorporating saxophone and organ, and the leader's walloping drums prominent in the mix. This formula propelled them through 1964, commencing with 'Glad All Over', which got to number one on 16 January; 'Bits And Pieces' and 'Can't You See That She's Mine' also made the Top Ten, but they began to lose direction a little in the autumn with the uncharacteristically R&B-flavoured 'Thinking Of You Baby'.

It was, as we have seen, a year of achievement for Cilla Black and

Dusty Springfield, whose haul of four hits during the year should really have been five. Her splendid account of Bacharach and David's 'Wishin' And Hopin'' was held back from release owing to the protracted chart run of 'I Just Don't Know What To Do With Myself' but in the meantime The Merseybeats had got in the Top 20 with their version, neutralising the Springfield single, when it came; it was, nonetheless, a US hit in July. Springfield's visual trademarks were her peroxide blonde hair and heavy black eye make-up, and for a time it seemed that any woman who wanted to succeed in pop had to possess some sort of gimmick or novelty appeal – Lulu with her extreme youth, Sandie Shaw, who sang in bare feet, not to mention the drummer Honey Lantree (The Honeycombs) and the bass-player Megan Davies (The Applejacks) whose gender obscured any talent they may have possessed as instrumentalists.

Among the men, one of the brightest prospects was Dave Berry who got away from covering material by his chosen namesake, Chuck, with 'The Crying Game', a haunting, mournful song that, almost 30 years later, inspired the film of the same name. Cliff Richard, who had ruled UK pop before The Beatles, rallied with three fine releases: the storming 'I'm The Lonely One', 'On The Beach' from the soundtrack of the otherwise unmemorable film *Wonderful Life* and the easy-paced, tuneful 'I Could Easily Fall'; the ballads 'Constantly' and 'The Twelfth Of Never', on the other hand, took him to the brink of schmaltz. At this stage his records were still being issued as by 'Cliff Richard and The Shadows', but his backing group had long since come out of the shadows, as it were, to make their own hits, the best of which in 1964 was the 'The Rise And Fall Of Flingel Bunt', an untypically punchy opus underscored by a biting riff, while their former drummer, Tony Meehan, had a fine solo hit with 'Song Of Mexico', as noted in Chapter 4.

But the scope of British mainstream pop encompassed more than stereotypical groups and singers. We have already seen how bands like The Rolling Stones, The Animals and Manfred Mann brought R&B and urban blues to the chart; there was also distinct jazz content in such contrasting records as the Migil 5's upbeat, ska-oriented 'Mockingbird

Hill' and 'Cast Your Fate To The Wind' by Sounds Orchestral, an atmospheric instrumental with constantly shifting moods and tempos. And The Barron Knights provided a welcome element of parody, sending up The Searchers, Freddie and The Dreamers, The Stones, The Bachelors, Dave Clark Five and The Beatles on 'Call Up The Groups'. Compared with what had been on offer a mere one year earlier, or at any other time in the history of British popular music, this was a rich and varied diet.

★ ★ ★ ★ ★

The pop music boom was symptomatic of a growing sense throughout popular culture that change had arrived and some of the conventions of the late 1950s and early 1960s could be cast aside. On television, for example, comedy was dominated by working-class characters who got laughs not only from their interaction with each other but from debunking the Establishment. The most popular sitcom, with over 22 million viewers, was *Steptoe And Son,* in which a rag-and-bone man tries desperately to better himself in the face of his unreconstructed father. Although in some ways it was a kind of comic sequel to the hopelessness portrayed in the kitchen sink dramas of the 1950s, the programme also celebrated the virtues of the working man. *The Arthur Haynes Show* also focussed on notions of class, a theme that its scriptwriter, Johnny Speight, was later to exploit in *Till Death Us Do Part,* but in this case the characters played by Haynes – tramps, burglars and other representatives of society's lower echelons – invariably got the better of authority figures such as policemen and petty government officials. (The Haynes show also showcased pop music talent: in one 1964 edition, The Rolling Stones gave an outstanding performance of 'You Better Move On'.)

At the other end of the spectrum there was *Seven Up,* a BBC documentary profiling fourteen seven-year old children; subsequently the same group were interviewed at seven-year intervals with touching, and at times harrowing, results. There were also a number of powerful dramas, none more controversial than *Lysistrata,* written by Aristophanes in the fifth century BC and translated from the Ancient Greek by Patric Dickinson. The story of a group of women demonstrating their opposition to the war with Sparta by occupying the Acropolis and refusing to have sex was shorn of some of its more extreme language but there were, as Amanda Wrigley has pointed out (*wordpress.com/2011/10/21*), still sufficient explicit references to elicit protest when it was screened by the BBC on 15 January 1964.

To some, *Lysistrata* symbolised the moral decay of broadcasting as a whole, and it was in response to such concerns that Mary Whitehouse launched her Clean Up TV campaign in the same month. January 1964 also saw the Director General of the BBC, Hugh Carleton Greene, receive a knighthood, and it was Greene who became the specific target of Whitehouse's invective. She proclaimed that the Corporation under his stewardship had spread 'the propaganda of disbelief, doubt and dirt' among the television audience. There is no evidence, however, that Clean Up TV had any impact on BBC policy – indeed in the years immediately following, censorship seemed to go in the opposite direction. Another pressure-group was formed in 1964, but this one was rather more benign. The Society for the Prevention of Cruelty to Long-Haired Men was a spoof organisation featured by the BBC's current affairs programme, *Tonight*, in November. Its spokesperson, interviewed by anchorman Cliff Michelmore, was a confident seventeen-year-old called David Jones, later to become better known as David Bowie.

The most momentous broadcasting event of the year was the creation of a second BBC channel, BBC Two, which began transmitting on 21 April. This helped the Corporation to try out new ideas without alienating its traditional audience and give opportunities to a younger generation of programme-makers. It also employed a greater bandwidth – 625 lines UHF (ultra-high frequency) as opposed to the 405 lines VHF (very high frequency) being used by the other two channels. This made it possible to transmit in colour and three years later BBC Two became the first European channel to do so on a regular basis.

Another important launch took place in the newspaper industry. 15

September 1964 saw the first edition of *The Sun*, introduced by IPC (International Publishing Corporation) to replace *The Daily Herald*, which had been losing circulation. At the outset, it tried to cash in on the feeling of confidence prevalent across the country and, in particular, to reflect the reforming spirit of Wilson's election campaign which had begun three days before. As Dominic Sandbrook writes,

> As commuters studied The Sun's first front page, everything smacked of modernity and excitement. Here was the paper of the future: progressive, modern, free thinking and classless. (*BBC History Magazine*, September 2011, p. 33)

The Sun was, therefore – strange as it may seem today – a left-wing newspaper and it was not until Rupert Murdoch bought it in 1969 that the now-familiar recipe of sensationalism, sex and sport was established.

In the field of literature the 400th anniversary of the birth of William Shakespeare was greeted with extensive celebrations: the Shakespeare's Birthplace Trust hosted a festival in Stratford-on-Avon which included seven plays and a special exhibition on his life and work. At the same time there was sadness at the passing of Edith Sitwell, TH White and Ian Fleming whose *You Only Live Twice* and *Chitty Chitty Bang Bang: The Magical Car* were published during the year. There were debut novels for Ruth Rendell and AS Byatt, two writers who could scarcely be more different in style. *From Doon With Death* introduced Inspector Wexford, hero of 20 subsequent Rendell stories; its taut, economic narrative makes it a compelling read, although changes in social mores over the last 50 years make the denouement far more guessable today than it would have been at the time. The dense, at times almost unfathomable prose of *Shadow Of The Sun* is no less absorbing and like other 1964 novels by women writers – such as Iris Murdoch's *The Italian Girl* and *The Garrick Year* by Byatt's sister, Margaret Drabble – paints a depressing picture of middle-class family relationships and the way they thwart, in particular, female ambition and potential. More pessimism, if any were needed, was to be found in CP Snow's *Corridors Of Power*, a window on the frustrations and futilities of government, and the play *Entertaining Mr Sloane*, Joe Orton's grim portrait of a psychopath.

Such works did not reflect the general mood of the country. On the contrary, there was a positive feeling in the air – inspired, at least among the young, by the new wave of pop music, but also by the stream of good news stories that permeated the year. On 10 March, for example, the Queen gave birth to her fourth child, Edward, who became third in the line to the throne after his elder brothers Charles and Andrew; eleven days earlier, her cousin Alexandra, also gave birth to a son, James – the most popular boys' name of 1964 – and as a further sign of the common touch, the princess attended the premiere of the Cliff Richard film, *Wonderful Life*, on 2 July.

In September, the Queen opened the Forth Road Bridge – at that time, aptly, the fourth longest suspension bridge in the world, and just one of many infrastructure projects to stir up national pride. Work began in March on the road scheme of the Severn Bridge which, at 3240 feet, was just a few metres shorter than its Scottish counterpart, and July saw the completion of London's 626-foot Post Office Tower. The first cross-channel passenger hydrofoil went into service in May, but as if to trump even that, Britain and France reached an agreement to build the Channel Tunnel.

British women were constantly in the news in 1964, from the royal family to the latest pop stars. The crystallographer Dorothy Hodgkin received the Nobel Prize for Chemistry (the first woman to do so since Marie Curie in 1911) while at the other end of the achievement spectrum Ann Sidney won the Miss World title for the UK. There were also major developments in the fashion industry in which Mary Quant was leading the field with her mod designs. Quant created the first miniskirt in 1964, naming it after her favourite car, the Mini, itself a fashion item. Costing from £448 (£7400 today) this tiny vehicle was affordable – especially second-hand – for many young adults and soon became ubiquitous in films, television and publicity stunts ('How many girls can you get into a mini?' was a successful 1964 Rag Day fundraiser at Glasgow University). Elsewhere in fashion Barbara Hulanicki opened her first Biba store in Kensington and the market for ready-to-wear garments expanded dramatically. The vogue for topless dresses was, on the other hand, somewhat short-lived, owing to the arrest for indecent exposure of wearers in London and Sydney.

In short, Britain had become the centre of the fashion world, just as it had across every area of popular culture and, increasingly, in science and technology. With a General Election due by the end of the year, there was every reason to suppose that what we have come to describe as the 'feel-good factor' would assist the ruling party in their bid to retain power.

★ ★ ★ ★ ★

Sir Alec Douglas-Home, Prime Minister of the United Kingdom of Great Britain and Northern Ireland as 1964 began, had come into office rather reluctantly. As the 14th Earl of Home, he had been quite content with his job as Foreign Secretary in the Conservative government of Harold Macmillan and much preferred the more dignified atmosphere of the House of Lords to the hurly-burly of Commons debates. Yet he was a dutiful and conscientious politician and when pressed by senior colleagues to succeed Macmillan, he put Party, and country, first.

Macmillan had fallen ill in October 1963, just before the Conservative Conference in Blackpool. There were fears that he had prostate cancer and although these proved to be unfounded (and Macmillan lived on until 1986), he decided it was time to resign; the Profumo Scandal had taken its toll and he was also becoming concerned that a cabal was forming against him. His decision was communicated to the Conference by Home, who then expected to be a bystander as a successor was identified. There were two experienced and well-fancied candidates: Lord Hailsham, Macmillan's own choice, and the Deputy Prime Minister, Rab Butler, but neither commanded the unanimous support of the Tory grandees. Hailsham had also made a tactical error by declaring too early.

So it was that Home was persuaded to come forward. He certainly had many of the assets required to lead the Party, having served as Commonwealth Secretary and Leader of the House of Lords before his current post; he had also played first-class cricket for Oxford University, Middlesex and the MCC. His only stipulation was that a substantial majority in both Houses must indicate their support for him, and once that was achieved, there were no further obstacles. Home, in typically disarming and casual fashion, relates in his autobiography what happened next:

> I heard then that a bet had been struck at Blackpool which must be unique. It coupled at long odds Breasley to win the Flat Race Jockeys' Championship and me to be Prime Minister. It was a spectacular "Autumn Double". I did not have time to tell Elizabeth the final decision. She heard on the wireless that I was off to the Palace. Her comment to my son was, "Heavens – in that suit!" (*The Way The Wind Blows*, p. 182-183)

In order to sit in the House of Commons, Home needed to renounce his peerage and seek a constituency to represent. This came along in the shape of Kinross and West Perthshire, where a by-election was due, and Home was returned with a majority of 9328. But almost as soon as he became Prime Minister, his attention turned to another election, for at some point during 1964 he would have to go to the country. For this reason, surveys of Home's premiership tend to be brief – even his own account concentrates on the duties attached to the position rather than details of policy and debate. Understandably, as a former Foreign Secretary, Home highlights his overseas responsibilities, notably his attendance at the funerals of Presidents Kennedy and Nehru, in November 1963 and May 1964 respectively. But he is silent on the more complex foreign issues with which he was presented. In February, for example, clashes between the Greek and Turkish populations of Cyprus were coming to a head, but its President, Archbishop Makarios, rejected British military intervention. Home, a resolute opponent of Communism, was in all probability suspicious of the Archbishop, a member of the Non-Aligned Movement, but does not tell us so. We learn nothing, either, about his attitude to the increased tensions between Yemen and Aden, the former British colony that had merged into the Federation of Emirates of the South the previous year.

On the domestic front, too, the year was not without incident – even before the run-up to the General Election. March, for example, brought the second and most dramatic stage in the programme of railway closures proposed by the chairman of British Railways, Dr Richard Beeching, in 1963. Over 1,000 miles of track and 360 stations were closed during the year, much to the horror of the travelling public. On their 1964 live album, *At The Drop Of Another Hat* (produced by George Martin), Michael Flanders and Donald Swann lamented the disappearing railway landscape on the elegiac 'Slow Train':

No more will I go to Blandford Forum and Mortehoe,
On the slow train from Midsomer Norton and Mumby Row,
No churns, no porter,
No cat on a seat,
At Chorlton-cum-Hardy and Chester-le-Street
We won't be meeting again on the slow train.

I'll travel no more from Littleton Badsey to Openshaw,
At Long Stanton I'll stand well clear of the doors no more,
No whitewashed pebbles,
No up and no down,
From Formby Four Crosses to Dunstable Town,
I won't be going again on the slow train.

The 1964 cuts represented the peak of what came to be known as 'Beeching's Axe' and in retrospect much more was lost than a picturesque transport system and pretty rural stations. The policy was disastrous both economically and environmentally: the government has provided ever-greater subsidies to the rail industry and there has been a massive increase in air pollution with more and more travellers taking to the road. Admittedly a small number of lines have re-opened and an even smaller number have been converted to light rail systems, but almost 50 years on, the name Beeching still conjures up short-sighted, draconian blundering.

The month after Beeching's Axe began to fall, Home was the subject of a botched kidnap attempt by two students from the University of Aberdeen who were only dissuaded from their action when the Prime Minister explained that it would result in martyrdom for him and a resultant Election victory for the Conservatives. Ever the gentleman, Home did not reveal the details of the incident for another thirteen years for fear of tarnishing the reputation of his bodyguard.

But he could not avoid mass publicity in July, when another sex scandal reared its head. *The Sunday Mirror* claimed to have a photograph of a peer of the realm sitting on a sofa next to an infamous gangster, the implication being that there was a sexual relationship between the two men. At that time homosexuality was still illegal, and the paper claimed that it could not print the picture due to UK libel laws. Yet the German magazine *Der Stern* did print the photograph – in which the couple were identified as Lord Boothby and Ronnie Kray. This was a potentially explosive revelation for Home since Boothby had been a prominent Conservative for nearly 40 years and was well known throughout the country for his appearances on the BBC's *Any Questions* radio programme; Kray, although his notoriety had not yet reached its zenith, was a high profile underworld figure.

However the Leader of the Opposition, Harold Wilson, was reluctant to take full political advantage of the government's predicament, mainly because the Labour MP, Tom Driberg, was also a homosexual associate of the Kray twins, and having witnessed the witch hunt that accompanied the Profumo affair a year earlier he was afraid that Driberg would almost certainly be dragged into it. So Wilson asked his lawyer, Arnold Goldman (nicknamed 'Mr Fixit'), to get Boothby to write a letter of denial to *The*

Times and eventually *The Sunday Mirror* backed down, giving Boothby an apology and £40,000 in compensation. Fear of reprisal by the Krays was also likely to have been a factor – certainly many other papers were guarded in their reporting of the twins' activities for some time to come.

On the advice of the Tory Party chairman, Lord Blakenham, Home opted for an October, rather than June, election. This would at least allow the furore over Beeching and the Boothby scandal to die down; it would also give Home a chance to become better known to the general public. Unfortunately, however, Home did not present a good image. He was already off to a disadvantage owing to his aristocratic background – indeed his Cabinet colleagues Iain Macleod and Enoch Powell had expressed the view at Home's accession that it was certain to bring electoral defeat. But what was worse was that he projected so poorly, both in the House of Commons, where he was frequently outshone by the relaxed and witty Wilson, and, crucially, on television. Even in 1964 this was becoming an important part of electioneering: in the US, four years earlier, Nixon had lost many votes to Kennedy through his wretched performance in a TV debate, and now – as is so often the case with media matters – Britain was going the same way. By Home's own admission, his appearance counted against him:

> In 1963 I had an unpromising start when I was being made up for some Prime Ministerial performance; for my conversation with the young lady who was applying the powder and tan went like this:
>
> Q. Can you make look better than I do on television?
> A. No.
> Q. Why not?
> A. Because you have a head like a skull.
> Q. Does not everyone have a head like a skull?
> A. No.
>
> So that was that. The best that I could do for the cartoonist was my half-moon spectacles. Elizabeth always said that they lost the 1964 election. (Home, *op. cit.*, p. 201)

The result was that the principles and policies Home was offering to the electorate became obscured by his public persona. He was, for example, vehemently opposed to the use of race as an electoral issue – a serious risk, given the actions of some of his own Party members.

After a consciously encouraging Commonwealth immigration into Britain during the 1950s, mainly to fill vacancies for the unskilled occupations spurned by the indigenous population, the government now found itself having to deal with racial tensions as – at least in the minds of many white Britons – employment, and housing, were becoming scarcer. During the run-up to the election, all eyes were focussed on Smethwick, near Birmingham, an area with a high percentage of immigrant families: it was alleged that supporters of the Conservative candidate, Peter Griffiths, had published literature proclaiming 'If you want a nigger for a neighbour, vote Labour'. As it turned out, Griffiths won the seat, defeating Patrick Gordon-Walker, future Foreign Secretary in the Wilson administration. Four months later, Malcolm X visited Smethwick, where he gave his final television interview.

Meanwhile, Harold Wilson was having problems of his own. Labour's lead in the opinion polls was dwindling and by the end of August, according to NOP, the Tories had taken the lead. One of the persistent jibes – still invoked today by opponents of the Party – was that they were too close to the trade unions and, if returned to power, would allow them free rein to hold the country to ransom. There were already signs in the weeks before the election that the unions were flexing their muscles, with disputes on the docks, on the London Underground and in the car industry. Fortunately for Wilson, these were all settled before Election Day, but the Labour leader had not trusted entirely to luck: he had got Frank Cousins, General Secretary of the monolithic Transport and General Workers' Union (TGWU), to agree to join his first Cabinet – a crucial move in damping down, in particular, the dock workers' strike.

There was also the ever-present risk of scandals, guaranteed to poison the electorate against the perpetrating party, or Party. As we have seen Wilson successfully stifled the Kray affair, but could not do a great deal about the wild behaviour, invariably inspired by alcohol, of his Deputy, George Brown. Appearing on a TV programme honouring the memory of President Kennedy, for example, Brown had lapsed into drunken sentimental ramblings and on a more recent occasion had shouted down the President of the Board of Trade, Edward Heath. It was too late in the day to dismiss him, so instead Wilson made himself the focus of the media's attention and sent Brown off on a nationwide tour. Another source of discomfort was the continuing rumour that Wilson was having an affair with his secretary, Marcia Williams. This was being pressed especially hard by Quintin Hogg who, as Lord Hailsham, had been the front-runner to succeed Macmillan. But now, as then, he overplayed his hand and was rebuffed by the statesmanlike intervention of the former Labour Prime Minister, Lord Attlee. Wilson was therefore able to circumvent both of these banana-skins and no damage was done.

By 15 October, the day of the election, most polls had Labour slightly ahead and indeed this proved to be the case when the votes were counted: they had secured 317 seats, the Conservatives 304 and the Liberal Party 9. Notwithstanding its slim majority, the new government stuck with policies it had outlined in the Labour Manifesto as well as adopting some that were not: for example, a free vote was allowed on the death penalty resulting in its abolition. As Ben Pimlott has written,

> The change in atmosphere at No. 10 in 1964, affecting both initiation and response, was perhaps the most dramatic aspect of the transition. At the outset, the tone set by Wilson was one of activity and reforming zeal, in big things and in little, with an excitement and drive that infused the whole Government in the opening months, despite the limitation imposed by the economy. (*op.cit.*, p. 355)

The energy of the new administration was in tune with what was happening in the country as a whole: indeed, it seemed to encapsulate the widespread feeling that a fresh start was being made. Above all youth seemed to be in the ascendancy. Wilson was the youngest Prime Minister of the 20th century thus far and many of his policies reflected a commitment to the welfare of young people, especially those from non-privileged backgrounds; while conventional in appearance himself, he was interested in popular culture and, of course, had courted The Beatles during their rise to international prominence. His vision for scientific progress also had implications for the young – for who else would be taking up the new opportunities that the white heat of technology would bring?

In some respects, Wilson's victory was the UK's 'Kennedy moment' – a surge of optimism reinforced by British achievement on a whole range of levels. Certainly, pop music was at the top of the list, and what was remarkable here was that innovation in 1964 took place *within* the mainstream rather than at the periphery of it. The pop audience was, in other words, absorbing new ideas as they were being generated, not, as is normally the case, some distance later: the most radical music being made in the UK was in the charts. But, as we have seen, Britons were succeeding across the board – in film, in art, in literature, in science and in sport. One such achievement crowned the year and in so doing seemed to capture the zeitgeist: after breaking the land speed record on 17 July by reaching 403.10 miles per hour in *Bluebird*, Donald Campbell broke the water speed record, getting his boat – also called *Bluebird* – to 276.33 mph on 31 December 1964.

★ ★ ★ ★ ★

The picture was more complex, however, in the United States. Kennedy's assassination had created a pall over the country but this was starting to disperse. The British Invasion helped turn heads, especially those of the young, in a new direction and Johnson's ambitions for social reform augured well for oppressed minorities – success at the Olympic Games also boosted morale and re-emphasised the contribution young people were making to the well-being of the country as a whole. As the year drew to a close, there seemed plenty to feel hopeful about.

At the same time, this promising outlook seemed to be threatened by storm clouds on the horizon and, again, young people were in the vanguard – whether burning their draft cards, writing protest songs, experimenting with hallucinogenic drugs or dropping out. All of these activities took place in a world outside mainstream culture – indeed, they came to be recognised as central features of the *counter*culture – and so threatened to undermine what the vast majority of its citizens believed their country stood for. Yet within their apparent negativity lay the seeds of something new – a way of thinking and behaving that may not have been what Johnson had in mind for his Great Society but which, unlike that pipe-dream, would genuinely enrich the American way of life in the years to come.

CHAPTER 9:

It's All Over Now

1964 was a special year for a great many reasons. That, I hope, has been demonstrated over the preceding chapters. The task now is to analyse the themes that emerge from the year's events and to assess their impact in the short, long and medium term. As the reader will be well aware, I have chosen to concentrate on music and politics: the developments in those areas seem to me to be both the most interesting and the most significant. But I also believe that the directions they took were indicative of a wider movement that embraced the Western world. Part of this defies exact definition – it is best described as a feeling, a mood or an atmosphere – whereas other parts are easier to get hold of since they can be charted by tangible landmarks. In either case, the connections are clear between music, politics, the arts, broadcasting, sport, science and technology.

Furthermore, each of these can connect bi-laterally. As I have tried to show at various stages in this book, the relationship between music and politics was especially strong in 1964, not just in Britain and the USA, but in Africa and the Caribbean. This was by no means a new phenomenon: Mozart's *The Marriage Of Figaro*, for example, first performed in 1786, contains more than a hint of the impending French Revolution while Disraeli's anti-Russian stance in the Eastern Crisis of 1875-8 attracted unequivocal support in the music halls through compositions like 'MacDermott's War Song'. But there was no precedent for the scale and depth of commitment evinced by, for instance, the protest singers. At a time when – as Marina Hyde has pointed out (*Newswipe,* BBC 4, broadcast

2 February 2010) – political engagement is used as a fashion accessory by vacuous celebrities, it is chastening to look back to 1964 when so many singers not only understood what was happening in the world but were capable of mobilising others to make it better. What *was* new, however, was the deliberate courting of pop stars by the leader of a political party, an eventuality which would have repercussions in the succeeding decades.

These examples immediately suggest two themes for our analysis: firstly the transformation or intensification of ideas which had gone before, and secondly features that were genuinely new. Pop music provides a template for such an approach; in *From Blues To Rock*, David Hatch and I argued that its history is characterised by – indeed, is dependent for its existence on – continuity and change. This is demonstrable both in the generality of musical idioms and in the detail of specific songs. So in terms of styles,

> Each set of performances which has been perceived, at the time or with hindsight, as crystallising a new tradition, invariably blends new elements or structures with recycled ones. Thus the transformation of one or more traditions typically combines the exploitation of and contributions to existing traditions. (*From Blues To Rock*, p.42)

Such traditions are expressed in terms of musical descriptors – country music, blues, rhythm and blues, rock and roll, rock, and others – but also in the very material that defines them, the songs themselves, which frequently migrate across genres and, as a result, occasion the processes both of continuity and change. In order to provide the evidence and illustrate how this works in practice, we coined the term 'song families' and showed how numerous songs had travelled through styles and through eras. Scions of the 'Minglewood Blues' song family, for example, are to be found in the work of such disparate artists as Gus Cannon's Jug Stompers, Charlie Patton, Muddy Waters, Neil Young, Dr Feelgood, The Grateful Dead, and Captain Beefheart.

Furthermore, we argued that almost all pop musicians begin by listening to and learning from records – that is, through aural transmission. Their attempts at copying them are, as a consequence, inevitably imperfect; even the use of sheet music or guitar 'tabs' seldom leads to exact reproduction of the original source material. The result, albeit in most cases involuntary, is change. Once that process is consistently adopted by the same artist, their identity is formed; once adopted by a group of artists, you have the beginnings of sub-style; finally, universal adoption results in an idiom – rockabilly, skiffle, Mersey Beat, punk, house, hip-hop, and many others were created in this way.

So for all of these reasons, while not doubting that pure innovation is possible, we concluded that change in pop music tends be a function of its past.

How, therefore, does such a template apply to the music of 1964, and is it relevant more generally?

★ ★ ★ ★ ★

At first sight, the pop music of 1964 seems to conform to the pattern of continuity and change as outlined above. In Britain, the coming trend was rhythm and blues, with an undercurrent of interest in blues itself. The results correspond precisely with the definitions proposed in *From Blues To Rock*:

> There are at least three possible stages available to new generations of pop musicians in the development of their musical competence. A recognisable first stage is that of song/performance reproduction (or copying) of examples taken from selected musical types. A second stage requires the competence to improvise on given patterns (usually manifested as song-family extensions). A third involves the writing of new songs composed of elements derived from the material in 'stage one', which thus can be described as musical family extensions. This appears to be a generally applicable model in pop song development, as stages one to three are constantly repeated. (p. 4)

291

Prominent recordings by British bands in 1964 would be categorised as follows:

Band	Stage One	Stage Two	Stage Three
The Rolling Stones	It's All Over Now, Little Red Rooster	Not Fade Away	Tell Me
The Animals	Baby Let Me Take You Home	The House Of The Rising Sun	
Manfred Mann	Do Wah Diddy Diddy		
Them		Baby Please Don't Go	
The Kinks			You Really Got Me
The Who			I'm The Face

The first point to note is that, in the case of an artist appearing at all three stages of the model, there does not have to be a chronological sequence – some performers regress to unadorned cover versions after periods of creativity and, in the example given here, The Stones' 'Not Fade Away' came before the records identified at the first stage. So taking the stages in turn:

- 'It's All Over Now', 'Little Red Rooster', 'Baby Let Me Take You Home' and 'Do Wah Diddy Diddy' are not significantly different from the originals by The Valentinos, Howlin' Wolf, The Mustangs and The Exciters respectively.
- The records cited at Stage Two certainly satisfy the requirements for that category. 'Not Fade Away', though a cover version of a Buddy Holly song, achieves much of its impact from Bo Diddley's 'hambone beat', while the electrifying arrangement of 'The House Of The Rising Sun' converts this traditional piece into a practically new composition. 'Baby Please Don't Go' belongs to a song family that seems to originate in 1927 with 'Don't You Leave Me

Here' by Papa Harvey Hull and Long Cleve Reed and also comprises versions by Muddy Waters and Big Joe Williams, to whom it is credited by Them: their explosive version, however, adds several new dimensions to the piece.

- 'Tell Me', 'You Really Got Me' and 'I'm The Face' are all original pieces but are closely related especially in structure, to rhythm and blues. Moreover the best of three, 'You Really Got Me', is, according to some sources including the composer himself, Ray Davies, a variation on one particular song – Richard Berry's 'Louie Louie', even if The Kinks' version is nearer to that of The Kingsmen in both instrumental and vocal delivery.

The same pattern applies to many of the leading American artists of 1964, yet some of them, such as The Beach Boys and Bob Dylan, had already gone beyond the first two stages and were producing music which was now less tenuously related to an existing musical family. Dylan's album *The Times They Are A-Changin'* was a conscious attempt to represent him as the heir to a tradition, so naturally there is much that derives – or seems to derive – directly from folk song. But in reality, Dylan was creating music which in terms of its imagery, imagination and moral authority had never been heard before. The follow-up, *Another Side Of Bob Dylan*, entirely lacked the gravitas of its predecessor, but instead was reaching for something else that was new: folk-rock. Both records see Dylan at the outer limits of Stage Three – almost, but not entirely independent of tradition, a position he has occupied for the greater part of his subsequent career.

Other protest singers, like Phil Ochs, Buffy Sainte-Marie and the Johnny Cash of *Bitter Tears*, went straight to Stage Three, Tom Paxton achieved a similar sleight of hand to Dylan – songs like 'A Rumblin' In The Land' and 'Ramblin' Boy' *sound* ancient but in fact are original compositions. In contrast, Pete Seeger made recordings at all three stages, but over a longer time period.

The music that emanated from the Brill Building, since it had been established for some years by 1964, does not fall within the scope of the model, and the same applies to artists working exclusively within a musical tradition, such as blues artists like BB King, Buddy Guy or Muddy Waters – especially the latter who, as we have seen, was positively encouraged to regress. On the other hand, Sam Cooke, who had spent years at Stage One as the gospel singer Dale Cook, scored a notable success in 1964 at Stage Two with 'Blowin' In The Wind', by then a permanent fixture in the folk tradition (and hence an example of how the cycle is repeated), and at Stage Three with 'A Change Is Gonna Come'.

Of all the pop musicians operating in 1964, on either side of the Atlantic, The Beatles were stretching the model to the greatest extent. They were clearly still making records at Stage One, as the multiple cover versions on *Beatles For Sale* attest. 'Matchbox' is an interesting example since it is one of those songs that migrated through styles and generations. Originally recorded in 1927 by blues singer Blind Lemon Jefferson, it was later adapted by the white country artist Larry Henseley (1934) and the rock and roller Carl Perkins (1956) on whose version The Beatles' was based. Yet there was nothing much at Stage Two (unless you believe – as Ian MacDonald suggests – that 'Mr Moonlight' is a parody), nor at Stage Three. In other words, The Beatles had, in 1964, made the transition to a Stage Four – complete independence of any tradition. Songs like 'If I Fell', 'Things We Said Today', 'You Can't Do That', 'And I Love Her', 'Any Time At All', 'I Should Have Known Better' and 'Can't Buy Me Love' belonged to a brand new epoch of song writing. It was almost as if Cole Porter, probably the greatest individual pop composer of all had, at his death on 15 October, passed the baton to John Lennon and Paul McCartney.

★ ★ ★ ★ ★

Although not designed for any other medium than pop music, the above model does have some implications for jazz, in that it helps us to identify the distinction between those who adhered to the standard rules of improvisation and composition and those who ventured into new territory. Yet in other ways it is more difficult to apply, since progress was being achieved not just by a new generation of musicians but also – unlike pop – by the more established figures like Miles Davis, Charles Mingus and John Coltrane. Furthermore, because improvisation is such a fundamental part of jazz, it is sometimes problematic to find a dividing line between Stages Two and Three.

A record like *The Complete Concert (1964)* exemplifies the dilemma. Here Davis displays outstanding improvisatory powers. Time and time again he goes off in surprising directions, but these are not random, disconnected outbursts. Like few other jazz musicians before or since, he conveys the meaning of a composition through his playing – his solos thus have interpretational as well as structural logic. On the other hand repertoire is unadventurous, consisting largely of standards, especially ballads, or pieces he had first introduced some years earlier and which consequently must be considered as material at Stage One. On the face of it, then, recordings like 'My Funny Valentine' and 'Stella By Starlight', despite their outstanding quality, can only be considered as at Stage Two. Yet in every case the themes are dispensed with swiftly, often in a matter of a few seconds, before Davis gets on with the serious business of soloing. In so doing he is creating what are in effect new works – which might just as easily be categorised as Stage Three.

Mingus's appearance at the Monterey Jazz Festival shows him operating at all three stages. Indeed, the Ellington medley can be seen to straddle Stages One and Two: by retaining the concept and spirit of their sources the treatment of 'I Got It Bad And That Ain't Good' and 'Mood Indigo' in particular go beyond mere copying. 'Meditations On Integration' is undoubtedly at Stage Three, being an eclectic mix of idioms both internal and external to jazz which Mingus coheres into a work of dazzling originality. Indeed, there is a case for placing it into Stage Four, since it is unprecedented in its musical and thematic scope. Earlier Mingus pieces, such as 'Fables Of Faubus', were characterised by political invective but 'Meditations' is a multi-layered composition which takes as its subject the polarised positions on racial integration held by Malcolm X and Martin Luther King, itself a metaphor for the wider conflict between violence and non-violence and between war and peace.

John Coltrane's *A Love Supreme* might also be regarded as a Stage Four record, but what was essentially new about it, the elevation of a jazz record on to a higher spiritual plane, first made itself felt beyond 1964. However *Out To Lunch* by Eric Dolphy undoubtedly transcends the model. In effect it recasts the roles and relationships of what had been the building blocks of jazz since inception:

- Composition and improvisation
- The ensemble and the individual
- The frontline instruments and the rhythm section

All these were clearly delineated in earlier forms of jazz, including the most experimental: even Ornette Coleman's 1961 album *Free Jazz* consisted of solos punctuated by a clearly distinguishable theme. On *Out To Lunch* these components are interchangeable. Written passages merge into extemporisation, with combinations of two, three or more musicians as likely to take a lead as a single soloist, and bass and drums are given licence to dictate direction. And what is more miraculous, given the potential complexities involved in such a project, is that the resultant music is perfectly accessible, laden with humanity, humour, elegance and pathos – underlining the terrible sense of loss that came in June with Dolphy's death.

Dolphy represented the link between the likes of Mingus, Coltrane and Coleman with a younger school of jazz musicians, two of whom, Archie Shepp and Albert Ayler, took the history of the tenor saxophone to new places with a way of playing that relied more on raw emotion than musical virtuosity. Both made their recording debut as leaders in 1964 but of the two only Ayler's *Spiritual Unity* was consistently at Stage Three, retaining some connections with music at Stage One while at the same time dispensing with the jazz improviser's rulebook entirely; for all

Shepp's potency, his *Four For Trane* consisted almost exclusively of variations on themes composed by his distinguished mentor.

Other forms of music discussed in this book – contemporary classical music and styles from Africa, for instance– undoubtedly evolved during 1964 but the more gradual pace of their evolution makes it hard to apply the model in-year. Ska, on the other hand, is a better fit: initiated by the reproduction of an earlier idiom, it improvised upon it and finally became a new musical entity. This demonstrates that the model can be extended beyond individual examples to whole genres – but can it have any function outside music?

★ ★ ★ ★ ★

Politics, like pop music, depends on novelty. All political parties like constantly to come up with new initiatives and ideas to solve what are very often ancient and intractable problems, although in reality very few are anything other than old ideas dressed up to appear innovatory. 1964 was an exceptional year in which the theme of new beginnings seems all-pervasive, so the task is now to examine whether politics – perhaps the second-oldest profession and certainly related to the oldest – was genuinely part of that picture.

When, in July 1935, Lyndon Baines Johnson took up the post of Texas Director of the National Youth Administration, he had already had substantial direct experience of poverty and its effects. He had also seen how President Franklin D Roosevelt, elected two years previously, was already starting to make a difference with his New Deal programme. By the time Johnson himself reached the Oval Office 28 years later, however, he was better known as a consummate wheeler-dealer than as a champion of the poor and disaffected – in fact, as a senator in the early 1950s he opposed Civil Rights legislation, a stance which helped his campaign to lead the Democrats in the Upper House.

As a result, one difficulty with Johnson's career is to assess the extent to which his stated beliefs were genuine, or motivated by political exigency.

This is nothing unusual – it is a question to be asked of almost every politician. What makes it relevant to the present discussion is whether his vision of the Great Society as articulated in 1964 was merely a cynical rerun of the New Deal designed to capture votes, an adaptation of that program to suit contemporary conditions, or a brand new policy, based on principles and past experience. In other words, does the Great Society fall in Stage One, Two or Three in our model of continuity and change?

Despite doubts about Johnson's sincerity, it would seem inappropriate to place the Great Society at Stage One. Admittedly there was an element of copying – and not just of the New Deal. Kennedy had also planned an anti-poverty strategy as part of his suite of domestic reforms and Johnson found it expedient to go along with it, both to preserve continuity and to represent himself as the heir to the much-loved President. But the New Deal was closer to his heart: as Dallek (*op. cit.,* p. 157) relates,

Johnson himself had little idea of what a Great Society or a war on poverty meant beyond "fulfilling FDR's mission". His objective, [Johnson staff member] Bill Moyers says, was to finish the Roosevelt revolution. Johnson "never really liked the term Great Society," Moyers adds. "It didn't come easily to him." But it gave the press a "bumper sticker. He didn't like it as much as he liked the New Deal. That's really what he saw himself doing."

Such a judgement makes it hard to see the Great Society as a Stage Three initiative. But nevertheless there were aspects of Johnson's programme that went beyond what FDR envisaged. Roosevelt, while he ensured access to welfare would be equally available to African-Americans, had not dealt with segregation, whereas Civil Rights were at the centre of what Johnson was advocating. Johnson also introduced the notion of publicly-funded health care (resulting over the next two years in Medicare and Medicaid, designed to support the aged and the poor respectively). So irrespective of its impact there is no denying that the Great Society was an enhancement of the New Deal – perhaps not all new, but to those who it (at least potentially) affected, new enough to engender a spirit of optimism.

Both of the Civil Rights figureheads advanced their cause considerably, and heroically, during 1964. Martin Luther King had already demonstrated by the Birmingham protests and subsequent March on Washington that he was a magnetic campaigner and the dignity of his words and deeds did much to accelerate Civil Rights legislation. But his doctrine of non-violence was not new – indeed King gave full credit to Mahatma Gandhi for teaching him the strategy of passive resistance which proved so effective in mobilising huge numbers of African-Americans. In the model of continuity and change, therefore, King's actions are characteristic of Stage Two.

Although his beliefs were not new in themselves, Malcolm X took matters further. Stage One in his case was achieved many years earlier when he joined the Nation of Islam; he reached Stage Two when he began to speak out independently of the Nation; finally, by the end of 1964, he had evolved a coherent philosophy which placed black nationalism and self-determination into a global context. He was also seen, in contrast to King, as someone who would not shrink from violence if it were necessary in the pursuit of his ideological goals. This, too, was unprecedented in such a high profile African-American leader and did nothing to dent his charisma: while Islam had historically appealed to – mainly obscure – African-American jazz musicians, no-one of the status of Cassius Clay had joined the Nation until now. In short, it is safe to say that no-one in 1964 embodied political change better than Malcolm X and as a consequence he justifies categorisation at Stage Four.

In Britain, events seemed to be unfolding at a gentler pace, at least in the first part of the year. The Home administration had only a few months to run before a General Election, so there was no time for spectacular initiatives. The big news in politics was the challenge being presented by the Labour Party with their formidable leader and radical manifesto. How much of Wilson's programme was new is another matter. Most of the policies outlined in *Let's Go With Labour For The New Britain* had been prominent in all of the post-war election manifestos. Nationalisation and Britain's role as an international peace-maker had been in them all and health, housing and education had featured in the last three; leisure and youth had been themes in 1959. The structure of the manifesto also reflected the experience of the Labour leader, who had learned the importance of planning from his previous bosses Sir William Beveridge and Sir Stafford Cripps: now there was a National Plan for Britain and Plans for the Regions, for Transport, for Stable Prices and for Tax Reform.

Yet there were also elements of Labour's programme that were unprecedented, particularly the emphasis on new technology and, crucially, the theme of fair access to opportunities for all, irrespective of social background. It was as if earlier socialist policies of universal health, housing, employment and benefit provision had not quite gone far enough, since they had not materially affected the British class structure. What Wilson was promising was an end to the system of privilege that governed advancement and using the new industries as his template. This was certainly a departure and shows that his policy-making had progressed to Stage Three in the model of continuity and change.

Such policies were, of course, also in tune with what was happening in the country at large, where established hierarchies were being overturned with some regularity. Working-class heroes were emerging in music, television and film, while in photography David Bailey, himself from humble origins, published his *Box Of Pin-Ups* containing pictures of the likes of The Beatles, Terence Stamp and the Kray twins alongside figures from higher social strata such as Cecil Beaton and Rudolph Nureyev. The whole project symbolised the parity of esteem that Wilson was looking to enshrine in law and typified the innovatory and iconoclastic spirit within popular culture in 1964. Mod fashion, the miniskirt, pirate radio, BBC Two – all were instances of developments at Stage Three. But by now the reader will be sufficiently familiar with the model to apply it to other examples: it is time to move on from seeing the year 1964 as a function of its past, and to consider the question – where did it all lead?

★ ★ ★ ★ ★

By the mid-20th century, political ideology – and specifically, Communism

– had replaced religion as a major cause of war between nations. The unresolved Korean conflict of 1950-53, in which the boundaries between the Democratic People's Republic of Korea and the Republic of Korea were much the same at the end of the war as they were at the beginning, should perhaps have warned the backers of the two countries, China and the USA respectively, to keep out of such internecine struggles. Yet the lessons were lost on America in particular, where the fear of the spread of Communism was so great as to justify their support for the South Vietnamese regime less than a decade later.

In 1964, that support began to turn into full-scale intervention – henceforth Vietnam would be like a quagmire in which each successive move led to deeper involvement from which there was no escape. As a consequence of the Tonkin Gulf Resolution, President Johnson had the authority to deploy US forces in Vietnam without making an official declaration of war. At first, he seemed reluctant to do so; for one thing the Presidential Election was imminent and there was evidence that the gung-ho policies of his opponent, Barry Goldwater, were not finding favour with voters. A Vietcong attack on Saigon's Brinks Hotel, home of many senior US officers, on Christmas Eve, 1964, went unanswered for fear of disturbing seasonal celebrations back home.

But it was becoming increasingly clear that the strategy of providing technical, financial and moral support to the South while conducting a bombing campaign in the North was not working. The South Vietnamese leadership was as weak as ever, the Vietcong as tenacious, and Hanoi showed no sign of buckling under the bombardment from American planes. So Johnson came to believe that, as Stanley Karnow has put it, (*op.cit.*, p. 422), 'the choices were simple: either the United States plunged into war or faced defeat'. The Tonkin Gulf Resolution gave him the opportunity to take the first option without panicking the American people.

In early 1965, US ground troops went into action in Vietnam for the first time, and as their numbers multiplied so did the range of measures to exterminate the Vietcong – whole South Vietnamese villages were destroyed in an attempt to root out insurgents and thousands of rural peasants driven towards Saigon where, it was felt, they could be more easily monitored for infiltration. In spite of Johnson's attempts to damp down fears that America was in too deep, news of casualties – as well as the atrocities being perpetrated by both sides – was arriving back with ever greater clarity and regularity. Even an operation which on the face of it was a success, such as the rebuttal of the Tet Offensive in 1968, seemed like a failure, such were the gruesome pictures shown on American television screens.

The arrival of combat troops in Vietnam re-ignited protest music which – subject, like any other style, to the vicissitudes of fashion endemic to pop – had begun to wane a little, due, at least partly to Dylan's rejection of it. Now protest songs were firmly located within rock music. Some referred directly to Vietnam, notably 'The "Fish" Cheer/Feel-Like-I'm-Fixin'-To-Die Rag' by Country Joe and The Fish, written in 1965, but not released until two years later; others took a more pragmatic course by expressing anti-war sentiments without making specific mention. By the late 1960s, both of these variants were part of the wider peace movement which played a huge role in the eventual withdrawal from Vietnam by the US in 1975. Since then the war has continued to figure prominently in the imagination of musicians; most – such as Bruce Springsteen ('Born In The USA', 1984) and Paul Hardcastle ('19', 1985) – excoriate America's involvement; some, such as Big and Rich ('8th November', 2006), are more equivocal.

Sadly, the whole American effort in Vietnam including the deaths of nearly 60,000 military personnel not to mention the devastation suffered by Vietnamese on both sides – was to little avail. Saigon fell shortly after the Americans left and a year later the country was unified as the Socialist Republic of Vietnam. As for Johnson, the Tonkin Gulf Resolution of 1964, which appeared to give him so much freedom, led to his downfall. Unable to bring the war to a conclusion – indeed, seen as someone who had unnecessarily prosecuted it – Johnson announced on 31 March 1968 that he would neither seek nor accept, if offered, the Democratic nomination for another term as President of the United States.

It had all seemed so different in 1964 when Johnson was riding high in the public estimation. No-one could possibly have imagined that it was his opponent, Goldwater, who would leave the more lasting legacy. For in Goldwater's candidacy lay the origins of what became the New Right, a major force in US politics in the years to come. He had gathered round him true believers in conservatism – not moderates like Rockefeller and Romney, whom he disparaged as crypto-Democrats – but adherents of a more fundamental right-wing doctrine. These included activists such as J William Middendorf II as well as politicians such as Ronald Reagan whose speech *A Time For Choosing* was one of the few highlights of Goldwater's campaign: indeed, Middendorf (*op. cit.*, p. 257) states that, 'I truly considered Reagan the ideological successor to Goldwater'.

After Goldwater's demise, Richard Nixon became the leader of the Republican Party once more. But although Nixon supported Goldwater's bid for the presidency he did not entirely fit the conservative profile matched so exactly by Reagan. Despite a streak of ultra-conservatism, Nixon had liberal tendencies – his willingness to treat with Communist China, his concern for the environment and his extension of the American social security system hardly endeared him to the Right and made him, at best, a moderate; much the same could be said of Gerald Ford, who took over the reins when Nixon resigned as President in August 1974.

Reagan, on the other hand, was a hero to the conservatives with his belief in small government, tax cuts and individual freedom; he was also a resolute and active opponent of Communism. Many of the backroom officials who had helped Reagan get elected in 1980 had worked for Goldwater, notably F Clifton White, who had led the Draft Goldwater Committee which secured his candidacy. Reagan was also much assisted by a diverse group of activists known as the Second New Right who had picked up the baton of conservatism after Goldwater had lost the 1964 election: more savvy than their predecessors, they polished his populist policies to make them more acceptable to the wider electorate, and with spectacular success. It is said of Reagan's debt to Goldwater that following the latter's failure in 1964 it took sixteen years to count the votes.

No fewer than three Presidents were inspired by Goldwater and benefited from his groundwork – after Reagan came George HW Bush and George W Bush, both in the same mould. The latter in particular conjured up memories of the Texas senator with his propensity for making unvarnished and impolitic comments. One former Goldwater acolyte, however, turned in the opposite direction – Hillary Rodham, a devout Young Republican and former Goldwater Girl, married the Democrat Bill Clinton in 1975 and became First Lady of the United States when he took up office as President in January 1993.

★ ★ ★ ★ ★

The struggle for African-American Civil Rights has been long and hard and some would argue that there is still a long way to go. It is undeniable that the Civil Rights Act of 1964 was a significant milestone – even allowing for the fact that making something illegal, in this case, racial discrimination, does not necessarily produce an immediate change in attitudes. Yet it failed to alleviate the tensions that had bedevilled US race relations in the run-up to legislation. Paradoxically, things seemed to get worse, with riots in Watts, Los Angeles, in 1965 and two years later in Detroit, Michigan. Both were sparked off by relatively minor incidents but below the surface there was deep seated resentment that the Act was not being fully adhered to and that some States, including California, were actively trying to block some of its provisions.

Martin Luther King, who had done so much to bring the Act about, continued to campaign fiercely. In 1965 he became concerned at the turn of events in Vietnam and spoke out vehemently against American involvement there. The following year he was active in Chicago, coming together with likeminded individuals and organisations under the aegis of the Chicago Freedom Movement and in early 1968 he spearheaded the Poor People's Campaign, designed to secure government resources for the nation's poorest citizens. On 4 April Martin Luther King was assassinated at the Lorraine Motel, Memphis. Though only one of many Civil Rights martyrs of the 1960s, King's death was one of the defining moments of the decade and he is now considered one of the greatest Americans of the 20th century. Guido van Rijn has calculated that almost 200 songs include mentions of King, as opposed to only one about Malcolm X.

Had Malcolm lived longer, then perhaps there would have been more. As we have seen, by the time of his murder in February 1965, he had developed a philosophy that, in its way, was just as convincing as King's and in certain respects, complementary to it. It is possible to link some of the more violent disturbances, such as those in Watts and Detroit, to the uncompromising statements made by Malcolm in 1964 – part of the 'American nightmare' he referred to in his speech in Cleveland on 3 April. Similarly, he may be seen as the inspiration behind Black Power, an expression coined in 1966 by Willie Ricks and Stokely Carmichael following the shooting of James Meredith at the March Against Fear. While it was a broad term – little more than a concept – covering multiple ideologies, Black Power certainly encompassed the notions of black nationalism and black separatism promoted by Malcolm. Nonetheless, in retrospect it is clear that what he was advocating most of all was the right of African-Americans to self-determination and the consequent formation of a movement that would be open to all his countrymen, irrespective of ethnic origin, and link with nations across the world, especially in Africa.

Partly perhaps because of Malcolm, Africa occupied a special place in the consciousness of jazz musicians. On a purely technical level there were clear connections between jazz and the music of West Africa (sometimes known as 'African retentions' and a subject of academic study). But of still greater appeal were the spiritual links first evoked by pieces like John Coltrane's 'Africa' and 'Dahomey Dance' (both 1961) and followed up in 1964 by such diverse releases as Yusef Lateef's *Jazz 'Round The World* – which included the Babatunde Olatunji composition, 'Abana'

– Randy Weston's *African Breakfast* and *Juju* by Wayne Shorter.

But neither Lateef nor Weston possessed the gravitas of Coltrane – his successor in that respect was Archie Shepp. As we have seen, Shepp recorded four of Trane's compositions on his 1964 debut album as a leader, together with one of his own, implying that he saw himself as his *musical* heir. But from 1965 onwards he rivalled, and eventually surpassed, Coltrane in terms both of raw emotionalism and political commitment. It was almost as if he now took Malcolm X for his role model rather than the visionary saxophonist. Three days after Malcolm's murder, Shepp began work on *Fire Music*, which included the tribute, 'Malcolm, Malcolm, Semper Malcolm'. On the follow-up, *On This Night*, he dedicated the title track to WEB Du Bois and this, and subsequent, albums contained compositions by Duke Ellington.

But together with these expressions of respect came unfettered, ferocious free improvisation which seemed to encapsulate both his anger at the continuing injustice being perpetrated on African-Americans and the violence of the riots in Watts and Detroit. It was almost as if his music was a continuous tone poem reflecting the progress (or lack of it) of Civil Rights since the 1964 Act. Increasingly, too, Shepp focussed on Africa: in 1967 there was 'The Magic Of Ju-Ju', in 1968, 'New Africa', and in 1969 he travelled to the Pan-African Festival in Algiers where he recorded a live album accompanied by North African musicians.

By this time Shepp had begun to work with members of the Art Ensemble of Chicago, a group that had grown out of the Association for the Advancement of Creative Musicians (AACM), its name an ironic twist on the National Association for the Advancement of Coloured People (NAACP). Formed in May 1965, the AACM mirrored the communal and co-operative spirit among African-Americans fostered by both Martin Luther King and Malcolm X. Musically, the Art Ensemble were just as radical as the likes of Shepp, Eric Dolphy and Albert Ayler, but their work was characterised by a greater sense of space and a greater sense of humour. Like Shepp they began to dress in tribal costumes and, in addition, employ a huge variety of African melodic and percussion effects, creating a musical fusion with jazz and other idioms from around the world that has continued into the 21st century.

★ ★ ★ ★ ★

Regrettably, the real Africa of 1964 and beyond did not measure up to the images so lovingly fostered in the USA. Although aid, loans and investment from the West were on the increase (motivated, at least, in part by the potential return to be gained from the continent's rich natural resources) much of it would never benefit the investor, nor indeed the vast majority of the people in the country concerned. For by then, the newly independent nations were locked in a cycle that would repeat itself as more and more countries escaped colonial rule:

INDEPENDENCE>DEMOCRACY >
CORRUPTION>DICTATORSHIP>MILITARY COUP/REVOLUTION

So many African countries can be plotted on to this continuum at any given time. In 1964, for example, Ghana had reached the stage of Dictatorship: in 1966 there was a Military Coup. Corruption in Nigeria had begun almost immediately after independence: by 1966 there was a Revolution, led by the Military. Malawi and Kenya became one-party states in 1964 – in the former, Hastings Banda declared himself president for life in 1971, crushing any challenge with the utmost brutality and even in the latter, one of the more successful African nations, an outspoken opponent of the Kenyatta regime, JM Kariuki, was murdered by the president's henchmen.

Much of the corruption in Africa centred on the particular head of state and his friends and relatives, but government officials also tended to benefit. According to Martin Meredith (*The State Of Africa*, p. 171),

Senegal's budget for 1964 shows that 47 per cent of the total was allocated to civil service salaries. In the Central African Republic and

Côte d'Ivoire the figure was 58 per cent; in Congo-Brazzaville, 62 per cent; in Dahomey, 65 per cent.

With such lavish protection, government employees were not about to sponsor any attempts to unseat their president.

Of all the African nations trapped in a downward spiral, none plummeted faster than the Congo – indeed the pattern shown above was completed in a matter of five years, from independence in 1960 to the rule of President Joseph Mobutu which began in 1965. Furthermore, Mobutu presided over a repeat of the cycle – but this time it spanned no less than 32 years. In 1971 he renamed his country Zaïre, part of a sequence of measures designed to dissociate it from the era of colonisation under the Belgians. But it had no impact on the way in which the country was run – Mobutu remained a corrupt, repressive and egomaniacal dictator who, nevertheless, had the good sense to win American support by his anti-Communist posturing – indeed as late as 1989 Mobutu was being described by President George HW Bush as 'an intelligent, open and sensitive man … one of our most valued friends' (Meredith, *op. cit.*, p.308). As Carolyn Henson reported for the *Seattle Times* on 3 January 1997, just weeks before he fled the country, Mobutu had amassed a fortune of at least $5 billion,

> most of it allegedly taken from state coffers … Despite great natural wealth in diamonds, gold, cobalt and other precious resources, in the thirty-one years of Mobutu rule Zaire has become one of the most corrupt and impoverished countries in Africa.

Given the repugnant nature of the Mobutu regime, it would be reasonable to suppose that the top Congolese musician Franco, not known for hiding his feelings, might have been moved to speak out in protest. Yet, no doubt aware of how the president treated his critics, he took care to be on the right side of Mobutu. The programme of 'Authenticity' under which the Congo became Zaïre was good for native musicians in that it reaffirmed their faith in their own music and Franco lent his support by taking the name L'Okanga La Ndju Pene Luambo Makiadi. As Graeme Ewens has written (*Congo Colossus*, p. 237):

> Franco was always clear about his obligations to the state. "It is my job to explain Mobutu's actions to the public," he once said. "The songs are not political, but we use music to spread information, for the government and on other topics."

But as ever, it would be unwise to accept Franco's songs at face value:

> Even such a piece of overt propaganda as Candidat Na Biso Mobutu, the campaign song for the 1984 presidential election, contains a kind of back-handed praise. The inevitability of the result in a single-candidate election is made clear; and to repeat the song on two sides of an album could also be interpreted as a sly joke or casual devaluation of the message. (*ibid.*)

In a strange sort of way, Mobutu's attitude to traditional culture was not so very different from that of the South African regime. Both saw it as a means to prevent external influences from contaminating their people and trap them into a restricted, submissive and backward-looking mindset; and in response, like Franco, South African songwriters looked for double-meaning and innuendo to convey their message of resistance.

Yet in 1964 it was difficult to sustain morale. The exodus of the country's foremost musicians continued unabated and in June the African nationalists were dealt what seemed like a fatal blow with the incarceration of Nelson Mandela and other members of the MK hierarchy. The ANC and PAC were banned and although they both set up offices in exile their ability to spearhead opposition and insurrection was much diminished. Slowly but surely, however, the resistance effort got back on track, encouraged by a combination of factors.

Firstly, Hendrik Verwoerd was assassinated on 6 September 1966 and replaced as the head of the National Party, and hence Prime Minister, by John Vorster. While an implacable believer in apartheid, Vorster was marginally more liberal than his predecessor and initiated a series of enquiries into economic and constitutional matters, all of which suggested he was open to the possibility of change. His successor, PW Botha, who had chaired one of these commissions, was still more interested in reform, even if apartheid remained non-negotiable. His twelve-point plan of August 1979 aimed, among other things, to improve the housing, education and employment opportunities for black South Africans.

In the meantime, though, the government continued to clamp down on any opposition. In 1967 the Terrorism Act had banned all non-racial political parties, the effect of which was to squeeze any protest into illegal gatherings on the street. And as young South Africans looked to the United States for their example these became more militant. In Soweto, on 16 June 1976, what began as a student protest at having to be taught in Afrikaans turned into a full-scale riot which spread outside the immediate area and, in time, to other areas of the country. By the time the sequence of disturbances, known as the Soweto Uprising, came to an end over 500 people had been killed.

Such demonstrations reflected a growing sense of dissatisfaction among young people that also found expression in the Black Consciousness movement centred around the leader of the South African Student Association, Steve Biko. The central tenet of Black Consciousness was self-determination for black South Africans – a clear echo of the philosophy of Malcolm X. Indeed, Biko was a comparably gifted orator whose eloquence posed as great a threat to the government as violent protests. No doubt that was why he was murdered in a police cell in September 1977, an episode which generated a wave of international outrage and did as much as anything to bring about the downfall of the South African regime.

Another crucial factor was the cultural boycott of South Africa that reached its climax in 1981 when the Associated Actors and Artists of America forbade its members to work there. That some high-profile singers, notably Frank Sinatra, continued to do so served, in many eyes, only to publicise the country's isolation. Yet for others it was an excuse to keep visiting the country and collect the substantial rewards for doing so, and it was this – as well as Ronald Reagan's policy of appeasement – that in 1985 inspired Bruce Springsteen to write 'Sun City', a condemnation of such morally-bankrupt performers and the eponymous glittering venue that attracted them.

1985 proved to be a pivotal year in South Africa's history. In January, Botha announced that he was prepared to release Nelson Mandela if he were to renounce violence. Mandela rejected the offer, calling for Botha to do the same, but it was an important signal. Then, in response to a series of disturbances now termed the Black Uprising, Botha declared a state of national emergency. And in June, the ANC held a successful conference in Zambia which reaffirmed their vision of a transformation in South African society and rejecting any notion of a settlement with the Government.

Above all it was becoming manifestly clear that Botha's reforms had not worked and that his administration was in disarray. Even the Bantu leaders, erstwhile collaborators on the homelands policy that had herded black South Africans into ancient, and mostly fatuous, tribal groupings, were no longer acquiescent puppets. For example, Gatsha Buthelezi, who back in 1964 had played his great-grandfather, also a Chief, in the film *Zulu*, had become an outspoken critic of the Government and was now an important political player, presiding over both the semi-independent state of KwaZulu and the Inkatha Freedom Party. Though no supporter of the ANC, Buthelezi kept contact with Mandela during his imprisonment and argued for his release.

By the late 1980s, national and international demands to free Mandela had reached a crescendo, culminating in the Wembley Stadium concert on 11 June 1988 to celebrate his 70th birthday. Introduced by Harry Belafonte and featuring a host of stars including Miriam Makeba and Hugh Masekela, it was broadcast to 67 countries and an audience of 600 million. It is not known whether FW de Klerk was one of them, but on 2

February 1990 in his first speech to parliament as President of South Africa, he announced that all bans on political parties were lifted, that the ANC was now legal again and that the policy of apartheid had failed. Ten days later, Mandela was set free. His imprisonment in 1964 had become a totem for the struggle against oppression both in his own country and throughout the world.

De Klerk's speech had the effect of transforming South Africa – it was almost as if a new nation was being created. But that brought with it a host of new problems, some of which only set in after the initial period of euphoria. That had been Jamaica's experience, too, following independence in 1962. For the first couple of years times were good: the ska boom of 1964 symbolised the spirit of optimism that bathed the country. Yet a divide was growing between rich and poor which neither of the main political parties seemed concerned about in their push to boost the middle classes. In time the disaffection of the rude boys became endemic to the city ghettoes and it was symbolic that, just as enthusiasm for independence slowed down, so did the music in the dance halls.

The frenetic pace of ska morphed into the more ponderous beat of rocksteady – a result not just of musical progress within Jamaica but of the influence of American soul in which the ballads of Otis Redding and Curtis Mayfield were an important feature. The texture of the sound was also changing with greater prominence given to bass guitar and less to trumpets, trombones and saxophones. While acknowledging both of these factors in the emergence of rocksteady, Lloyd Bradley additionally draws attention to the 'atmosphere of trepidation in the dancehalls … patrons, whether rudie or not, needed to be on their guard':

> And as for the effect on the music, it meant less fancy footwork, shuffling or jiving as couples, and more remaining rooted to the spot, moving from the hips and shoulders. You know, rocking steady, either by yourself or locked tight to your best girl, but staying strictly in your own space, ever alert to what was going on around or managing to look detachedly menacing. (*op. cit.*, p.164)

At the same time, Rastafari was taking root. It appealed both to the poor and to disenchanted intellectuals, since it combined the belief in spiritual deliverance common in oppressed communities with a robust ideology, albeit at times shrouded in mysticism. Although there had been Rastas in Jamaica since the 1930s, their morale, and numbers, were bolstered by the visit to Jamaica in 1966 of the Emperor of Ethiopia, Haile Selassie, whose pre-regnal name Ras Tafari gave the movement its title. The Emperor's visit also conferred respectability on the Rastas, who had been regarded up until then as social outcasts. Yet the government continued to view them with suspicion and 1968 refused the readmission to Jamaica of the black nationalist Walter Rodney who had helped bring Rastafari to the island's ghettoes.

By then, there was a new trend in Jamaican music, reggae, and Rastafari would provide a good part of its vocabulary. Just as rocksteady had been a reaction to ska, so reggae was a reaction to rocksteady. More flexible and diverse than its predecessor, reggae was characterised by a quicker beat and the use of new sounds and sound effects. To begin with, reggae lyrics were innocuous but before too long they became permeated by social and political comment and/or Rasta themes and their associated Biblical allusions. This applied equally to some of the biggest hits of the genre, including 'The Israelites' by Desmond Dekker (1969) and 'Blood And Fire' by Winston Holness (also known as Niney The Observer) in 1970. For many, the ultimate expression of reggae came in the early 1970s with Bob Marley and The Wailers, who had married music and politics so effectively with 'Simmer Down' back in 1964.

★ ★ ★ ★ ★

The popularity of reggae was widespread and almost instantaneous – even The Beatles got on the bandwagon with their 'Ob-La-Di, Ob-La-Da' of 1968. But reggae was just one of the musical genres interwoven into the double album set *The Beatles* (otherwise known as the White Album) which came out in the November of that year. It is in many ways hard to believe that the musical progression evident in this release had taken place in the four short years since *A Hard Day's Night*.

In 1964, The Beatles had produced a blueprint which it seemed would endure forever, but it is now clear that the innovations they introduced then were just the beginning of what was to become a golden epoch, both for them and for pop music as a whole.

To begin with, all of the songs on *A Hard Day's Night* were original compositions by members of the band (Lennon and McCartney) – a first not only for The Beatles but for British pop. This meant that they also had some conception of how they would like the recordings to sound, unlike previous generations of pop stars who were at the mercy of producers, arrangers and engineers – and, sometimes, the writers themselves. During 1964 we see the balance of power between The Beatles and George Martin reaching a state of equilibrium – a partnership which would flourish over the next five years and capitalise on the creativity of both parties.

Nowhere is this better illustrated in the search for new sounds which began in 1964. The jangly guitar sound on 'A Hard Day's Night', the fade-in on 'Eight Days A Week' and the use of feedback on 'I Feel Fine' were the first examples of sonic experimentation that was to culminate in tracks like 'Eleanor Rigby', 'Tomorrow Never Knows', 'Being For The Benefit Of Mr Kite!' and 'I Am The Walrus'. George Martin played a crucial role in all of these, giving shape and substance to the band's flights of fancy.

Control of the songs to be recorded also resulted in greater influence over the whole process of issuing an album, especially the appearance of the finished product. From 1964 onwards, the sleeve designs on Beatles records became more ambitious, culminating in the extravagance of *Sgt Pepper's Lonely Hearts Club Band* and its complete antithesis, the White Album, designed by eminent Pop Artists Peter Blake and Richard Hamilton respectively and both conforming to The Beatles' wishes. But more importantly, it gave them the authority to govern the content and theme of their releases, the high watermark in this respect coming in 1967 with the 'concept' single about Liverpool, 'Strawberry Fields Forever'/

'Penny Lane', and its follow-up on an appropriately larger scale, the 'concept' album about Britain, *Sgt Pepper.*

1964 was also the year in which The Beatles broke through internationally, commencing with their brief, but hugely important, visit to the US in February. The consequences of their worldwide fame were so far-reaching as to be almost impossible to quantify but certainly, whatever your point of view, they transcended the entertainment industry. For what The Beatles, albeit unwittingly, initiated was a shift in social mores, especially in the West, the repercussions of which are still being felt today. Their music, appearance and attitude led directly to the 'permissive' society which, while it ceased to be a reality 40 years ago, opened up freedoms of class, race and gender that once gained, cannot be reversed. Not everyone has regarded this as a good thing – subsequent governments in both Britain and America have blamed society's ills on the challenges to accepted behaviour that characterised the mid-1960s. Yet such pronouncements serve only to cement the belief that the events of the era were pivotal in shaping contemporary life.

As this book has endeavoured to show, The Beatles, though they may have been figureheads, were by no means the only influence on the changes that took place in, and resulted from, 1964. Indeed, it could be argued that in purely musical terms, The Rolling Stones were of comparable significance. That is because The Stones were the harbingers of the music that has dominated youth culture for the last 50 years, rock. By using the structures, sounds and songs of R&B and blues, they injected into popular culture a powerful stimulant to both mind and body – music with a respectable pedigree that appealed to intellectual and egalitarian leanings but which you could also dance (or generally shake about) to.

In 1964 The Stones went for blues in a big way, from the Bo Diddley hambone beat that drove 'Not Fade Away' to the Muddy Waters, Jimmy Reed and Slim Harpo covers on their debut album to 'Little Red Rooster', written by Willie Dixon for the quintessential bluesman, Howlin' Wolf. Aside from the music was their attitude – unsmiling, rebellious and threatening – which took The Beatles' disregard for authority to the level of contempt. This was just the image to captivate young people increasingly disillusioned with the world constructed by their parents and remained the stance adopted by rock artists from that day to this.

Behind The Rolling Stones came a queue of bands looking to emulate them by digging into the blues back catalogue. Them, for example, formed in Belfast in April, came up with their incendiary version of 'Baby Please Don't Go', while The Animals had an enormous hit in the summer with 'The House Of The Rising Sun'. The Yardbirds, who had followed The Stones into a residency at the Crawdaddy, naturally had a repertoire drawn from very similar sources, but John Mayall, another regular on the London blues scene, wrote his own material, albeit hugely derivative of Chicago and the Mississippi Delta.

It was The Yardbirds and Mayall, both of whom made their first recordings under their own name in 1964, who were to have the biggest impact on the second phase of rock development, largely because they both employed Eric Clapton who as a musician in his own right and as a member of Cream came to define its guitar sound, effectively the core element of the music. Another member of The Yardbirds was Jimmy Page, a former session guitarist who had played on a number of hit records of 1964 including 'Baby Please Don't Go', The Nashville Teens' 'Tobacco Road', 'As Tears Go By' by Marianne Faithfull and PJ Proby's 'Hold Me'. Together with Robert Plant, John Paul Jones and John Bonham, Page formed The New Yardbirds, re-named a short time later as Led Zeppelin.

Despite a myriad of subsequent trends and fashions, rock music has not gone away – in the 1990s, for instance, there was an enormous revival when grunge, spearheaded by Nirvana, and the Britpop of Oasis ruled the roost, and today bands like The Foo Fighters and The Red Hot Chili Peppers continue to appeal to legions of fans around the world.

As for the originators of this music, the blues artists themselves, they too benefited from the popularity of rock music, if to a much smaller extent. Some received royalties for songs they had written many years before (though in some cases, not without a fight: Willie Dixon had to sue

Led Zeppelin for basing 'Whole Lotta Love' on his song 'You Need Love'); others enhanced their income by touring Europe; only a tiny number, including John Lee Hooker and Buddy Guy, achieved success commensurate with even a second division rock star.

Subsequent generations of African-Americans who built on the blues and R&B tradition fared much better. 1964 saw the first Motown record to reach number one on both sides of the Atlantic – The Supremes' 'Baby Love' – and thereafter Berry Gordy's label became a part of the American entertainment mainstream.   For the remainder of the 1960s it blended aesthetic excellence with commercial success through recordings like The Four Tops' 'Reach Out I'll Be There', The Supremes' 'You Keep Me Hanging On' and Marvin Gaye's 'I Heard It Through The Grapevine', but the formula became too constraining for artists like Gaye and Stevie Wonder whose music became more social aware and, at times, overtly political.

Soul music had begun to take that road in 1964 and continued to do so in a seamless line of development that led ultimately to funk and hip-hop. As we have seen, Curtis Mayfield started the ball rolling with 'Keep On Pushing' and followed it up with the yet more explicit 'People Get Ready' (1965), 'We're A Winner' (1968) and 'Move On Up' (1970). But it was James Brown who was the major figure in this transition. His 1964 record 'Out Of Sight' virtually defined funk (and, for that matter, pointed the way to hip-hop), and from 'Don't Be A Dropout' (1966) onwards his music was infused with social and political comment. 'Say It Loud – I'm Black And I'm Proud', released after the assassination of Martin Luther King, may have damaged his prospects of crossover stardom – he never made the US Top Ten again for the rest of his career – but it endeared him to the African-American community to whom he remained a hero, and a huge musical influence, for the rest of his life.

Despite a reputation as one of the greatest jazz artists of all time, Miles Davis looked on Brown's career with envy. Following the recruitment of Wayne Shorter to his quintet in 1964, the trumpeter released a superlative string of albums which combined compositional and improvisational originality – indeed this group were, and still are, considered on a par with any in jazz history. Yet most of the people who bought his records were middle class and white; jazz, in addition, was fast becoming a minority interest, with a market polarised between nostalgia and the sort of relentless experimentation that was emptying the clubs with great rapidity. Davis set out to broaden his appeal to include the African-American audience that had eluded him, while at the same time aspiring to the record sales and earnings of rock musicians. Arguably more successful in the second objective than the first, Davis did, however, create a new form of music, jazz-rock, which – albeit often in its diluted form, fusion – became ubiquitous in the 1970s and 1980s.

In the UK, soul music inspired a trend of a very different kind. In 1964, the priority for the mods had been their clothes. Indeed it was something of an obsession, marking out the 'faces' from their followers, the 'tickets', and distinguishing them most of all from their adversaries, the rockers. But as media interest in the mods began to wane and their favourite bands, such as The Who and, subsequently, The Small Faces, moved into mainstream rock music, what was left of their music became equally (and ultimately more) important.

Typically, though, it was not the well-known artists from Motown or Stax that attracted the mods but the more obscure performers on the more obscure labels – indeed the cachet of discovering a great record by a singer no-one had heard of ranked with setting a new sartorial fashion – that is, the ultimate accolade for a mod. This tendency was most apparent in mods from the north of England, hence the epithet for the music, Northern Soul. It flourished in clubs such as the Wigan Casino and the Twisted Wheel in Manchester (originally located on the aptly-named Brazennose Street), characterised by their marathon, all-night sessions. Against all the odds, Northern Soul has not only survived to this day but has played a crucial role in the growth of British dance/DJ culture.

★ ★ ★ ★ ★

Together with musical change came political change, the two bound together in a complex web of reciprocal influence. For music was affecting society which in turn was reflected in politics. At the same time politics, and specifically governmental decisions, created the environment which enabled and/or inspired musicians to flourish. Although it is not always possible to distinguish the chicken from the egg, this interrelationship was dynamic, highly tuned and constantly fluctuating in its emphasis. In short, it led to the Swinging Sixties.

The newly-elected Labour government of 1964 pursued its programme with vigour and attracted almost universal praise. As Ben Pimlott has written (*op. cit.*, p.356):

> Labour kept ahead in the polls for all but four months during the 1964-6 Parliament, while Wilson's personal rating stayed above 50 per cent almost throughout ... The new Government was judged a success – bright, energetic and symbolised by Wilson. Foreigners acknowledged it, and so even did the Tories.

And so did the electorate: at the General Election of 31 March 1966, Labour were returned with an increased majority.

A major priority was to eliminate discrimination on grounds of race, class and gender, and so making a reality of the equality of opportunity heralded in the manifesto.

As early as the House of Commons debate on the Queen's Speech, less than three weeks after the 1964 Election, Wilson stated that the Conservative MP, Peter Griffiths, whose campaign in Smethwick had been shaped by the racism of his supporters, would 'serve his time there as a Parliamentary leper'. Within a year, the Race Relations Act was passed outlawing racial discrimination in public places, strengthened in 1968 to cover housing and employment.

While stopping short of abolishing fee-paying schools, Labour also expanded the provision of comprehensive education and created a new type of higher education institution, the Polytechnics, which were to specialise in vocational subjects and award degrees which, at least in theory, would be on a par with the traditional 'academic' universities. And, a pet project of Wilson's, an 'Open' University was created at which adults who had not, for various reasons, been unable to get a degree could now do so by studying in their own homes.

Finally, and in the face of opposition both from employers and trade unions, came the Equal Pay Act of 1970, which gave parity of earnings to men and women doing the same job.

The government also took on the moral issues of the day – homosexuality and abortion were legalised, the death penalty abolished and legislation amended to allow divorce to take place for reasons of marital breakdown. They also ended censorship in the theatre and pursued constitutional reforms including the devolution of powers to Scotland and Wales.

All of the above had an impact on young people to some degree, and the result of the education and employment reforms was that the gap between rich and poor was reduced, also a positive factor in the welfare of the young. But the key measure came in 1968 when the voting age was reduced to eighteen. Wilson's conscious effort to woo young people had come a long way in the four years since he had appeared with The Beatles at the Annual Luncheon of the Variety Club of Great Britain. Now he saw the band as generators of revenue for the British exchequer and ensured that, in 1965, the Queen repaid them by awarding them each an MBE. Such direct contact between the leader of a country and pop group was unprecedented but much imitated – both in the US by Jimmy Carter, Bill Clinton and even George W Bush as well as in the UK where, shortly after becoming Prime Minister in 1997, Tony Blair famously invited Oasis to his celebratory party at 10 Downing Street.

Unfortunately for him, Wilson's extension of the franchise to eighteen-year-olds did not bring victory in the General Election of 1970. By then, culture, society and politics were very different – but that is a subject for another book.

★ ★ ★ ★ ★

At that luncheon at the Variety Club, Harold Wilson had unwittingly hit on one of the factors that made 1964 a turning-point for pop music: indeed he mocked the fact that the music correspondent of *The Times* (William Mann) had applied the vocabulary of classical music criticism to The Beatles. Yet this was a development of enormous significance – for the first time in its history, pop was being taken seriously. Indeed, as the writers Gestur Gudmundsson, Ulf Lindberg, Morten Michelsen and Hans Weisethaunet point out (*Pop Music And The Press*, p. 41), 'The period 1964-69 marks the genesis of rock criticism proper'.

But naturally enough, this only reflected what was going on in the music itself. Bob Dylan and the protest singers, the darker themes creeping into The Beach Boys' records, Sam Cooke and Curtis Mayfield with their allusions to Civil Rights, the iconoclasm of The Rolling Stones – all of this merited a more rigorous analysis than the fanzines of the time were able to give. And of course there were The Beatles – worthy of scrutiny on a sociological and cultural as well as musical level. Yet this was just a part of the study of popular culture more generally that was formalised at Birmingham University's Centre for Contemporary Cultural Studies and in books such as Marshall McLuhan's *Understanding Media: The Extensions Of Man*. Thus it was not just the substance of popular culture that was changing in 1964 but the means of describing it.

As we saw earlier in this chapter, not everything that happened in 1964 was completely new – each period in history is inevitably a function of what came before. But such was the surge in energy, flair and imagination that any innovation, perceived or real, seemed to stimulate another, often across disciplines. Alongside major musical and political developments there were massive advances in almost every sphere of human endeavour – fashion, film, art, broadcasting, science and technology – all of which symbolised the spirit of the age: a New Beginning with young people at the forefront, young people who were educated, inspired, liberated, at times provoked, not just to wish and hope but to do – to create and to achieve.

Times were changing: it was the start of an era in which anything seemed possible.

Bibliography

Gwen Ansell – *Soweto Blues* (Continuum, 2005)

Michael Archer – *Art Since 1960* (Thames and Hudson, 2002)

James Barber – *South Africa In the Twentieth Century* (Blackwell, 1999)

Steve Barrow and Peter Dalton – *Reggae: The Rough Guide* (Rough Guides Ltd, 1998)

The Beatles Anthology (Apple Corps, 2000)

Chuck Berry – *The Autobiography* (Faber and Faber, London, 1988)

Bill Birch – *Keeper Of The Flame: Modern Jazz In Manchester 1946-1972* (Self-published, 2010)

Rudi Blesh – *Shining Trumpets* (Alfred A Knopf, 1946 – Da Capo, 1980 edition cited in this book)

Lloyd Bradley – *Bass Culture* (Viking, 2000 – Penguin edition cited in this book)

Bill Brewster and Frank Broughton) – *Last Night A DJ Saved My Life* (Headline Book Publishing, London, 2000)

British Hit Singles And Albums, 19th Edition (Guinness World Records Limited, 2006)

David Brun-Lambert – *Nina Simone: The Biography* (Aurum Press, London, 2010)

H. Joseph Carnie – *Talking To The Centre: Different Voices In The Intellectual History Of The Centre For Contemporary Cultural Studies* (University of British Columbia)

Ian Carr – *Miles Davis* (Quartet Books, 1982 – Paladin, 1985 edition cited in this book)

James H Cone – *Martin & Malcolm & America* (Orbis Books, 1991)

Robert Dallek – *Lyndon B Johnson – Portrait Of A President* (Oxford University Press, 2004 – Penguin edition cited in this book)

Dave – *The Manchester Wheelers: A Northern Quadrophenia* (Soul Publications, 2008)

Miles Davis with Quincy Troupe – *Miles: The Autobiography* (Simon and Schuster, New York – Picador, 1990 edition cited in this book)

Susan Douglas – *Where The Girls Are* (Penguin, 1995)

WEB Du Bois – *The Souls Of Black Folk* (first published 1903 – Paperview, 2005 edition cited in this book)

Max du Preez – *The Rough Guide To Nelson Mandela* (Rough Guides Ltd, 2011)

Graeme Ewens – *Congo Colossus* (Buku Press, 1994)

Betty Friedan – *The Feminine Mystique* (WW Norton, 1963 – Penguin, 1992 edition cited in this book)

Jonathon Green – *All Dressed Up* (Pimlico, 1999)

John Greenway – *unpublished memoir*

Peter Guralnick – *Feel Like Going Home* (Omnibus Press, 1978)

Peter Guralnick – *Sweet Soul Music* (Harper and Row, 1986 – Penguin, 1991 edition cited in this book)

Lionel Hampton with James Haskins – *Hamp* (Robson Books, 1990)

Michael Haralambos – *Right On: From Blues To Soul In Black America* (Eddison Press, London, 1974)

Jeff Hannusch – *I Hear You Knockin'* (Swallow Publications, Ville Platte, Louisiana, 1985)

David Hatch and Stephen Millward – *From Blues To Rock: An Analytical History Of Pop Music* (Manchester University Press, 1987)

Richard Hoggart – *The Uses Of Literacy* (Chatto and Windus, 1957)

Lord Home – *The Way The Wind Blows* (William Collins Sons and Co. Ltd, Glasgow, 1976 – Fontana, 1978 edition cited in this book)

Steve Jones (editor) – *Pop Music And The Press* (Temple University Press, Philadelphia, 2007)

Stanley Karnow – *Vietnam: A History* (The Viking Press, New York, 1983*)*

Ashley Khan – *A Love Supreme: The Creation Of John Coltrane's Classic Album* (Granta Books, 2002)

Miles Kington – *The Jazz Anthology* (HarperCollins, London,1992 – 1993 paperback edition cited in this book)

Let's Go With Labour For The New Britain (The Labour Party, 1964)

John Litweiler – *The Freedom Principle: Jazz After 1958* (Blandford Press, 1984)

Joe Levy (editor*)* – *Rolling Stone: The 500 Greatest Albums Of All Time* (Wenner Books, 2005*)*

Mark Lewisohn – *The Complete Beatles Recording Sessions* (Hamlyn, London, 1988)

Mark Lewisohn – *The Complete Beatles Chronicle* (Pyramid, London, 1992)

Ian MacDonald – *Revolution In The Head: The Beatles' Records And The Sixties* (Pimlico, 1998)

Dave Marsh – *Before I Get Old: The Story Of The Who* (Plexus, London, 1983)

Martin Meredith – *The State Of Africa* (The Free Press, 2006)

J. William Middendorf II – *A Glorious Disaster* (Basic Books, New York, 2006)

Philip Norman – *The Stones* (Elm Tree Books/Hamish Hamilton – Pan Books, 2002 edition cited in this book)

Paul Oliver – *The Meaning Of The Blues* (Macmillan, 1960 – Collier Books edition cited in this book)

John Pidgeon – *Eric Clapton* (Panther Books, 1976)

Ben Pimlott – *Harold Wilson* (HarperCollins, London, 1993)

Keith Potter – *Four Musical Minimalists* (Cambridge University Press, 2000)

Brian Priestley – *Mingus: A Critical Biography* (Quartet, London, 1982)

Ron Ramdin – *Martin Luther King, Jr* (Haus Publishing, London, 2004)

Guido van Rijn – *President Johnson's Blues* (Agram Blues Books, The Netherlands, 2009)

The Rough Guide To World Music (Rough Guides Ltd, 1999)

Sheila Rowbotham – *Promise Of A Dream: Remembering The Sixties* (Verso, 2001)

Anthony Scaduto – *Bob Dylan* (Abacus, London, 1972)

Dale Spender – *For The Record* (The Women's Press, London, 1985)

Gary Stewart – *Rumba On The River* (Verso, London, 2000)

Frank Tirro – *Jazz: A History* (JM Dent, London, 1979)

Joel Whitburn – *The Billboard Book Of Top 40 Hits (Guinness Superlatives, 1983)*

Dave van der Vat and Michele Whitby – *Eel Pie Island* (Frances Lincoln, London, 2005)

Richard Williams – *Out Of His Head* (Abacus, 1974)

Mary Wilson – *Dreamgirl* (Cooper Square Press edition, 1999)

Tom Wolfe – *The Electric Kool-Aid Acid Test* (Farrar, Strauss and Giroux, 1968 – Bantam edition cited in this book)

Joe Wood (editor) – *Malcolm X In Our Own Image* (St Martin's Press, New York, 1992)

Malcolm X with the assistance of Alex Haley – *The Autobiography Of Malcolm X* (Grove Press, New York, 1965)

Acknowledgements

At various points in this book I have quoted from other authors, giving the name of the work concerned and the page number of the edition I have used. Publication details of these works can be found in the Bibliography.

Details of Beatles itinerary and recording dates are derived from the Mark Lewisohn books listed in the Bibliography.

Elsewhere, information on records, when not obtained directly from the releases themselves, comes from:

- the Joel Whitburn and Guinness World Records books cited in the Bibliography
- *www.discogs.com*
- *www.sixtiescity.ca*
- *www.wikipedia.org*

Information on the release date of films is derived from *Halliwell's Film Guide, Ninth Edition* (HarperCollins, 1993) edited by John Walker. All details of Academy Award nominations and winners come from *www.oscars.org.*

The quotes in Chapter 2 from Harold Wilson's speech at the Twelfth Annual Luncheon of the Variety Club of Great Britain and from the interview with The Beatles following their first visit to the USA both derive from the bonus footage accompanying the VHS release of *A Hard Day's Night* (VCI VS 6509).

Reference is made to the following DVDs:

- *British Movietone News: The Golden Years: 1964* (PMI/C21C)
- *The Jazz Icons series (Reelin' In The Years Productions)* – *Charles Mingus* (DVWW-JICHB), *Dexter Gordon* (2.119002), *Chet Baker* (2.119006)
- *Masters Of Jazz* (Metrodome MTD5199)
- *Pathé News: A Year To Remember: 1964* (Pathé)
- *Six Quick Ones (*Spitfire Pictures/Universal*)*

Grateful acknowledgement is made for permission to use the extract from *Eel Pie Island* by Dave van der Vat and Michele Whitby in Chapter 4.

As regards song lyrics, permission to quote has been obtained from the song publishers listed below. According to the database of PRS for Music, the publishers of the remaining songs from which I quote in this book cannot be traced and/or are unknown.

'The Times They Are A-Changin''
Lyrics by Bob Dylan
Copyright ©1963; renewed 1991 Special Rider Music
Administered by Sony/ATV Music Publishing
All rights reserved. Used by permission.

'Universal Soldier'
Written by Buffy Sainte-Marie
Published by ALMO MUSIC CORP. on behalf of CALEB MUSIC

'Can Blue Men Sing The Whites'
Words and Music by Vivian Stanshall © 1968
Reproduced by permission of EMI Music Publishing Ltd, London W8 5SW

'Dancing In The Street'
Words and Music by Ivy Jo Hunter, Marvin Gaye and William Stevenson © 1964
Reproduced by permission of EMI Music Publishing Ltd, London W8 5SW

Acknowledgements

'(I Read It In The) Daily News'
Words and Music by Thomas Paxton © 1964
Reproduced by permission of EMI Music Publishing Ltd, London W8 5SW

'Keep On Pushing'
Words and Music by Curtis Mayfield © 1964
Reproduced by permission of EMI Music Publishing Ltd, London W8 5SW

'Mississippi Goddam'
Words and Music by Nina Simone © 1964
Reproduced by permission of EMI Music Publishing Ltd, London W8 5SW

'Remember (Walking In The Sand)'
Words and Music by George Morton © 1964
Reproduced by permission of EMI Music Publishing Ltd, London W8 5SW

'(Walking) In The Rain'
Words and Music by Barry Mann, Phil Spector & Cynthia Weil © 1964
Reproduced by permission of EMI Music Publishing Ltd, London W8 5SW

'Wish Someone Would Care'
Words and Music by Irma Thomas © 1964
Reproduced by permission of EMI Music Publishing Ltd, London W8 5SW

'Baby Please Don't Go'
Words and Music by Joe Williams
© Copyright 1944 Leeds Music Corp. Universal/MCA Music Limited.
All Rights Reserved. International Copyright Secured.
Used by permission of Music Sales Limited

'Talking Union Blues'
Written by Lee Hays, Mill Lampell and Pete Seeger
Published by Harmony Music Limited on behalf of Stormking Music
Used with permission

Acknowledgements

'Apache Tears'
Words and Music by Johnny R Cash
Chappell & Co (ASCAP)
    All Rights Reserved

INDEX

Names in parentheses are those to which the person or organisation are referred elsewhere. Page references in italics denote use in a quotation, diagram or note.

Index

Index

Manne, Shelley, 201
Mansfield, Mike, 81
Many Characters Of Oscar Brown Jr, The (stage show), 210
Marcels, The, 40
Margulis, Max, 203
Marie Antoinette (film), 63
Marley, Bob (Bobby Martell), 33,240-1,242
and The Wailers, 313
Marsh, Dave, 117,119
Martin & Malcolm & America (book), 162
Martin, Dean, 137
Martin, George, 11-13,54-56,62,64,282,314
Marvelettes, The, 170
Mary Poppins (film), 264
Masekela, Hugh, 30,31,237,311
Mason, Dave, 274
Mathias, Mildred, 267
Matshikiza, Pat, 237
Matthew, Brian, 16
Matthews, Dave, 234
Maxwell-Davies, Peter, 48
May, Phil, 145
Mayall, John, 142-4,*147,*148,316
John Mayall with Eric Clapton, 186
Mayfield, Curtis, 165,187,312,317,321
Mead, Margaret, 39,153
Meaden, Peter, 119,120
Meat Joy (happening), 251
Medley, Phil, 14,62
Meehan, Tony, *147,*148,275
Mehegan, John, 30,31
Memphis Slim, 184
Méndez, Rubén Jaramillo, 97
Meredith, James, 305
Meredith, Martin, 307
Merrill, Bob, 263
Merry Pranksters, The, 87-9
Merseybeats, The, 70,275
Metzger, Gustav, 121,250
Metzner, Ralph, 89
Michelmore, Cliff, 277
Michelsen, Morten , 321
Middendorf III, J William, 257,303
Middlesex County Cricket Club, 281
Midnighters, The, 42
Migil 5, The, 275
Miller, Bob, 76
Miller, Glenn, 35
Miller, Roger, 258
Miller, Ronnie, 177
Milton, John, 224
Mingus, Celia, 35
Mingus, Charles, 31,35,36,187,193,195-8,206,208,*209,*219,295,296
Mini, Vuyisile, 233,234
Miracles, The, 13,121,168,178
Mittoo, Jackie, 239
Mkaba, Zinakile, 233
Mobley, Hank, 204
Mobutu, Joseph-Désiré,

24,27,229,231,308,309
Mock, Jerrie, 266
Modern Jazz Quartet, The, 214
Mods, 115-119,122,123,124,138,140,300,318
Moeketsi, Kippie, 30,31
Moholo, Louis, 31
Mojos, The, *147,*148
Monk, Thelonious, 188,193,199,203,6
Monkees, The, 1
Monterey Jazz Festival, 197
Monty Python's Flying Circus (TV show), 131
Monument Records, 259
Moody Blues, The, 146,*147,*4
Moog, Robert, 267
Moon, Keith, 119,120,121,122
Moore, John 'Dizzy', 239
Moore, Roger, 264
Morecambe and Wise Show, The (TV show), 44
Morgan, Derrick, 33,122
Derrick and Patsy, 122
Morgan, Lee, 205,206
Morgenstern, Dan, 206
Morricone, Ennio, 265
Morris, Eric 'Monty', 244
Morrison, Van, 63,140,*147,*148,149,150
Morse, Wayne, 93
Morton, George 'Shadow', 59,60,64
Most, Mickie, 145,*147*
Mothle, Ernest, 237
Motown Record Corporation, 168
Motown Records, 133,136,168-172,*176,*180,243,260,263,317,318
Movement, The (book), 210
Moyake, Nick, 31, 236
Moyers, Bill, *298*
Mozart, Wolfgang Amadeus, 289
Mthembu, Patrick, 235
Mtolo, Bruno, 235
Muhammad, Elijah, 160,161,270
Muléle, Pierre, 229
Murdoch, Iris, 278
Murdoch, Rupert, 278
Murphy, Mark, 214
Murray, Alex, *147*
Murray, Mitch, 13
Murray, Sunny, 203
Musekiwa, Isaac, 25
My Fair Lady (film), 264

NAACP (National Association for the Advancement of Coloured People), 36,154,158,189,195,306
NCNC (National Council of Nigerian Citizens), 228
NMU (National Miners Union), 76,77,104
NPC (Northern People's Congress), 228
Nashville Teens, The, *147,*149,316
Nasser, Gamal Abdel, 234
Nation of Islam, 160,161,164,270,299
National Jazz and Blues Festival (music festival), 184

Index

Price, Alan, 144,145
Price, Lloyd, 174
Prince Andrew, 279
Prince Buster, 33,238,243
Prince Charles, 279
Prince Edward, 279
Princess Alexandra, 279
Princess Margaret, 10
Proby, PJ, 146,*147*,149,316
Professionals, The (TV series), 148
Professor Longhair, 144
Profumo, John, 19,22,127,280,283
Promise Of A Dream (book), 164
Prospect Of Immortality, The (book), 267
Psychedelic Experience, The (book), 89
Psycho (film), 107
Pukwana, Dudu, 31,236
Pulp Fiction (film), 173
Puttnam, David, 19
Pye Records, 123

Quang Duc, 81
Quant, Mary, 134,279
Queen Elizabeth II, 67,72,279,319,320
Queen Elizabeth The Queen Mother, 10

RCA (Radio Corporation of America), 2,245
REM, 262
Race Relations Act, 319
Rachabane, Barney, 237
Radio Caroline, 16, 128-9,140
Radio Luxembourg, 16,73,128
Ragovoy, Jerry (Norman Meade), 63,175
Ramsey Jr, Frederic, 125
Ranglin, Ernest, 238,239
Rau, Fritz, 183
Ray, Eddie, 175
Rayber Records, 168
Raymonde, Ivor, 43
Ready Steady Go! (TV show), 16,117,139-140,180
Reagan, Ronald, 303,304,311
Rebel Without A Cause (film), 4
Record Mirror (pop music weekly), 138
Red Bird Records, 59
Red Hot Chili Peppers, The, 316
Red Wedge, 5
Redding, Otis, 140, 175-6,312
Reddy, Helen, 58
Reece, Florence, 79
Reed, Blind Alfred, 76
Reed, Evelyn, 153
Reed, Jimmy, 137,179,182,186,315
Reed, Les, *147*
Reeves, Jim, 258,259
Reeves, Martha, 172
Martha and The Vandellas, 140, 171
Reflections, The, 123
Reich, Steve, 247,248
Reid, Duke, 33,242
Reisz, Karel , 222

Relf, Keith, 142
Renbourn, John, 144
Rendell, Ruth, 278
Reprise Records, 212
Republic of Congo (Middle Congo/Congo-Brazzaville), 24,228,230,*308*
Republican Party, 5,255,256,257,303,304
Reynolds, Malvina, 41
Richard, Cliff, 17,42,258,275,279
and The Shadows, 275
Richard, Keith (Keith Richards), 38,128,133,134,135,136,138,146,260
Richards, Ron, 12
Richardson, Tony, 222
Richmond, Dannie, 196
Ricks, Willie, 305
Right On: From Blues To Soul In Black America (book), 179
Righteous Brothers, The, 41,57
Riley, Bridget, 66,253
Riley, Terry, 247-9,250
Rivers, Sam, 200
Roach, Max, 35,36,187,*195,209,*210,219,220
Robbins, Harold, 266
Robbins, Marty, 61
Robinson, Earl, 76
Robinson, Ruby Doris Smith, 154
Robinson, Smokey, 14,168,5,5,5
Rock Against Racism, 5
Rockefeller, Nelson, 255,256,303
Rockers, 115,138
Rockin' Berries, The, 58
Rodgers, Jimmie (country singer), 76,108
Rodgers, Jimmie (pop singer), 127
Rodgers, Richard, 40,52,190
Rodney, Walter, 313
Roitelet (Augustin Moniana), 25,26
Rolling Stone magazine, 71,182,220
Rolling Stones, The (Phelge), 11,38,42,43,44,62,117,*119*,120,124,128,*129,*130,132-139,140,142,144,145,146,*147,*169,173,175,176,178,179,180,183,185,186,220,258,260,275,276,292,315,316,321
Rolling Stones' Rock And Roll Circus,The (film), 132
Rollins, Sonny, 202,215-6
Romero, Chan, 43
Romney, George, 255,303
Ronettes, The, 56,59
Ronstadt, Linda, 58
Roosevelt, Eleanor, 153
Roosevelt, Franklin D (FDR), 7,34,297,298
Roosters, The, 141
Ross, Beverly, *147*
Ross, Diana (Diane), 169,170
Rossi, Alice S, 153
Rothko, Mark, 253
Rotolo, Carla, 107
Rotolo, Suze, 86,107,108,
Rowbotham, Sheila, 65,164
Rowe, Dick, 11,135,146

343

Roy and Yvonne, 244
Rudd, Roswell, 201
Rush, Otis, 37,186,207
Ryan, Kris and The Questions, 273,274
Rydell, Bobby, 261

SANE (National Committee for a Sane
   Nuclear Policy), 83
SCLC (Southern Christian Leadership
   Conference), 155,157,158
SDS (Students for a Democratic Society), 83
SNCC (Student Non-Violent Co-ordinating
   Committee),
   154,155,157,158,160,189,210
SPU (Student Peace Union), 83
Sainte-Marie, Buffy, 100-102,103,293
Sakai, Yoshinori, 269
Sandbrook, Dominic, 278
Sandburg, Carl, 87
Sandom, Doug, 119
Santamaria, Mongo, 128
Santana, 245
Sarne, Mike, 42
Saturday Club (radio show), 16
Saturday Night And Sunday Morning (novel),
   66,222
Scaduto, Anthony, 106
Schaeffer, Pierre, 245
Schifrin, Lalo, 208
Schneemann, Carolee, 251
Schollander, Don, 269
Scott, Ridley, 19
Scott, Tommy, *147*
Scranton, William, 255
Seaga, Edward, 33,242-3
Searchers, The, 17,41,54,70,123,274,276
Seattle Times, The, 308
Sebastian, John, 97
Seeger, Pete, 76,78,79,80,104-106,293
Sellers, Peter, 67,264
Seme, Pixley, 28
Seven Up (TV documentary), 276
Sex And The Single Girl (film), 266
Shadow Of The Sun (novel), 278
Shadows, The, 275
Shakespeare, William, vii, 224,278
Shangri-Las, The, 59
Sharp Jr, Ulysses Grant, 92
Shaw, Artie, 35
Shaw, Arvell, 212
Shaw, Sandie, 42,61,275
Shearer, Hugh, 243
Shearing, George, 239
Sheeley, Sharon, 175
Shepp, Archie, 201-
   2,203,206,207,208,296,306
Shining Trumpets (book), 167
Shirelles, The, 13,58
Shirley and Lee, 166
Shorter, Wayne, 191,192,205,214,306,317
Shostakovich, Dmitri , 249

Shotton, Pete, 74
Shout Records, 63
Shuman, Mort, 61
Shuster, Earl, *147*
Sidney, Ann, 279
Silent Spring (book), 267
Sillitoe, Alan, 67,222
Silver, Horace, 204,205
Sinatra, Frank , 311
Sing Out! magazine, 104
Single Form (sculpture), 253
Simon and Garfunkel, 109,127,220,262
   Art Garfunkel ,109
Paul Simon, 109,237
Simone, Nina, 158,160
Sisulu, Walter, 29
Sitwell, Edith, 278
Six Quick Ones (DVD), 121
Skatalites, The, 239-40,243
Slick, Grace, 152
Slovo, Joe, 234
Small Faces, The, 124,318
Small, Millie, 239,244
Smith, Charles Edward, 125
Smith, Cherry, 240
Smith, Connie, 259
Smith, Ian, 231
Smith, Jimmy, 208
Smith, Mike (musician), 42
Smith, Mike (producer), *147*
Smith, Norman, 12
Snell, Peter, 269
Snow, CP, 279
Sometimes A Great Notion (novel), 88
Sonny and Cher, 262
Sounds Orchestral, 276
Spann, Otis, 185
Spector, Phil, 2,3,41,55,56-57,59,61,64,
   135,136,137,169,262
Speight, Johnny, 276
Spender, Dale, 154
Springfield, Dusty, 42,43,58,62,237,238,275
Springfields, The, 43
Springsteen, Bruce, 47,133,262,302,311
Stamp, Chris, 121
Stamp, Terence, 300
Stanislavski, Konstantin, 130
Starr, Freddie, 41
Starr, Ringo,
   15,45,50,51,53,54,56,69,70,74,120,133
Stax Records, 175-7, 318
Steely Dan, 204
Steinbeck, John, 77
Stephens, Geoff, *147*,148
Steptoe And Son (TV show), 276
Sterling, Lester, 239
Steve Allen Show, The, (TV show), 178
Stevens, Guy, 129
Stevenson, Mickey, 171
Stewart, Ian, 38,134,136
Stewart, Jim, 175,*176*

Music Index

The following records are referred to in this
   book – albums are in italics. NB They are
   not necessarily the original versions of the
   composition concerned.

Index

Index

Index